THE SALES PROFESSIONAL'S ADVISOR

Revised Edition

DAVID M. BROWNSTONE

IRENE M. FRANCK

amacom
AMERICAN MANAGEMENT ASSOCIATION

Library of Congress Cataloging-in-Publication Data

Brownstone, David M.
    The sales professional's advisor.

    Includes index.
    1. Selling. I. Franck, Irene M. II. Title.
HF5438.25.B747   1987   658.8'5   87-47713
ISBN 0-8144-7683-X

Printing number

10 9 8 7 6 5 4 3 2 1

PREFACE

Sales professionals today need a book that will help them to successfully pursue their careers in what for many are personally difficult times. For without paying greatly increased attention to astute career development, lifelong professional self-development, and careful medium- and long-term personal planning, many will find themselves trapped in exceedingly adverse circumstances as this period unfolds.

Our intent in writing this book has been to focus on such personal and practical career matters as career building, moving up, effective job changing, and developing a program of lifelong professional self-development. We have also focused on such very practical skills as selling, time management, and effective communication.

Please note that this book is an abridgment, with modest updating, of our previous work, *The Sales Professional's Advisor*.

Our thanks to Rosemary Guiley, whose thinking contributed substantially to the development of Chapters 6, 7, and 8; to Bruce Trachtenberg, whose thinking contributed substantially to the development of Chapter 6; and to Robert A. Kaplan, our publisher at AMACOM Books.

David M. Brownstone
Irene M. Franck
Chappaqua, New York
January 1987

CONTENTS

CHAPTER 1

CAREER-BUILDING ESSENTIALS

First things first: building a career in selling depends on being able to sell well, year in and year out, decade after decade, whatever and wherever you are selling. That is rather an old-fashioned thing to say in a world full of systems, prospecting aids, sophisticated promotion pieces, and a large variety of advice on how to persuade, negotiate, confront, wheedle, and generally sharp-angle your way to "the top." Perhaps it is so basic that it need not be said in an era of distribution and marketing majors, MBAs headed for marketing careers, and a good deal of portal, field, and refresher sales training.

Or perhaps it is so basic that it must be said again and again throughout a lifetime in selling—not by others, but by each of us to ourselves, as part of the indispensable and very personal self-analysis that is at the heart of all professional self-development and career building. It is an interconnected series, best expressed in these questions:

- Am I selling well and consistently?
- Are my attitudes to life and work "on straight"?
- Am I doing it all, and increasingly effectively?

- Am I putting in enough and the right kind of time?
- Am I avoiding the main traps? taking advantage of the main opportunities? consciously pursuing a course of lifelong professional self-development?
- Do I have long-term and very real personal and career plans, and am I working my plans?
- Am I taking my understanding of the selling process and my selling skills into every aspect of my business life?
- Am I behaving like the independent businessperson and professional that I really am?

All these are very straightforward, but all too seldom they are seen as an intertwined set of basics.

As seasoned sales professionals so well know, selling well and consistently most emphatically does not mean "having a good day" (or week, or month, for that matter). Certainly, to sell well today is indispensable; just as certainly, the person who does not habitually engage in the whole selling process and who does not develop a personally effective and comfortable selling style will be erratic, at best, with the bad days far outnumbering the good. To fail to prospect effectively is—sooner or later—to run out of qualified prospects, and thereby to run out of good days, no matter how effective you may be face to face. To fail to develop information and sell empathetically is to set up the conditions for failure after failure, no matter how strong a "closer" you are, and whether you try to close once, twice, or fifteen times. To come to where you have little respect for your company, management, and product, and are "sour" in a job, is to have overstayed and set up a personal disaster. To come to where you reflexively attempt to hide your distaste for a good many of your customers and prospects—and therefore for yourself, for being in the situation you are in—is at best an immediate and tremendous problem to be dealt with urgently, and at worst a career breaker.

We deal with the selling process at length in Chapters 3 and 4 of this book, and will not duplicate that treatment here.

What must be clear at the outset in any discussion of a career in selling, though, is that without demonstrated selling excellence, you have no real place in selling. You will not be able to build anything permanent in the way of a career, no matter what other personal and business skills you bring to that career. Also, you must realize that even the developed skills of a career sales professional will not withstand a long-term loss of effectiveness, although loss of effectiveness in one job should never be taken to indicate loss of professional skill and motivation; very often, what is needed is a job change, not a change of occupation. In straightforward and practical short- and medium-range terms, if you cannot sell effectively enough, then you cannot hold a job, or can hold it only so tenuously that the stresses involved make it clear that a change is advisable.

Most working sales professionals do not encounter problems that immediate and profound, though, unless they are in serious personal and career trouble. Far more frequently, it is a matter of doing the kind of job that you or your manager may characterize as fair, but know very well is mediocre, and far beneath your performance possibilities. It is even possible to hang on year after year, hovering around quota, inevitably growing less and less satisfied, and more and more trapped, as others move ahead all around you. Make no mistake about this: only excellence in the field commands the attention of management. Nobody wants a mediocre seller—no matter how experienced—to take training assignments, to handle national or key account responsibilities, to introduce new products and lines, or to become an assistant manager of a region or a field sales manager. Those things are for people who sell well and consistently—that is, they are openers. Nobody wants to hire someone with a mediocre track record, either; some will, for good people are always hard to find, and those hiring often have to settle, with regret, for less than the ball of fire they were looking for. And nobody reaches into someone else's organization to steal a mediocre seller, either; that, too, is reserved for top performers.

Bedrock, then: you have to sell consistently and well to be able to seriously pursue a career in selling. And equally basic: you have to understand what that career in selling is and what kind of commitment is needed to build it seriously.

THE SELLING PROFESSION

Folklore and even some modern stereotyping have it that selling is a lark, that people who sell are happy-go-lucky, smile a lot, work very little, and spend their little time on the job creating a tissue of lies to ensnare the unwary. Modern stereotypes often also include mea culpas every morning, *déjà vu* daily, and identification with Willy Loman on grey days in November. Nonsense, surely; and *Death of a Salesman* was scarcely about people who sell, being intended as a metaphor for the human condition in the American society of its time.

Yet stereotypes are interesting here, for they can mislead people within a profession or trade, as well as those without. Selling has traditionally attracted many people looking for a good, quick, and easy living. Most such people do not last very long, but their presence does testify to the impact of the stereotype. Beyond this obvious impact, though, there is a widespread misapprehension among people in selling that somehow it all ought to take less time, that selling should really be a nine-to-five kind of job, and that sales professionals should be able to look forward to a 35- to 40-hour week, like normal human beings—for example, like the people who work in the home office.

Which people? Certainly not professional managers, who work in company offices from nine to five or thereabouts and then proceed to work another 10 to 30 hours a week, and sometimes more, at home, on commuter trains, on weekends, and on the road. And certainly not those in other professions or businesses. Many doctors habitually work 60 to 80 hours a week, and sometimes more, as well as trying their best to keep up with advances in medicine. Most small-business owners are on deck 12 hours a day, six days a week, and spend many more hours on paperwork and planning at home. And try talking to a lawyer deep in litigation or a CPA during tax season about the 35-hour week!

In truth, field sales professionals need just as much independence and commitment as managers, doctors, lawyers, accountants, and small-business owners. Whether employed by others, as most are, or running their own selling businesses, they must behave like people in business for themselves. That means planning, preparing, prospecting, selling interviews, and successfully handling selling situations, often along with installation and some aspects of customer service as well. All of that requires a very considerable and absolutely necessary time commitment.

It also requires self-definition as someone capable of selling whatever, whenever, and to whomever, and a recognition of the need for continuous professional self-development. In other words, it requires self-definition as an independent sales professional, rather than as someone employed to sell a particular product or line of products. In selling, as in management, professionalism is a question of self-definition and a body of skills. Not buttressed by certification, selling is rather an apprenticeship occupation, as were so many of the currently certified professions in earlier times. But it is no less a profession, and recognition of that is as essential to sales professionals as is the ability to consistently sell well.

KEY ATTITUDES AND SKILLS

Career building, like selling, rests heavily upon a set of positive and growth-producing personal attitudes and skills. Some of these attitudes are precisely the same as those needed and cultivated throughout their working lives by successful sales professionals; that gives sellers some very significant career-building advantages, if they are able to recognize the strengths they carry over from the selling process into other aspects of their business lives. Among these are:

- personal integrity
- the will to win
- the ability and will to function entrepreneurially
- the ability to plan and execute, and to set, reach, and exceed personal goals
- the habit of skeptical and searching self-analysis
- the ability to refresh yourself from those around you
- the linked responsive listening, seeing, and empathizing skills that are so basic to long-term successful selling

No less important in career building is the ability to surmount the potential emotional problems caused by personal and business problems, especially in difficult times like these. Likewise, sellers must have the ability to overcome some of the hazards endemic to working with others in all seasons. Time wasters and rotten apples are to be found in every trade and profession, and are always quite ready to negatively color your attitudes, if you let them; the successful sales professional does not.

Not the least of these positive career-building attitudes is the will to win. No, not to be a carnivore, chewing up the people all around you in an unrelenting pursuit of fame and fortune; that is the stuff of bad novels and third-rate films, not the reality created by people who must work together in organizations. To be a winner nonetheless, one who wins most of the contests, plans well, quite visibly works those plans successfully, and is a natural for a difficult assignment—or a promotion.

The will to win on a bedrock of personal integrity, that is. For personal integrity is as much a bedrock career-building matter as are selling consistency and professionalism. It is odd to have to point that out, in a way; but we live in a world in which this most basic of positive personal characteristics is often perceived as something of a drawback in a business world that is sometimes—and sometimes properly—perceived as a "jungle."

When we think of others as possible business associates, colleagues, superiors, peers, and subordinates, we think first—and last—of people whom we can trust, "stand-up" people, people who "will be there when you need them"—in short, people of integrity. All the other positive things, too, but personal integrity most of all. For all our talk of jungles and competitive warfare, we value integrity most, and oddly enough, even while doing some things ourselves that give the lie to some of our most cherished self-images. It therefore seems apparent that personal integrity is the most important career-building personal characteristic of all. You are both what you are and what you make of yourself. The person who has a well-deserved reputation for personal integrity has the most important image a sales professional can have—and as actuality, not merely image.

That kind of observation seems hard to square with perceived corporate and marketplace realities. Advertisers routinely overstate, lying by omission and exaggeration and often by outright misstatement as well. Many books and articles counsel a wide range of cunning stratagems and artifices, claiming to instruct people on how to play all the possible games they can encounter in life and work. Some claim to have the keys to "powerful" professional and personal relations, others tout foolproof negotiating and persuading methods, and yet others offer sure ways to move ahead with enormous and unchecked speed and momentum. Indeed, people who sell professionally are sometimes urged to engage in a whole set of practices that add up to cunning manipulation of buying motives and buyers, to close deceptively and hard again and again, to use "every trick in the book" to make the sale. Nonsense, of course; those who buy are inured to tricks and deceptions, and the professional seller who develops a well-deserved reputation for being slippery and tricky soon needs to find another line of work.

That is easy to see in selling; sound sales professionals know all about the unique importance of integrity. Yet sometimes the same people who see the importance of perceived integrity in the field do not see it so easily when dealing with career-building matters. The person who habitually "cuts a corner" by covertly offering an "on approval" sale, to the house's considerable disadvantage in terms of shipping and installation costs, is making a serious personal error. So is one who pads an expense account every month because "everybody does it"; or engages in shady competitive practices; or badmouths a selling colleague in competition for a promotion. Those who do that sort of thing very often destroy both self-respect and the respect of others, to enormous personal and career detriment.

The truth is that all of us live in the same business and personal world, know the tricks as well as we know what we had for lunch ten minutes ago, and desire nothing quite so devoutly as to work with people we trust, who do not play manipulative games—precisely the games we are urged to play by some bogus experts. Most fully seasoned sales professionals know better than to habitually play such games, recognizing the professional and personal harm they can do to themselves and to others; a few do not. Some inexperienced people are taken in by bad advice, and do try to play manipulative games, harming themselves and others in the process, and doing themselves no good at all professionally. Certainly there is tactical maneuvering in the real world; certainly we do not always reveal everything we know to others; certainly we do things that hurt others—that is the inevitable result of any competition at all. However, habitual "gaming" is extraordinarily counterproductive personally and for organizations. And the person who is seen by his or her peers and superiors as lacking in personal integrity has nowhere to go but out, if personality and image cannot be repaired in place.

Integrity and the will to win are not the only positive personal characteristics needed to sell well and to build a career in selling. You also need—we almost hate to say it, for it conjures up a wholly unwanted image—a considerable measure of personal buoyancy or optimism, if you will. Ah, shades of the smiling idiot who wants to sell popsicles in a snowstorm . . . ? No, not really. It is just that to sell well consistently you have to be up and ready for every selling situation, so that you may give it your best with as little residual impact as possible from prior negative experiences. And that occasionally takes some doing, as when you have just come into an office on the hottest day of the summer, after being stuck in a traffic jam in a car with a broken air conditioner, after two busted appointments in a town 20 miles away, and missing lunch entirely. Or when you have been moving about in a city business district on foot in a snowstorm, unable to find a taxi, and carrying demonstration materials that weigh 40 pounds, which by now feel like 140 pounds, and you have failed to close a sale all week. Not an atypical situation, by the way, and sometimes quite unavoidable, no matter how well you plan. People who sell encounter stressful situations very often, and see rejection every day, and if they allow themselves to do so, they see it as personal rejection. Stress and rejection are intrinsic. They are part of the job, which means that survival alone demands a certain amount of self-confidence and personal buoyancy; consistent sales success and astute career building demand even more.

REFRESHING YOURSELF

But self-confidence and buoyancy do not flourish untended, nor can they be tended in isolation. You can pump yourself up for a little while by doing self-confidence exercises before a mirror every morning. However, in the long run you must have a sound, reliable means of refreshing yourself through others—like Antaeus touching earth mother, in a very real sense—and of growing professionally in a variety of ways.

There is nothing particularly wrong with looking at yourself approvingly in the mirror every morning, by the way. That may be a pretty good reflex, if you take the trouble to develop a sharply analytical and self-critical eye. Checking the externals is particularly important when you are pursuing a highly visible profession. At the same time, you may be able to develop the ability to check some of the internals, too, during that early morning look at yourself, and again and again as you go through the day. It is valuable to know what takes you up, and what pushes you down emotionally. You adjust, of course, and simply go on through ups and downs; but it is nice to be able to do a few modestly remedial things in a reflexive way when you find yourself down. For example, many people really do function much better at one time of day than another, which requires adjustment during the off times. For someone who functions well in the morning, that ritual mid-morning cup of coffee may be a waste of valuable selling time, as it so often is; but for someone whose metabolism is demonstrably sluggish until some time after lunch, that mid-morning coffee may be vital, its usefulness far outweighing the time spent. Yes, you can do without the coffee, or the few minutes spent freshening up between a hot parking lot and a waiting prospect, or, for that matter, a relaxing sit-down lunch occasionally. But it is far better to learn to reflexively schedule yourself so that such routine physical needs are routinely satisfied, if they are indeed needs.

Deeper refreshment comes from mutually supportive relationships with others, and with learning from others as they learn from you. It starts with the deeper personal relationships, really; the ability to interact fruitfully with co-workers, prospects, and customers reflects more your home and other deep personal relationships than the other way around. Putting it a little differently, a good home situation can take you through many adverse work situations, no matter how much impact these work situations have upon you and those you love. But it takes only one really adverse home situation to create a personal and professional disaster.

That argues strenuously for involving those you love in your work, as much as all of you can reasonably stand, and perhaps even a bit beyond sometimes. The best thing that can happen in this regard is for everyone at home to be interested—really interested—in your long, perhaps boring recountal of the day's events, or the week's events, if you have been traveling. Bear in mind that the converse must be equally true, for if you expect interested listening from them, but are not equally interested in their long, boring recountals, you will soon lose their interest in your doings. After all, it is not that these events are intrinsically interesting; it is that they are fascinating because they are part of your life and theirs.

That means a lot of talk, often at times when you and others are tired and perhaps have some office-at-home work to look forward to, besides. And it means some forethought. Whoever is on the road—and these days it may be either spouse or both—needs to thoughtfully provide the little presents and mementos that make the return home something of an event. The same holds true for those at home. Forethought, by the way, also means mutual forbearance; the best kind of family agreement on problems is to wait to take them up until all have had a chance to unwind and reaffirm relationships.

It also means taking every possible opportunity to travel with those you love. To sales meetings, certainly—most modern managements routinely provide these kinds of opportunities, and they should be taken advantage of. On personal selling trips, besides—a longish trip with a minivacation at its other end, timed to coincide with a school holiday, a spouse's vacation, or both, can be a superb family builder. And make no mistake about this: every family builder of this kind is also, in the long run, a career builder of no small importance.

Family involvement can yield a substantial additional benefit. Many Americans, not surprisingly, see selling as a low-status occupation, and not a profession at all. The stereotype of seller as a calculating and habitual liar has had considerable impact for some generations. In this sense, all those "traveling salesman" jokes—like all jokes depending upon occupational, racial, sexual, ethnic, and religious stereotypes for their "humor"—are in this sense very far from funny. That "Daddy sells brassieres," or "Mommy sells soap," is hardly likely to confer status upon children going to school with other status-conscious children. And when Mommy or Daddy (or both) are away from home a good deal on selling trips, it is possible for those left at home, including nonworking spouses, to feel neglected, as well. Involving family in work can go a long way toward preventing the development of problems before they even get a chance to get started. There are trinkets, travel notes, trips that the spouses and children of prosaic doctors, lawyers, and bankers do not get to share. And there is also the self-confidence that comes with a full sharing of your expertise and professional self-definition. Spouses share, if you let them. Children seldom seem to listen, but almost always emulate, whether you like it or not. Give your loved ones a chance to see what you are, what you do, and where you go, as shared family strengths; the benefits to all can last a lifetime.

We can also refresh ourselves daily, from customers, colleagues, and prospects. Such refreshment is a simple-seeming, perfectly obvious, positive attitude builder. Yet how you handle it can make or break your career. Lack of it is often at the heart of the problem of the "stale" seller, the "sour" seller, or the seller who's "over the hill." These are things that almost invariably have to do with how you see, feel about, and relate to your customers and prospects; they often have little or nothing to do with age, experience, and "selling skills." The truth is that no one can continue selling year after year, with empathy a precondition for achieving success, unless there is continual refreshment from, and growth with, customers and prospects.

Such refreshment is pretty central personally, as well. It can be extraordinarily painful to go out into the field day after day, detesting the work and the people, unsuccessfully trying to make it on technique without the substance of human relationship. "Liking to talk to people," of course, is not quite enough. Refreshing yourself with customers, colleagues, and prospects means asking a lot of the right questions about work, product applications, competition, company, industry and community affairs; it means listening hard and responsively; and it also means expanding your knowledge in a conscious, fully rounded way.

A solid sales professional learns a great deal from customers, colleagues, and prospects, and keeps learning afresh every day. For example, you can learn a lot about current business, industry, and specific company needs and conditions—valuable information that, as you pass it on, can help you in similar selling situations. People often look to sellers to carry this kind of general information, appreciate it, and, more importantly, develop a view of the seller as counselor, advisor, someone whose opinion is worth soliciting. The day your customers and prospects begin to look upon you as a valued business advisor is the day your future in selling is pretty well assured.

You can also continually test the strengths and weaknesses of your products under actual field conditions, as well as continually reexamine their market appeal. That is like taking a combined continual refresher course in product knowledge and sales appeal. The truth is that no home office can supply you with the kind of refresher that is yours for the asking from the very expert product users and sellers you meet every day in the field.

It is a question, though, of how you view those you are selling to and working with. If you think you can learn a great deal from them, and take the trouble to try to do so, you will learn. If you think they are objects to manipulate, you will not learn and, in the long run, you will not sell very well or build your career either.

That is one of the things that is wrong with excessively "sharp" (meaning fast, tricky, and unscrupulous) sellers. They cannot grow, their manipulative skills get progressively more empty, and they have nowhere to go but downhill, which is often an entirely avoidable personal tragedy.

So add now to this constellation of key personal attitudes and qualities the ability to consistently achieve understanding and empathy, whence comes a constant refreshment of personal warmth and continuing personal pleasure in face-to-face daily interplay with all kinds of people functioning in many different kinds of situations. "Being out there with people" is one of the chief wellsprings of pleasure for sales professionals, and for most that is the best part of the game. And game it is, in considerable part; without the game element, any profession or trade can become flat, stale, and ultimately personally distasteful.

STEADINESS

The will to win, integrity, well-founded self-confidence, and buoyancy: all these are required. Also steadiness, which is another way of saying that you must know for yourself and consistently convey to others that you are the kind of person who can do anything that needs to be done as well as or better than anyone else—that you are a man or woman for all seasons.

This describes a whole set of handling abilities and the attitudes consistently underlying those abilities. Sales professionals have to handle all kinds of situations and people every day, many of which involve problems that must be solved before a sale can be consummated; others involve difficult post-sales and servicing questions that may be of an emergency nature to those who raise them. In a single day, there may be potentially hostile receptionists and secretaries, personally difficult prospects, customer complaints, servicing emergencies, demanding home-office and sales supervisory staff, complicated reports to do, a balky automobile, and a sound film presentation that does not work. There may also be some sales, the opportunity to expand one or more of them, some valuable referral possibilities, a useful new home-office contact, and several firm appointments made for next week. And through it all, a sound professional maintains equanimity and demonstrates excellent people-handling and problem-solving skills, flexibility, balance, and warmth. And is extremely bright and quick, while seeming to take it all in stride, in what to others may seem a deliberately slow-paced style. Prospect and customer relations, home office/field matters and relationships, and scheduling problems all are treated as everyday matters, to be handled extremely well and without fuss.

That kind of steadiness stems from possession of the kinds of key personal qualities we have discussed so far, and also from firm possession of some very important personal skills, such as astute listening, careful and considerate questioning, close watching, and the ability to "put yourself in the other guy's shoes"—that is, to empathize. After all that comes the ability to skeptically and realistically analyze people and situations, while learning by engaging in critical self-analysis. These are the basic personal selling skills, and every sales professional has them and knows how to use them.

As selling skills, that is; their use by sales professionals in career building is, to put it gently, rather minimal. When that is so, it is a waste of some extraordinarily valuable skills, and something to put right. The sales professional who consciously and consistently adapts and uses his or her selling skills for career-building purposes can go very nearly any distance desired, in a career sense; and those who do not, often cannot. For sales professionals engaged in career building, the key understanding is that the selling skills that we sharpen every day are entirely usable as tools of persuasion in every other part of our working lives. The key activity, therefore, is to learn how to do all the things we know so well how to do in a wider context. All the steps of the selling process are involved in job seeking, promotion seeking, intracompany relationships, and personal network building; all the skills we use in the selling process are as equally well used in these matters as they are in selling. It is as necessary—and as fruitful—to develop and tell a benefits story in every other part of business life as it is in the field.

LISTENING

Listening is an extraordinarily important selling skill and an equally important career-building skill. Just listening—listening to what people say, and doing your absolute best to understand what they really mean. Listening to be able to understand well enough to empathize and, if desired, to persuade. As in field selling, it requires the habit of full concentration upon "the other guy" rather than upon yourself and your own needs and desires, no matter what else is happening, with as few preconceptions as possible. You have your problems; other people have theirs. To them, theirs are always far more important than yours. When a sales manager complains about how much time has to be spent on training new people, you may be hearing an attempt to divert you from your legitimate complaints about sales compensation plan changes, product defects, and territory adjustments. More likely, you are listening to someone who needs the kind of help you can offer—if you are interested in starting a move into management with successful sales training assignments under your belt. When a customer complains about the state of the business, you may be hearing a chronic complainer or someone setting up a stall or objection to buying what you are selling, but once in ten, you may be hearing someone who may need the kind of selling or sales management help you can offer.

Listening also goes beyond persuasion to self-development. We listen and learn and, if we listen well, we learn a great deal. Our associates and customers do more than refresh us; they teach us much of what we need to know to move forward. It goes far beyond formal education and product knowledge acquired from company-supplied materials. Our customers teach us about a whole field, composed of one or more industries. They also help us to keep up with a fast-developing business world, in which they function as working professionals. Our associates learn with us, and together we learn far more than any of us could learn alone, if we take the trouble to listen carefully to each other.

With listening comes astute questioning. Not adroit interrogation—that is for bad courtroom dramas and pushy people who tread on toes and alienate everyone in sight. The lifelong habit of successful questioning depends upon personal warmth and seeming indirection. We ask questions aimed at eliciting answers that inform and clarify, often as much by the way the question is answered as by the content of the answer. And the right questions almost always raise further questions, with all adding up to clues that can be used in persuasion and insight that can contribute to self-development.

If we listen and question well, then we inevitably also become very good at watching and seeing, as all good sales professionals do. We watch the entire verbal and nonverbal communications patterns of those with whom we speak. We reflexively watch the interplay between all the members of groups we are in; it quickly becomes second nature to do so. We see environments, people, and motion, and we develop the habit of picking up insights we will use to build a benefits story. This is true whether that benefits story has to do with selling goods and services or selling ourselves into a new job.

We empathize. People buy because we reach in to find their possible buying motives and then empathize with those motives; that is, understand those motives well enough to put ourselves into their shoes, show them how our products satisfy their wants and needs, and make it easy and completely logical for them to buy now. That is the process of selling benefits empathetically; in a wider sense, it is also the process of persuasion. Good sales professionals really do not need to read books on how to manipulate their way upward in the big, bad corporate world, or how to get others to do what they want. They handle people's wants and needs every day of every week.

LEARNING

To the list of career-building keys, add also now the ability to learn from experience and training, for without that, professionalism is only a dream. Learning requires the interlinked habits of analysis and self-analysis; these habits in turn are linked with skepticism and realism, those personally indispensable traits for all seasons and situations. Which is also another way of saying that self-confidence is wonderful only if accompanied by skepticism and realism; and that sales breed more sales and success builds success, but only professionalism can build long-term success and career.

From the first sales call we ever make right through a whole career in selling, we learn to sell analytically. We scribble notes on prospect cards in elevators and lobbies; have near-accidents in automobiles while reliving that last presentation, whether it went well or ill; and coffee ourselves into near-addiction in the course of "postmorteming" with trainers, managers, and often enough only with ourselves. That is, if we are any good at our trade; the sales professional who does not develop the habit of analysis and self-analysis is not worth much in the long run.

It is interesting, by the way, to watch and then postmortem with a home office visitor who has taken all or part of a presentation while visiting you in the field, whether to demonstrate something to you, try out something new on a prospect, or out of sheer desire not to lose touch. For underneath all else, and no matter how experienced, the home office visitor should be asking himself or herself the same basic personal questions you always ask yourself:

- How was I going in, and in those vital first few minutes?
- Did I see the right things, and ask the right questions?
- Did I get real contact and empathy?
- How was my presentation? my objection handling?
- Did I smoke out and handle the real objections?
- How was my timing and handling of the close?
- When was that sale made—or lost?
- If made, did I sell everything I could?
- If lost, what about next time?

If your home office visitor is or has been a sales professional, that is; failure to ask these key questions will be a clear indication, if not.

GOAL SETTING

Closely tied to analysis and self-analysis is the personal goal-setting habit, and the development of a pattern of reaching and exceeding the goals you set. This applies to sales goals, certainly, but goes beyond sales goals to career-building matters.

Sales professionals certainly get enough practice in goal setting and achievement. The budgeting process often seems to go on all year every year, with seller and management continually discussing and revising quotas of all kinds. Indeed, between quotas and contests, there are often all kinds of daily, weekly, monthly, quarterly, and yearly goals to meet, for sales, resales, lead conversions, and expansions, and even sometimes for the numbers of presentations, calls, and referrals you make. Often it all seems like far too much, and the paper it all generates seems part of a field paperwork blizzard.

Some of the paper generated by management really is excessive, the product of ineffective staff work and too many computer-generated information requests generated by cumbersome management information systems. Yet at the heart of the matter there are real needs here: management's need to know, control, and motivate; your need to feel that some people care about you and how you are doing out there, sometimes lonely and often rejected. Exceeding company quotas, winning contests, even writing some of those never-ending reports all provide a meaningful set of organizational attachments, even while you pursue your work as an essentially independent entrepreneur.

Company-provided goals also provide a minimum set of standards from which you can begin to set your own goals, your own quotas and standards. And that is an indispensable lifelong activity—indispensable in selling, and indispensable in career building. Yet in career building, you have none of the help so routinely available in selling. In career building, you are not an integral part of an ever-developing, continually reevaluated set of companywide plans. No one is there to help you analyze your personal career situation as managers, trainers, and home office people help you analyze sales. You get no leads, brochures, or planned presentations; you meet no quotas and win no contests. No one continually insists that you consistently sell benefits, sharpen your persuasive skills, continually update your knowledge, plan your career and work your plan, as you do in selling. In short, no one pushes you to apply all the enormously valuable things you know how to do to the question of building a career in selling and beyond if you wish.

It is necessary to do it all yourself, as any other independent professional does. There is a business and financial side to every professional career, and in the largest and longest-term senses, sales professionals are engaged in the development of their own businesses and professional careers, whether employed by others or operating independently. When sales professionals go fully into management, they pursue management careers; that is a whole different game, requiring new skills and approaches to be added to the existing sales career skills. When they go into their own selling businesses, they become small-business owners as well as sales professionals, and that, too, is quite another game, added to the existing selling career. For major lifelong professional planning, though, the main approaches are the same: it all really starts with the understanding that you need to do it all yourself and for yourself, just as if you were a much larger business entity.

Long-term planning is much easier and more effective if, early in your career, you have developed a pretty good idea of the directions in which you want to go. Fairly early, anyway—it is rather difficult to make a meaningful long-term plan, with interim goals along the way, if you are terribly uncertain about main personal drives and goals. That is what we are discussing here: overall personal plans five, ten, and twenty or more years out, with rather carefully thought-through and specific plans year by year that are fully reassessed at least yearly and, in some respects, as often as monthly. Yes, that can sound somewhat unrealistic to those who rely upon their companies to plan their business lives for them, and who plan their personal, business, and financial lives hardly at all. But it will seem only rational to those who understand that the difference between sound planning and poor planning can also be the difference between a life full of as many satisfactions as living can bring and a life that consists of a long, frustrating, exhausting stumble uphill, punctuated by endemic financial and personal crises, with one's later years spent as a de facto ward of an uncaring state. So we do our level best to plan as well as we can, trying to learn how to reflexively ask ourselves as many of the right questions as possible every step of the way, and counseling with ourselves as we would counsel with others.

These are difficult times for American business organizations. That has been so for well over a decade now; it will in all probability continue to be so for many more years. We have watched the dismantling of considerable portions of the American industrial system, the erosion of much of the once-superb American infrastructure, and the partial demoralization of much of the American management cadre, as most American companies have turned more and more toward the pursuit of short-term profits, rather than pursuing the traditional goals of both profit and growth. We can expect that pursuit of short-term profits to continue, with continued adverse effects. We can also expect international competitive pressures in most industries to accelerate that process of adulteration of materials and shoddiness of workmanship known as "hidden inflation," which daily debases American products and services, thereby worsening competitive positions and providing sales professionals in many industries with goods that create ever more problems and are ever more difficult to sell. Increasingly, the American economy, in both private and public sectors, fails to renew its industrial base and large portions of its infrastructure—and becomes in several very important ways antique and uncompetitive.

It may get worse, it may get better; but it will not change very substantially for quite some time. Yet, at the same time, there are very healthy American industries as well as many sick ones, and many healthy American companies—and many opportunities for career building in sales. But they are harder to find, and cannot be taken for granted. It is no longer realistic to expect to work for a few companies early in your working life, one or two more in your thirties and forties, and set yourself into a job in your late forties or early fifties, to move only for an extraordinary opportunity. That can happen; it will happen for some who are working in healthy industries and companies. For most, it is far more realistic to assume that one who enters upon a career in selling also enters upon a perpetual consideration of multiple job opportunities, inside and outside of the place of current employment.

That means considerably more heightened sensitivity to career opportunities and pitfalls than was necessary when the perceptions of those now in senior sales jobs were formed. This, in turn, means that some advisors who have kept up with new realities can continue to be enormously useful, but that other advisors should be looked upon with new skepticism. It means that recruiters who yesterday might have been thought to be terrible time wasters today should be looked upon as indispensable adjuncts to astute career building. It also means that professional meetings, courses, and contacts of all kinds take on a new career-building significance, for each is also a job mart. One should burn no bridges at all, if possible. The need to build a web of long-term business friends—now called networking—is more important than ever. And the interpersonal and political skills underlying all this must be kept sharp as never before. Upward career mobility can happen almost by accident, a happy combination of being in the right place at the right time and doing an excellent job. But it is, as it always has been, rather unusual for it to happen that way. Normally, it takes a good deal more than that. And today, as never before, it takes careful and constant self-assessment and astute opportunity seeking to protect your career and help it grow.

PROFESSIONAL SELF-DEVELOPMENT

Professional self-development is by far the most long term, and also one of the most important, of the career-building essentials. We refer to professional self-development, rather than professional education, deliberately. For professional education has come to be widely used as synonymous with *formal* professional education, that which is *taught,* whatever the teaching form adopted. And from a personal point of view, that tends to stand the matter on its head, to the detriment of consistent and lifelong self-educational efforts, the success of which must be measured by what is learned and applied successfully in life, rather than by what is taught. To say this does not denigrate the role of the teacher or of the school in which teaching takes place; it is only natural for institutions to measure success in their own institutional terms, rather than attempting very seriously to go deep into the subsequent practical careers of their students in order to measure what has been learned. In truth, that would be too much to expect—institutions should be expected, alas, to self-justify, rather than self-criticize, for that is intrinsic to their natures.

From the individual's point of view, all selling education is self-education, whether secured formally or informally, and at whatever stage of one's career. Whether you follow a course of study eventuating in a marketing or distribution degree, take a refresher course in or out of your company, or accrete on-the-job experience, the extent of your resulting development depends upon how well you learn the material at hand. Putting it a little differently, it is quite possible to take courses, secure degrees, work in the field, and learn relatively little. It is also possible to spend relatively little time in formal courses, accrete experience, and learn a great deal. For, although selling skills and attitudes can help be developed by formal courses, selling is still, and will be in the foreseeable future, one of the few great remaining apprenticeship occupations, with its most important skills and life-long attitudes learned on the job.

We should distinguish here between education and credentials. A bachelor's degree is a necessary credential; it is now openers for most beginning professional selling jobs. But that degree, by itself, is nothing more than a credential; its holder may or may not have acquired much that will prove useful in the pursuit of a selling career.

For those who sell, professional self-development is mainly a matter of sustained lifelong attention to the self-development that can come from day-to-day practical experience, if that experience is seen as a source from which learning can flow. If, on the other hand, day-to-day experience is treated so pragmatically that generalizations are not habitually drawn from it whenever possible, very little learning results. Then it scarcely matters how much formal training is joined to practical experience, for little personal development takes place.

It is not really usual for us to think this way. We tend to think of learning as something for the classroom; the practical world is somehow different. That, too, is only natural. After all, most of us spend our early years embedded in educational establishments that develop that point of view, with very little opportunity to develop self-generating learning attitudes. Yet, as working professionals, we desperately need self-generating learning attitudes if we are to grow as we can and should in a fast-changing world. That central contradiction between early educational modes and lifetime educational needs haunts most of us all our lives. It need not; but it requires clear understanding and considerable initiative to surmount the early disabilities we carry.

Yet even while recognizing the primacy of experience, we must also recognize the need for lifelong continuing formal education to keep up with the pace of change in a world characterized by accelerating technological changes and a worldwide information explosion. In addition, people who visibly pursue lifelong formal continuing education are perceived as more hirable and promotable than those who have not; that is one of the facts of life and work. Also, if you may want to move into management or into your own selling business, you can profit greatly by preparing yourself for such a move with appropriate formal courses, which you will join with practical experience later on.

Many professions in this period are faced with similar continuing professional self-development needs. In some professions, such as medicine, that need stems from the enormously swift pace of change in medical science and related areas; the doctor who does not keep up may literally lose lives that might otherwise have been saved. In other areas, such as law, it is the interplay of legislative, regulatory, and judicial materials that makes it absolutely necessary for lawyers in many substantive areas to keep up or fail to represent and advise their clients properly. In profession after profession, it becomes increasingly clear that competence depends much upon continuing professional self-development. For some professions and in some jurisdictions, such professionals as doctors and lawyers are legally required to take continuing professional education courses. California is one state that has been a pioneer in this area.

Sales professionals, as of this writing, face no such legal requirements. But selling shares with other professions the momentum created by both an accelerating pace of change and rapidly developing public attitudes as to the desirability of continuing education. That is why continuing education is such a widespread movement in American business, with many organizations offering it in various forms—including the American Management Association, a large number of graduate and undergraduate colleges and universities, and several thousand independent educational organizations of all kinds. They offer everything from hard-knowledge courses in computers, mathematics, and financial analysis to highly questionable courses and traveling seminars on the latest fads in the manipulation of yourself and others.

Once again, it is desirable to distinguish sharply between credentials and useful learning. In the area of continuing professional education, the overwhelming emphasis is upon learning; yet even here, credential seeking often plays a part. Someone who takes courses part-time as a matriculant in pursuit of a business degree can and often does pursue learning and credentials simultaneously, with the courses completed—even well short of a degree—counting considerably in promotion plans on a present job and in a résumé. Someone who secures an advanced marketing degree often finds doors opened, even on a current job, that were closed before, although the level of knowledge and professionalism achieved the day before the degree was earned is much like it is the day after. The degree, in that respect, then becomes a matter of status—not your perception of self, but how you are perceived by others.

Many courses yield credits called Continuing Education Units. Such credits do not, at this writing, lead toward any kind of generally recognized degree, in the sense that the BA and MBA degrees are widely accepted degrees, granted by institutions of higher education, operating within a whole accrediting and legitimizing apparatus. Courses are given by thousands of organizations unaffiliated with accredited institutions of higher education. Many of these courses are very useful indeed; some are not. Yet even in this area credentials are often gathered, with companies viewing current and prospective employees more favorably if such courses are part of a work history and résumé.

As a practical matter, however, the relative utility of such courses is the most important thing about them. Someone who takes a relevant professional education course is very often informed and made more valuable to his or her company by that course. Such courses are particularly useful where practical experience has been light, and when the student is not a recent business graduate who has just taken relevant courses. The sales professional who wants to move into management can be helped a good deal by showing current interest, aptitude, and knowledge, as evidenced by relevant completed courses.

A very practical note here: Many companies will finance or help finance continuing professional self-development efforts on your part, all the way from the company that routinely sends top and middle managers to a business school summer seminar, all expenses paid, to the company that matches your tuition contributions in pursuit of a graduate marketing degree. Company practices in this area are important to explore when considering a job offer. And such matters can also be part of the substance of negotiation between you and a prospective new employer or your current one.

Professional association memberships also have a role to play. Although they are most often seen as career-building tools, they can also be self-developmental tools. The extent to which that can be true varies greatly; an individual chapter may be moribund, or it may be an active organization, with useful exchanges of ideas and experiences, interesting speakers, and in the long term provide a good deal of valuable material. A national organization may do little more than run a showy convention once a year; or it may run a large body of continuing professional education meetings, seminars, and large formal courses, by itself or in conjunction with colleges and universities. Alert modern companies normally encourage their people to participate actively in appropriate professional organizations, and often pay membership fees, encourage attendance at meetings and conventions at company expense, and act as sponsors of association educational activities. It is useful to encourage your company in this, and to participate actively yourself, as part of both continuing professional self-development and career building.

THE LANGUAGES OF BUSINESS

Professional self-development also very much includes understanding and using the changing language of modern business. As a personal and practical matter, sales professionals must have excellent speaking, reading, and writing skills in standard (sometimes called "university") English. Let us hasten to add that we are not practicing "elitism" or "cultural imperialism" when we urge this. We strongly urge those who for good reason want to be expert in such special languages as Black English, the several regional English dialects spoken in the United States, and for that matter the different languages spoken by the many ethnic groups comprising our culture and people to pursue that goal, agreeing that plurality and diversity are essential to the unfolding of the unique American experience. At the same time, we must very strongly say that the language of business, as is true of most of the professions, is standard English, and will be standard English for the foreseeable future. All the main ideas expressed in business, all the main information, and all the sublanguages developed by specialists use standard English. All memos, reports, studies, proposals, letters, and promotion materials are written in standard English, and evaluated by people who accept standard English as "correct." The sales professional who does not have a wide vocabulary and flexible command of all the modes of expression in standard English is, in professional terms, considerably disadvantaged. And one who has poor standard English skills must either sharply improve those skills or be substantially and perhaps fatally disabled in professional terms.

There is considerable change in the language of business, even from year to year, as old techniques and objects are described in new ways, and as new processes and technologies call for new descriptors. Much of it is ephemeral, here today and changed tomorrow, and it is tempting to dismiss most of it as gobbledygook, and the new terms as buzzwords.

That is a mistake, for new language, however ephemeral, must be learned, if only for the purpose of communication with those who use it, pretentiously or otherwise. And very often new language does usefully describe new processes and technologies, although sometimes several different terms will be used to describe the same thing, as language evolves.

For example, a generation ago the term describing marketing efforts directed at selling goods and services to discrete, determinable, and relatively small markets was *spe-*

cial interest marketing. That became, in due course, *special marketing.* At this writing, the main term describing exactly the same thing is *narrowcasting,* with some also using the term *segmented marketing.* In this period, all four terms are worth knowing, and any one of them is useful in describing the marketing processes involved.

Or take some terms out of the special sublanguage of computers, that fertile source of new and often terribly awkward synonyms for perfectly usable existing terms. During the course of a single selling interview, or in a single communication, you may be exposed to any one of the following related terms: terminal, computer terminal, editing terminal, layout terminal, video-editing terminal, videotext terminal, video-layout terminal, video display terminal, cathode ray tube, or the initials VDT or CRT, which are used even more often than video display terminal and cathode ray tube, for which they stand. The problem is that all those terms may be used imprecisely, and cause complete confusion. For a video display terminal (VDT) is a kind of cathode ray tube (CRT), which is often familiarly called a terminal or, somewhat more formally, a computer terminal. All the other terms are possible video display terminal uses, depending upon the programming involved. Later on, more sophisticated and therefore much simpler language will evolve; right now, you have to be able to communicate with the imprecise and overlapping set of terms available.

You must be able to move easily in standard English and on through to the appropriate sublanguages. You must also have a couple of good reflexes. One is the dictionary reflex; when an unfamiliar term comes up, that reflex calls for turning to a large standard dictionary, a general business dictionary, or a special dictionary for your industry or business.

A second reflex is the keeping-up reflex. One of the most important functions performed by current business and general periodicals is to keep you abreast of relevant current language, language that is so new that it is not to be found in the dictionaries you consult. Very often, language that new is not really defined in the periodicals you read, but can easily be understood in the context of the work in which it appears, and then used and understood as necessary in other contexts.

An old saw has it that understanding the jargon is half the battle in any field. Taking away the wryness implicit in the observation, and replacing the term *jargon* with the word *language*, that old saw has it exactly right. Mastering the language of business is part of being a sales professional.

In sum, astute lifelong professional self-development provides much of the basis for sales professionalism, and helps make it possible to move freely between companies and between industries, as well as into your own business or into management.

CHAPTER 2

ASSESSING CAREER GROWTH

We face the same basic career direction questions all our working lives: Where do I want to go? How do I want to go about getting there? The contexts and answers certainly change a great deal for most of us during the course of our lives and careers, but the basic questions remain the same. As age, experience, and accomplishment grow over the years, some of us come to prefer these questions cast in terms of processes: What do I want to be doing for the next five years? The next ten? For the rest of my career? For the rest of my working life?

After basic career choices have been made, many—or perhaps most—working professionals do not ask those kinds of questions systematically and repeatedly. If faced with personal or career crises, they may be forced into a reexamination of basics. But systematic and repeated reexamination of career choices is not a habit that can only develop out of a set of self-analytical reflexes. Yet without asking and re-asking those basic questions, there can be no serious career planning. There is only a reach for each successive promotion or seemingly advantageous job change, even though our personal desires and needs may change enormously over the years, and even though career survival itself in these times may depend on careful long-term analysis and reanalysis of goals and personal situations.

Sales professionals have a wide variety of career and personal goals, and the two are intertwined. The most dedicated young college graduate determined to subordinate all to career is merely failing to see personal goals. Even the youngster who announces that he or she is determined to sell up a storm, make a million dollars a year, and go on to preside over a major corporation usually carries a rather romantic view of corporate and personal power, prerogatives, and status, and secretly wants to impress his or her loving family and all the kids on the block.

These basic personal-goals questions underlie all the rest. For the answers to the host of questions that add up to "How am I doing?" must always be related to the basic goals questions, if they are to make any sense at all. Personal goals change in rapidly changing world; grabbing the brass ring on the merry-go-round does not mean much if you have decided that the merry-go-round is not where you want to be. That promotion into sales management working out of the home office of a New York-based company may not turn out to be what you really wanted if, between the time you started trying for it and the time you received it, you have decided that New York is not the place for you, and that the Southwest is where you want to put down roots and stay. The decision to put down roots anywhere may change the basic career game for you so much that you want to reexamine some seemingly basic goals. Maybe you want to find a company headquartered in the Southwest and settle into it, with a view toward developing your own independent representative operation there in later years.

Sometimes your choice of industry will restrict your mobility, overriding other concerns. Perhaps you above all want to work with books, even though you know that many portions of the publishing industry are desperately sick, that many companies will not survive, and that you could make a lot more money now and have far better future prospects as a sales professional in another, healthier industry. Then the decision to stay in publishing, which makes no sense at all without the desire to stay with books, may not only be defensible, but the only one you should make. You will still look for a relatively healthy company to work with, and try to grow with it as best you can under considerably adverse circumstances, but your basic decision has been to stay with books, and to try to get where you want to go in an admittedly difficult vehicle, the publishing industry.

People have all kinds of reasons for developing and then changing these kinds of basic desires as the years go by. What is indispensable is to develop the ability to recognize your own basic desires, assume the ability to reach them, and continue to reassess them as they change, for change they will. Concentrating as Americans do upon personal relationships, it is easy for most of us to see that relationships change quite naturally as life patterns develop. We easily see that marriage relationships, sibling relationships, and all kinds of other personal and family desires and relationships change. What is not so easy to see is that, by the same token, it is entirely natural that career matters are also deeply affected by life experience and changes in personal goals. The key thing is to recognize the attitudes and to assess the changes in them that do occur. How? By engaging in more or less continual self-analysis. By that we mean not psychotherapy, but rather developing the habit of continually asking oneself the right questions, again and again, throughout a lifetime. "Where do I want to go?" then properly becomes "Where do I want to go as I see myself, my needs, and my desires now?" "How do I want to go about getting there?" then properly becomes "How do I want to go about getting there as I see myself, my needs, and my desires now?"

In business, we routinely develop five- and even ten-year development plans, revising those plans yearly or even every six months. And we routinely do yearly forecasts that become budgets, reassessing those budgets quarterly, sometimes even monthly, or whenever extraordinary business developments make such reassessments necessary.

A career cannot be planned quite as easily as that. Yet it can be planned. The principles of periodic and systematic questioning and reassessment are the same; the need to do a rolling revision of plans based on current outside and inward realities is the same. So, too, is the need to recognize the interpenetration between the "How am I doing?" questions and the more basic "Where do I want to go and how do I want to go about getting there?" questions.

This leads us to the whole body of questions that, for serious and continuous career building, must be asked of oneself periodically. By periodically, we mean at least yearly in a formal sense; as a practical matter, these are the kinds of questions that should recur reflexively and quite naturally as career and personal events occur. Once we get into the habit, these are the kinds of matters that are under perpetual review as we do whatever else we normally do. All are in a very real sense "How am I doing?" questions; all are inextricably intertwined with the basic "Where do I want to go and how do I want to get there?" questions.

REVIEWING CAREER STATUS

Most career-related questions are incapable of being answered in hard, precise ways; in this they differ greatly from sales performance and personal financial growth questions. That is a key reason for focusing first on the easiest to answer and therefore easiest to assess career question: "How am I doing financially?" Although progress in this area, year by year, is not necessarily a crucial determinant, in the long run money tells us a great deal about how we are doing. In a very real sense, we sell our time and talent in an overlapping set of national and world markets, composed of all those who might buy the use of that time and talent. In the long run, therefore, marketplace supply and demand factors tend to deeply affect levels of pay; comparative pay within an indus-

try, and among those doing similar jobs in different industries, provides most revealing information as to how we are
doing in the national and international marketplaces in
which we work. And in addition to comparative pay, we can
measure how we are doing in real dollars, very specifically
and unsentimentally.

During the last 18 years, prices as measured by the
Consumer Price Index have just about tripled, meaning that
the dollar we spend today is worth about one third of what it
was worth 18 years ago. (As you read this book, these basic
facts may have changed somewhat, but they are unlikely to
have changed very much for the better.) Therefore, a sales
professional who is now making $60,000 per year is—in real
pre-tax, or gross income, dollars—earning about as much as
one who was making $20,000 per year 18 years ago.

That is a pretty staggering fact; it means that many
people who have spent their whole careers moving up from
$20,000 to $60,000 (or whatever the equivalent tripling of
income has been) have in fact turned out to be marking time
financially; even though they may carry far larger responsibilities now, they are making no more real money than they
did 18 years ago. It is not quite that simple, of course; many
made real gains until the mid-1970s, and then lost all their
gains and often much more as the pace of inflation leaped
ahead of increases in most incomes. Others who did not keep
up with the pace of inflation as well as this have suffered
quite substantial losses during most of the 1970s and 1980s.
Someone who is now making $40,000 is making $13,000–
16,000 in the real dollars of 18 years ago.

These are difficult facts for most of us to face. But
without facing them, there can be no realistic answer to
"How am I doing financially?" That your income went up
10% last year may signify a real increase in pay, if the
inflation rate last year was 6%. But if the inflation rate was
10%, that was only a cost-of-living increase. And if the inflation rate was 12–14%, that was no real raise at all, but a loss,
no matter how large the congratulations that came with the
seeming raise, or how many sales contests you won.

If all those working in the American economy gained or lost equally, this would be an empty question. But that is not the way it works; varying rates of real increase or decrease occur, often relating less to individual merit and progress than to company, industry, and career choices. A company that is doing badly may not be able to significantly raise the compensation level of even its most successful sales professionals; it may indeed require pay cuts, which have a multiplied impact in periods of rapid inflation. In this period, many whole industries are sick; sellers working in those industries are often disadvantaged vis-à-vis managers in other industries. Sometimes whole professions are more or less advantaged than others. For example, sales professionals as a group have not kept up with the incomes and tax-advantaged practice-building possibilities of people in the health care professions, but they have stayed well ahead of the general income levels of people in such professions as social work, urban planning, and writing.

With all that in mind, "How am I doing financially?" is a little harder to answer. Certainly, if your cash compensation is growing at a faster rate than the pace of inflation, you are at least making some progress. In more sophisticated terms, more important for those with higher incomes, if your total compensation package is growing significantly faster than the pace of inflation, you are making some progress—but that is somewhat harder to assess than direct cash compensation. What a pension or profit-sharing plan will be worth at some future date is often hard to evaluate, especially in difficult times; and whether or not today's strong-looking company will be there to honor its long-term commitments when you retire may be questionable. With cash compensation needed more than ever, and with tomorrow's ability to honor today's promises shakier than ever, it is surely most realistic to look hardest at cash compensation—cash in hand now—when assessing financial progress in your career each year. Cash compensation is, therefore, by far the firmest and most determinable single aspect of career progress in this period.

That emphasis on increasing the amount of real dollars you are paid each year has some very significant career-building implications. Among other things, it means that a job move within one's current company that does not result in significantly higher immediate real-dollar income is to be regarded very warily indeed; we can no longer expect that moves into management from field selling, or moves to greater responsibility within a field organization, will more or less automatically result in higher real incomes, even when they are accompanied by moves to higher compensation grade levels within a company. More than ever before, higher compensation in current companies under these conditions becomes a matter of negotiation, rather than acceptance of a presumably beneficial status quo, in terms of established salary and organizational structure. For we are now in a time when many companies can reasonably be expected to strongly resist routine real-dollar salary increases, making every attempt to substitute status for money and promises for real dollars now.

As sales professionals are very much on their own in compensation negotiations, a new stress must be placed on job mobility. Certainly job mobility is a must for defensive purposes in difficult times; it is also a must for those of considerable talent and skill, who can do better elsewhere than in their present companies. Putting it a little differently, we are in a period in which many companies are not willing or able to hold their best people with real-dollar compensation increases, and in which each of us must be ready to move to other companies for real-dollar compensation gains. Under these circumstances, moving from job to job rather frequently is no longer as clearly inadvisable as it was in an earlier day; instead, it becomes a necessity for many people, as companies and whole industries falter and become unable to move their people up as well as do other companies and industries.

No, we do not suggest moving every year or two to a different company; that is still properly described as sterile job-hopping, leaving you with too little time to really build anything anywhere, and raising a serious question as to whether or not you are capable of doing so. We do suggest a far more serious attempt than ever before to keep other company and industry job options wide-open, to spend time adroitly increasing those opportunities, and to come to regard job moves as quite natural and healthy, rather than fearing each move as a step off into an unknown world full of hazard. But never burn a bridge. The number of companies that see former employees as somehow disloyal grows smaller every year, as current business realities change old attitudes. More often than ever before, a move to greater real pay and responsibility in a different company or industry ultimately results in a return to a previous company at a higher level. Somehow, those who could not see you for a desired promotion when you were an employee can easily see you for a job two steps up from that a few years later, when you are returning from a more responsible job in a different company. The career-building logic of our time is not "Stay put, and grow it where you are," but "Move, move, and keep moving until you find something to grow, unless you are lucky or skillful enough to find that early in your career."

REVIEWING COMPANY STATUS

The next career assessment question would, in other times, have been the question of one's own excellent performance. But in these times, a prior question is "How is my company doing?" Excellent personal performance, even if well perceived, no longer can be relied on to bring desired rewards; companies and portions of companies must be doing relatively well to reward excellent performance. It must often be seen even more narrowly than that, down to "How is my division doing?" and "Does my management have the power to reward my excellent performance, or are they in such difficulty that we are all likely to be swept away in the debacle that is about to occur here?"

In a way, the larger questions are rather easier, although most of us do tend to stick our heads into the sand and refuse to recognize when our companies or operations are in trouble. For example, American industry is full of sales professionals who have had the experience of working within a company that was losing money, or was clearly vulnerable to takeover because it was not making enough money, or was about to be sold by owners anxious to retire, and who refused to recognize that their business environments were about to change, dramatically and sometimes adversely, because of a change of ownership. It is not so hard to study company balance sheets and operating statements to see how your company is doing relative to other companies in its industry, or to keep up with your company's stock as it fluctuates. It is fairly easy to keep up with ownership possibilities in a family-owned company, or with acquisition and divestiture movements within a larger corporate structure; that is some of what home office friends are for. And it is essential for your long-term career that you do all those things. If you are doing rather well, and everyone else is doing very badly, you may be seeing opportunity—but you are far more likely to be seeing a disaster shaping up, in which you will be deeply involved, unless you take early and decisive preventive steps. Not that what you do, or try to do, will always be correct or work out well; but the worst possible error is to make of yourself an uninformed ostrich caught in a corporate sandstorm.

It may be hardest of all to recognize that you are associated with a failing situation. Hope springs eternal; and inertia strongly prevents movement, especially when you are selling well and would, in normal circumstances, be enjoying good income, job security, and excellent future prospects. But it can happen that a seemingly good job situation is, in truth, anything but that—and never more so than in difficult times.

There are no easy answers in this area. Good professionals become identified with their own operations, and develop group goals and loyalties, whether or not things are going well. It is the rare person, indeed, who is able to stand back and coolly recognize that the situation all are trying so hard to save is in fact unsavable, and that it is time to add some distance, to transfer, to change jobs—in short, to move on. It usually happens far too late, when choices have already been severely limited. Yet, in career terms, it is desirable to cultivate just that sort of analytical ability in all seasons, no matter how deeply involved you are in the efforts of the moment or period. And in this season—a season of prolonged and intractable economic and, therefore, company difficulties—that kind of analytical stance becomes an absolutely necessary career-building and career-saving tool.

How your company is doing and how it is likely to do in the near future is an important estimate to make. You are best able to make job moves when you are doing very well, in a company that itself seems to be doing at least rather well. When a company is visibly doing badly, it often becomes much harder to move up out of it, to the kind of job that is a substantial promotion and increase in real dollar pay. Your desirability and therefore your negotiability are always best when moving from a strong company, and almost always weakest—unless you have recognizably unique or valuable things to offer—when moving from a troubled or failing company.

REVIEWING SELLING SKILLS

And then, in estimating how you are doing, there is you, your attained level of selling skills and demonstrated excellence of performance. Learning how to sell increasingly well is a lifelong enterprise, and one that continuously refreshes those who sell. To some extent, the way that ability is developing is a matter of subjective analysis, of feel, rather than only a matter of how well you are selling. Selling well is certainly basic and indispensable, but no matter how well we are selling, we are best advised to be our own most severe critics; that is the way to continuing excellence. That requires a well-developed habit of self-analysis, of taking a long, cool, critical look at personal performance, day by day, year in and year out. "I'll do that even better next time" requires the ability to make some pretty informed estimates as to how well you did it this time, whether or not a sale was made.

Selling excellence is demonstrated to others by how well we sell and how well we perform all the other tasks associated with selling, including such matters as prospecting, customer service, referral selling, paperwork, and home office relationships. We want to perform excellently, for ourselves and for our own professional development most of all. We also want our excellent performance to be recognized by our superiors and peers, and that requires exceeding quotas, winning contests, and demonstrating sales leadership in every possible form.

Beyond that, making sure that our excellence is recognized is partly a matter of politics and positioning within an organization. How one is currently doing within a company is more than that series of basic and indispensable matters having to do with demonstrated sales excellence, real pay, and the esteem of superiors and peers. Those things are musts; without them there is no progress possible or discernible, and no amount of skill in personal maneuver is likely to prove very helpful in career terms. There are exceptions, of course; only the blind would maintain that American business is free of nepotism, favoritism, sexual exploitation, and assorted bigotries. Yet they are exceptions; the general rule is that, at least, recognized competence and, more often, demonstrated relative excellence are openers when dealing with questions of career advancement in most substantial business organizations.

Yet once those basic matters are in place, a substantial number of what can only be called political skills come into play in every organization, as formal and informal organizational structures interpenetrate to form the real motor forces at work in every organization. Therefore, "How am I doing in my current company?" must also be answered in terms of essentially the same kinds of questions that occur to those involved in any other kind of political life. These are questions that involve business friends, mentors, rivals, influences, promises given and received, and the whole web of relationships that characterize every organization.

Therefore, political skills are to some extent part of the career-building side of selling, as they are in other professions, as well. The curricula of our colleges and universities are strikingly deficient in this regard; although Machiavelli is seen and taught as an historical figure, little or no attempt is made in any of the professions to develop those indispensable skills that have to do with motivating and moving the people and organizations we work with in desired directions. We teach a little about propaganda, something of selling, and sometimes (in speech departments) focus on the techniques of persuasion, but hardly at all on intraorganizational persuasion and the skills associated with that practice. It is an enormous gap in the formal education offered the overwhelming majority of professionals, sales professionals among them. True, the skills involved are hard to quantify, graph, program, and otherwise massage with mathematical tools. And true, these skills are all too often rather sanctimoniously viewed by many in academe as somehow indecent, often as the unwelcome underside of American public, commercial, and professional life. But they are indispensable skills, nonetheless; without them, one cannot in the long run function very effectively in a world full of emotional, self-interested, often irrational people, carrying all sorts of conflicting attitudes—in short, ourselves and our co-workers.

In this context, "How am I doing in my company?" requires a sober periodic counting-up of friends and foes among peers and superiors, and an equally sober comparison of relationships now with those of a previous time, probably a year before. And along with that counting-up go some questions:

- Have I maintained and strengthened relationships with my friends?

- Have I done anything for each one of them in this last period, or they for me?
- Have we continued and strengthened our information sharing and mutual day-by-day support?
- Have I paid attention to their wants and needs as I would want them to pay attention to mine, or have we let our relationship slip somewhat, assuming quite erroneously that we will "be there" for each other when needed?
- Have I added any friends?
- Have I acted as a mentor for others?
- Have I, in short, properly recognized that friendships must be worked at and have I continued to strengthen mine within the company?

The same sorts of questions apply to superiors, some of whom may be your long-term, in-company sponsors, champions, and advisors—your mentors. All lasting relationships are two-way streets, matters of give and take, of caring about those who care about you, and that applies to those who, at first glance, might seem to want or need nothing from you while being willing to help you in any way they can. With a mentor, it is often as little as a note or clipping; some seemingly irrelevant talk about the weather and current state of each other's health when you get together at a sales meeting; a baby picture; a golf score; a restaurant recommendation; a shared complaint about the air conditioning—a set of tokens, signifying that you face your world together, rather than apart and at arm's length. It may also involve such matters as information sharing—many a wise, corporate-level old-timer understands the value of networking at least as well as younger and less experienced people who are rapturously discovering, applying, and writing about the technique. Early, sound information delivered by those we trust can, and often does, make all the difference between timely action and far-too-late attempts to piece things together after a costly set of errors. And those who deliver timely information coupled with their own sound insights are demonstrating excellence and are seen quite properly as comers by astute people farther up the corporate ladder.

A subsidiary question that should accompany this kind of periodic in-company personal evaluation has to do with somewhat intangible—and therefore more difficult to assess—positioning matters. Formally recognized sales leadership is clearly a career builder. But to a lesser extent so are such things as training assignments, new presentation field tryouts, field visits from home office managers, and key account troubleshooting assignments. These bring contact with matters important to management, and considerable exposure to management, exposure that may be worth as much as any other accomplishment in a given year, even though it may be only two or three days in the field with a home office marketer anxious to try out a new presentation. Therefore, further proper questions are: Have I had any kind of fruitful or potentially fruitful special assignments and exposures in this period? How have they worked out, in career-building terms? If still in progress, what should I see and do to help them work out to my best personal advantage?

CAREER MOVES

The answers to all these kinds of questions make it possible to arrive at a reasonable evaluation of how well you and your company are doing now, and as compared with the last such evaluation. They provide the necessary basis for asking such questions as:

- Should I be actively seeking an in-company move right now?
- Am I doing all that I can to build my career in this company at this time?
- Is this still the right company for me, given my own changing wants and needs, and given internal company, industry, and general economic developments?

- Or is it really time to move on, to very actively seek affiliation with a different company, in view of current possibilities in my present company, my demonstrated skills and performance level, and the level of opportunities available elsewhere?

The answers to these kinds of major career questions rest in part upon your answers to some other questions that deal with somewhat wider professional and personal matters.

Here we turn to lifelong professional self-development, seen from the viewpoint of practical career mobility. For it is when you encounter questions like these that you really begin to see the importance of keeping up with the industry and function within which you are currently working, with the broad contexts within which you and all other sales professionals are working, and with the profession of selling as selling. When you make a move, you may present yourself as expert in a field or industry; of at least equal importance, you present yourself as a wholly mobile sales professional, to whom "selling is selling." And to the extent that you have consistently pursued lifelong professional self-development, you are able—by demonstrating who and what you are to a prospective new company—to back up your central claim to being a professional.

That is particularly important when moving from the field into management, or from one industry to another. Then all the questions about in-house and outside courses, degrees, professional association activities, and the breadth of view demonstrated in that all-important set of face-to-face hiring interviews come up; the question of lifelong professional self-development becomes central.

YOUR OWN NETWORK

When we are considering the big question of whether or not to try for an intercompany move, we also find ourselves exploring how well we have pursued our network of outside contacts during our current employment. And it is extraordinarily important that we do just that, quite formally, at least once a year, as part of a substantial "How am I doing?" evaluation. Unless carefully scheduled, this question can and does easily get away from most sales professionals, who quite naturally focus on current collegues and job-related matters, rather than making the effort to keep up with and further develop a wide network of career friends and contacts far beyond their present companies. The person who does let this kind of networking activity slip away, despite good early intentions, is in a very poor defensive position should anything go seriously wrong with current employment. Even if a decision to move has been made from strength and the realization that better opportunities exist elsewhere, such a person is in a seriously deficient job-seeking position.

This is when you test the network of professional friends you believe you have built up over the years and find out whether the potential job contacts you have cultivated are really worth anything. This is when you see if the customer or recruiter who sought you last year meant it when he or she begged you to "get in touch" if you ever changed your mind and decided to make a move. This is when you find out that you should have developed a network and cultivated job contacts, if you had not previously done so.

When the will to do so is present, it is very easy to build a network of potential career builders, and the ways of going about it very easy to see. Many of our best lifelong career contacts are those with whom we have previously worked, people who were part of our internal networks over the years and who have moved up or on to other companies. It is often as simple and direct as following a mentor to another job; the new marketing director reaching back into a previous company or division for key sales personnel is a common phenomenon in the business world. Often the connections are considerably more circuitous, however. Peers who once worked together and have remained friends over the years may inform and recommend each other for job after job in an ascending spiral for decades.

So, too, can our customers and competitors become part of our network of potential career-building contacts. A satisfied and admiring customer is often, later on, an equally satisfied and admiring employer or source of employers. A competitor who has every reason to respect your work over the years may be very happy to lure you away from your current employer. A standard caution applies here, though: never engage in job-changing conversations with customers or competitors unless you are very serious about considering a move, for no matter what people tell you about confidentiality, the word soon enough gets around in an industry that you are considering a move. And that can hurt your company, and your own sales performance. People buy you, your company, and your products, all mixed together in their minds; and if you no longer think enough of your company to want to stay, and will not be there when they need you to handle a problem, they will not buy nearly as readily from you as before.

Excellent career contacts can also come from outside professional contacts. People who find themselves sharing and enjoying a weekly or monthly table at a periodic professional luncheon quite often expand their contact and become valuable professional friends.

And then there are the recruiters. Not those who will take anywhere from several hundred to a couple of thousand of your dollars to run tests and perhaps help you find a job if you are involuntarily unemployed, but those who are engaged by companies to find excellent sales professionals to fill vacant or soon-to-be-vacant selling and sales management positions, and therefore call you. They are all too often pejoratively described as headhunters, the implication being that they will do anything to steal good people from their loving companies. Nonsense; let yourself be headhunted, recruited, or whatever you want to call it. There is no better way to turn up good opportunities; you are never in a better negotiating position than when a company comes to you regarding a new job, rather than vice versa.

Even if you have no intention of making a move, it never

really hurts—and can help a good deal—to talk to recruiters. In immediate terms, you may find yourself confronted with an offer too good to turn down, one that you had no idea at all you might receive at this stage of your career. Also, you may very possibly learn a good deal about pay and conditions in other companies and throughout your own and other industries. Recruiters come to know a great deal about many things that sales professionals—and especially excellent professionals who do not move about very often—may not learn so easily in any other way. And in less immediate, but often even more important, terms, every recruiter you talk to is a potential job contact should you decide to make a move in the relatively near future. By all means, take the time to meet and talk with recruiters. Let them talk; listen hard; ask questions. Each such contact can, in the long run, amount to a considerable expansion of your network of job contacts.

Recruiters can be particularly valuable for a very special reason having to do with the difficult nature of the times. Many of them do tend to specialize in one or two industries, but many work in several industries and keep files reaching across many industries. In this period, characterized as it is by faltering companies and even whole industries in trouble, when you may very much need to be able to reach into other industries as well as into other companies for stable jobs, recruiters can play a considerably enhanced role. An experienced recruiter who knows you and believes in your experience and demonstrated talents can in these times become a prime career-building asset for you, as are all the key people in your network of business and personal friends and contacts.

In difficult times, most of us tend to focus on defensive career moves, as when we try to anticipate personal trouble in a failing corporate situation and attempt to make a job change while still employed and doing well, so that we can move from employed strength rather than from a visibly failing situation or an unemployed position. That is proper—but it is far from the whole story, nor should it be. In good times or bad, there will always be many selling professionals who have the ability to move ahead in desired directions, for excellent selling skills are in great demand in every season. In some ways, it is easier to move ahead in hard times, for then many companies are making sales organization changes, as they try hard to boost lagging sales. Easier, perhaps, but more chancy. To move from a good situation to another, perhaps more promising, situation in hard times may also mean a move from strength to weakness. For when you are doing well in a strong company, you may be attractive to many potential employers, but if you have moved into a new situation that does not work out and need to make another change, that change may be much more difficult to accomplish.

Still, many of us do make changes in pursuit of career goals, rather than purely defensively. Rather thoughtfully, usually—almost all of us are well aware of the potentially disastrous personal problems that can come with an ill-considered change, as when someone with small children who sells in a major metropolitan area and is home almost every night takes on a travel territory and sees the family thereafter mostly on weekends. Yet, with sufficient thought, many make quite substantial job changes in pursuit of career goals. A strong travel territory may mean a good deal more money and far better opportunities for sales leadership than a relatively weak city territory. That can be very important for someone who has children soon headed for college or who is driving toward management. A territory in one region or selling group can be far better positioned than one currently worked, if only because someone is about to retire in the new region.

Similarly, a move to special account handling, or to become part of a national account group, may be much desired, and seen as a necessary move up in terms of career goals, even though a great deal of traveling is involved.

On the other hand, someone who does not particularly want to move into management, and who wants to set down roots in an area and perhaps later move into business as an independent, may be better advised to stay put and develop wide-ranging and deep relationships throughout the business community in the area, and in the process become a well-recognized and valued part of that community. For someone with those kinds of goals, there is no particular value in moving about the country, servicing widely separated accounts, or being part of sales management. Far better then to join every local club in sight, to take probably much-needed small-business management courses locally to prepare for eventual small-business ownership (if that is what you want), and to keep on selling, more and more effectively and lucratively as the years go by. You will, by the way; as you become a fixture in an area, the whole business of selling in that area becomes easier and easier, even aside from the fact that you are getting better and better at it.

Small-business ownership, even as an independent sales representative, is a whole other thing; that is not recognized as often as it should be. Aside from capitalization needs, there are a wide range of financial and business skills that are little needed when employed by a company, even though you are an entrepreneurially minded sales professional employed by that company. Very good sales professionals can easily fall flat on their faces as independent sales representatives running their own organizations, unless they take the time and trouble to learn what they need to know as small-business owners. That is partly a matter of apprenticeship and partly a matter of formal preparation. The best possible course of action for a sales professional headed for a personal independent representative's business is to go to work selling for an established independent representative organization and to work at that for at least six months, or better a year, paying close attention to how the business side of the independent representative business works, including the smallest operational details. At the same time, courses at a local business school will be an excellent idea, aimed at helping you to understand how to start and operate a small business.

THE MOVE INTO MANAGEMENT

So, too, a move into management is a very different thing from selling—and this is fully recognized far too seldom by those who want to make that move. To a significant extent, that is a matter of relative professional prestige in organizations that are, after all, run by managers. The organizational expectation is that a very good sales professional will quite naturally want to become a field sales manager and then perhaps move into general management. That expectation is, to some extent, often also carried by family, friends, and the world at large, as management is a profession carrying considerably higher prestige value than does selling in this culture at this time.

But there is no particular reason, other than prestige, for someone who enjoys selling and is very good at it to change careers—for that is what a move into management is—unless there is real desire to do so, rather than the expectation of others to satisfy. Some management people—those up at the tops of substantial organizations—make more than do all but a very few sales professionals, but those sales professionals who move into management are usually far less equipped to move to the tops of organizations as managers than are those trained as professional managers. That will be more and more true as time goes on. Most field sales managers, and even many national sales managers, make less than the top producers in their own sales organizations, work at least as hard, see their families a good deal less, and have less job security than do their top sales producers. Indeed, since most sales managers were top producers before they became managers, many actually earn less than they did as field representatives. And they are often low people on management's totem pole, quite overshadowed by home office people of all kinds, although as top sales producers they were treated with little less than adulation for being the geese that laid the golden eggs for the whole organization.

The necessary skills are quite different, too. Ideally, a

top producer is made into a sales manager so that replication can occur, with the selling ability of one turned into the selling skills of many. But the truth is that not terribly many people who are very good at selling are also very good at training and leading a sales organization. And even fewer are very good at home office relations and policy matters. Selling is selling, but management is management. It requires a considerable body of quite different training, people-handling, supervisory, and leadership skills than does selling, and a great deal more tolerance for intracorporate matters and the development of necessary intracorporate political skills. The truth is that many superb selling professionals operate as entrepreneurially minded independent businesspeople in their own territories, but are entirely misplaced as cogs in a large corporate wheel, and have little in the way of management skills when they make the mistake of becoming part of management.

So—look before you leap. And if you do decide to leap, be prepared to learn a whole new profession on top of the selling profession. A sales management person is a dual professional, just as is a computer designer, engineer, accountant, or copywriter who moves from any other functional skill into management. In a very real sense, moving into management involves a new period of on-the-job apprenticeship; it should also involve a good deal of additional formal training and the cultivation of quite new self-development reflexes.

If you do decide to try to move into management from selling, your move is most likely to be in-company, rather than directly into another company, unless it is into a much smaller company in which you both sell and manage, typically growing a selling organization from scratch. If it is directly into another company in a full managing position, though, then you are attempting the most difficult of tasks, for you are moving into a new profession and a new company or even industry simultaneously, and have an enormous amount to learn very swiftly, all while you are charged with producing sales. Within your own company it can often be done a little more gradually, using your own demonstrated sales excellence and your web of intracompany supportive contacts—your network, that is—to help you make the move you want.

Sales excellence first, of course—without that, there is no real hope of a move into sales management, no matter how good your supportive network might be. There is no better way to bring yourself to the attention of top management than to be a consistent sales leader and contest winner. It guarantees that you will be talked about by everyone in the home office marketing group, right up to and including top marketing management. And beyond—many top management people want to know everything they can about sales results and sales leaders, quite correctly understanding that nothing at all will go right without sound and consistent selling.

Sales leaders are also those in the field force who get direct access to top marketing and general management. A sales leader who wins an all-expenses-paid trip to a watering place is also usually presented with an opportunity to spend some very personal time with top management. In that kind of situation, top management is always sizing up the winners with sales management in mind, now or in the future. Sales meetings present similar opportunities, but of a lesser nature.

Sales leadership also carries with it the top management field visit, to try out a new presentation, to get a first-hand look at how all is working in the field, or to look you over with sales management in mind. Such a visit brings with it both major opportunity and major hazard for those seeking management positions, and should be treated with extreme care. Which means being on your best behavior as regards such potentially disabling factors as overdrinking and complaining, and making very sure that you sell something—or several somethings—while you are working together in the field. That means setting up as many promising appointments as possible before the visit, even if it means a certain distortion of activity in the period before your visitor arrives, and a certain amount of possible overbooking during your time in the field together. Work extremely hard and effectively, do not worry about tiring your visitor, and make some sales. There is nothing quite so satisfying to a visitor (especially a top management visitor) as to be able to tell everyone in the home office, in loving detail, about the sales you made together in the field. Your visitor is likely to remember those live field sales—and you—for years, as he or she goes through all the obligatory meetings, briefings, performance appraisals, paperwork storms, and marathon telephone conversations that so characterize the life of the modern American manager.

Never ask for a move into management during a field visit. Never complain, no matter how justified your complaint about policy or personnel might be. Never attack anyone else in the company. Nobody wants to bring a pushy complainer, whiner, or backbiter into management. If asked about management aspirations, answer directly. If not, say nothing about them; your feelings will usually be quite apparent to experienced people. If not, and they want to know, they will find some way to gently ask, without necessarily offering.

If you do want to move into management, there are likely to be people who will help you along the way, some of whom you will have cultivated and some of whom came quite naturally, without much prior cultivation. First among them is likely to be your manager, who may recommend you for training assignments that train you as much for management as they prepare your trainees for selling. Your manager is also very often able to recommend a successor on transfer, promotion, or retirement, and will be listened to very closely.

Help will also come from those of your peers who have moved into management before you, and from such sources as home office trainers and marketing people you have worked with over the years. If you do want to move into management, and are a sales leader, there are always many ways to make your desire known and listened to, and a very good chance that you will be able to move in that direction.

CHAPTER 3

THE SELLING PROCESS

This chapter could just as easily be called "The Buying Process" as "The Selling Process," for buying and selling are two sides of the same coin. We focus here on the selling process because that is what you are able, to some extent, to control, to move; but it is easier to understand what is happening between buyer and seller if we first examine buying motives and then examine selling approaches and actions.

Don't be alarmed. We are not now going to embark upon a long, tedious, and ultimately sterile discussion full of psychological jargon—what has so aptly and cuttingly been described as *psychobabble*. Our approach is not theoretical, either. We are concerned here with discussing lifelong successful selling, rather than with the development of a body of motivational and marketing theory, however useful that may or may not be in other contexts.

Sales professionals can benefit greatly from the operations of economists, market researchers, psychologists, corporate planners, direct marketing people, marketing managers, advertising people, public relations practitioners, and a wide variety of other professionals engaged wholly or partly in analyzing buying behavior. It is broadening and refreshing, in the long run, to keep up with what is being done in related areas. But at the same time, it is necessary to "keep your eye on the ball"; for sales professionals that means focusing sharply on the essence of the individual transaction between buyer and seller, understanding it so well that it can be applied to scores and perhaps hundreds of different situations encountered in the course of a selling career. For if, indeed, "selling is selling," it is because the essence of the sales transaction can be captured, and we are therefore able to generalize well enough to have and apply insights reaching all selling situations.

People do seem to buy for all kinds of reasons. They buy insurance against potential catastrophe and sports vehicles that cannot help but bring catastrophe closer. They buy foods that they know will make them fat and chemical preparations aimed at making them thin; paintings of great beauty as investments and extraordinarily ugly bric-a-brac of no artistic merit because they think it beautiful; sound houses to live in and absurdly uncomfortable and expensive houses for show. They soberly shop for bargains in order to save, while conspicuously consuming luxury goods. They buy because they need, and they buy because they want—quite rationally and entirely irrationally. They buy on a hard sell and they buy on a soft sell. They buy for a very wide and mixed variety of emotional and rational reasons that intertwine and move toward purchase or rejection in what can be called either the buying process or the selling process, depending on the point of view adopted.

In the end, they buy because they feel—consciously or unconsciously, and often a little of both—that their purchase is somehow satisfying, the right thing to do, something they want to do, something from which they derive benefits. That, not at all oversimplified, is the essence of the matter.

SELLING BENEFITS

The essence of the matter to sellers, therefore, is to convert all the features of what they are selling into benefits that, on some conscious or unconscious level, will be regarded by the prospective purchaser as reasons to buy. In shorthand, the essence of the matter is therefore to sell benefits.

Consistently selling benefits is one of those very easy things that can be extraordinarily hard until mastered, and then you wonder why others have any trouble at all understanding a concept that is so obvious or mastering such an easy approach to selling. And consistently selling benefits is also the single most important key to lifelong selling success.

All it really takes is the ability to "put yourself in the other guy's shoes," and to do so reflexively and completely, time after time, with much of your attention devoted to gaining the information and insight necessary to make that possible. Among other things, it requires understanding what the benefits are in each situation, and not confusing product features with your prospective purchaser's benefits. It requires reflexively asking yourself the same question about your prospect in each selling situation: "What benefits can you get out of what I'm selling?"

That is a very simple, direct question, and consistent selling success requires that you be able to answer it fully and well in the vast majority of selling situations. Oh, there will be a few situations in which you make the sale without the answer to that question—the prospect who "takes it away from you" before you even get halfway through your presentation, or the prospect who buys for reasons you cannot fathom after you have quite given up and are ready to pack it in—but those situations are few and far between. To be able to identify and sell benefits is the simplest, most basic skill in selling, and the most important.

Features are not usually benefits, though occasionally they are so perceived by prospects and therefore become so in fact. A loving description of all of the outstandingly advanced technical features of the small-business computer system you are selling will very rarely sell that system; you must convert those features of the system into benefits recognizable by your small-business owner prospect, such as ease of use, economy, increased speed of collection, and improved inventory control. There may seem to be exceptions; the small-business owner who is also a computer buff may be fascinated by your technical descriptions and be eager to describe the advanced features of that system to his or her envious computer buff friends. You still will probably need to convert features into benefits to make the sale, but the features then are also benefits, for the status the system brings becomes a buying motive, which is a synonym for benefit.

It is very easy to confuse features with benefits, and thereby confuse the selling situation as well. It happens most often in technical areas, but in all other selling areas as well, and is the hallmark of the novice. Unfortunately, it is also a habit into which experienced professionals can and do also slip on occasion. The computer system seller who is entranced with hardware, software, and the rest of the jargon of the computer world has an exact counterpart in the life insurance seller who loses sales with interminable talk about settlement options, cost per thousand of term versus life and vice versa, and new interest rate schedules—all after an easy close could have been effected.

Benefits must be put simply and clearly to prospects. We must remember that we are extremely familiar both with our products and the kinds of selling situations that develop around our attempts to sell them. Our prospects are not; it is all new to them. Even the most astute prospect needs the clarity provided by our interpretation of features into benefits. To state features and benefits in complex, difficult-to-understand language does not elevate the product being sold in any way; rather, it normally betrays a lack of the kind of complete product knowledge that is needed for simplicity of statement. As all writers and teachers understand, you have to know a great deal about a matter to put it simply and clearly, yet fully and correctly. In this, as in so many other things, simplicity is the essence of sophistication.

PRODUCT KNOWLEDGE

Product knowledge consists of a great deal more than the ability to demonstrate and explain the workings of your products. Certainly you will be able to present effectively, answer basic questions, and compare product or products presented with other products in your line, if any. You also, however, often have to discuss product uses and possibilities far beyond the limit of your prepared presentation, and be ready to discuss very knowledgeably the products of your competitors as well. In almost all instances, those who sell must know their products intimately, in terms of real strengths, weaknesses, uses, and competitive position.

In a fast-changing world, you must also keep up—certainly with your own products, as they change and develop, but also with those of your competitors. Beyond products, it is quite necessary to keep up with developments in your field. There are a number of ways to accomplish this. One of them is through careful study of company-provided materials, such as sales materials, technical manuals, and house-generated newsletters and magazines directed to internal staff and to customers. You should read and reread these materials very carefully until their contents are fully understood, for sales will often depend on your understanding of them. That means the company has a stake in your understanding them; therefore sales management, production people, and home office staff will, in most companies, be responsive to questions from the field, which you should not hesitate to ask.

Company training and retraining sessions can be excellent sources of updated product, competition, and industry knowledge. Many companies run such training sessions as ongoing schools, passing field staff through retraining courses periodically. Many others include training sessions in regular sales meeting agendas. Experienced professionals use these sessions for the accretion of needed information, and therefore often regard sales meetings as opportunities—which they usually are—rather than as necessary evils.

If you work out of an office with others, those you work with and report to can often be excellent sources of information, particularly on selling approaches that are working well and on competitive matters. For some, this opportunity turns into a trap, consisting of endless talk over second breakfasts and too-long lunches, while prime selling time is wasted. But it need not be so; controlled exchanges with co-workers can be very useful.

Customers and prospects can be extraordinarily important sources of information and insight, if you take the time to listen to what they have to say. These are people in your field who are spending a great deal of time using your products and those of your competitors in the field. They can be an endless source of competitive information, third-party selling material, new selling ideas, and practical knowledge as to the strengths and weaknesses of your own products.

When it comes to customers and prospects, sometimes it is hard to separate the useful material from the rest, and it can take a good while to learn what is worth your attention. It is very easy to block out the chronic whiner and complainer, ignoring the kernel of information buried in the mass of minor complaints. Sometimes that is the right thing to do; chronic complainers waste a great deal of valuable time, and are best treated as briefly as possible, as long as their real complaints are satisfactorily handled. But there are also many customers and prospects from whom you can learn a great deal, if you listen.

It is also a good idea to keep up through subscription to one or more industry publications; such periodicals normally keep up rather well with industry developments and trends, and also include new product and service announcements that can prove useful. Many people in selling also take formal courses, such as those offered by local adult education courses and area colleges, in order to better understand the basics of their fields. Many companies encourage this, and provide tuition assistance or even full tuition payment in recognition of the value of such outside self-development activities.

EMPATHETIC SELLING

One can be extremely well armed with up-to-date product knowledge, understand the importance of identifying and selling benefits, know the difference and be able to sharply distinguish between features and benefits—and still not be able to sell. And without the ability to consistently turn it all into sales, this is all interesting, but merely academic. The proof of this pudding is wholly in the selling, which largely depends on the interaction between buyer and seller, an interaction that must be generated and controlled by you, the seller.

Face to face with a prospect in a selling situation, the probable general sequence of events is predictable. With minor variations and transpositions within the sequence, you will try to develop information about the prospective purchaser and his or her relevant needs and desires; present your product or products; attempt to handle stalls and objections; and ultimately attempt to move into a successful close. But if it is as mechanical as all that, you are hardly likely to close successfully very often. That is scarcely selling, and is about as useful as some of the canned presentations handed to sales professionals by a small number of relatively unskilled marketing management organizations.

Successful selling, like all successful persuasion, is what is happening underneath all that. The mechanical moves are easy to see; the interaction and processes underway between the players—seller and prospective buyer—require more insight. Observing seller and buyer at work with each other, you may see the seller speaking, and strongly reinforcing and amplifying what is said with body language, relaxation and tension, pace, and timing. Meanwhile, you may see the buyer saying one thing and nonverbally showing that something else is so; you may see a buyer back away, not necessarily knowing why. An experienced seller will reach forward to find out why—often to help the buyer find out why—so that whatever is really there can be made explicit and can be dealt with, and perhaps be handled as a lever with which to move toward the close.

If you are watching a good sales professional, you will see someone at work who understands very well that it is crucial to be able to put yourself, as much as possible, into a prospect's thought processes, to understand how another is thinking and feeling in the middle of the situation. The essence of the matter is to be able to move with your prospect toward solutions of problems, toward satisfaction of needs and desires, adding your own insights so that you share in the process and reach conclusions together. That is, after all, the essence of all face-to-face persuasion; it is also a description of the processes involved in empathetic selling. It works somewhat differently with groups, and very differently with multitudes. We are speaking here, and in the main throughout this book, of face-to-face, one-to-one persuasion, the processes involved when one seller attempts to persuade one prospect to buy.

Empathetic selling—or, to put it a little differently, successful selling—is the ability to put yourself into your prospect's shoes every step of the way and move ultimately to the close in complete agreement. It requires early *concentration* on the prospective purchaser and his or her expressed problems, needs, and desires, rather than on yourself and your own need to present and sell. It requires the ability to concentrate while projecting—and feeling—*relaxed,* so that you may best be able to draw out your prospect. It requires the ability to *see;* yes, literally to pick up visual clues from your prospect's appearance and business or personal environment. It requires the ability to *listen,* to really hear what your prospect is saying to you. An astonishing number of sales are lost because sellers do not bother to listen to the basic information and clear selling clues that prospects provide early in the interview. And most of all, it requires feeling and projecting personal warmth and real interest in what your prospect has to say, so that you find yourself developing a *sympathetic stance* and *empathy* with your prospect. And it better be real. On the one hand, people are very used to detecting phony sympathy and rejecting it; on the other hand, and much more important, it is in the long run extraordinarily dangerous and self-defeating to try to project a false image rather than to develop long-term empathetic attitudes. There is no surer way to turn yourself sour, and ruin both your career in selling and your personal outlook. But when the approaches and techniques that add up to achieving empathy with your prospects are fully accepted and become reflexive, the act of selling can become the rewarding fun it can and should be.

PROSPECTS AND CUSTOMERS

People who sell goods and services face to face outside and by telephone spend a good deal of their time identifying and finding prospective purchasers who are qualified to buy by virtue of their needs or desires, and who are further qualified by their ability to buy. Some astute retail sellers—especially those selling rather specialized goods and services—also prospect, seeking to find and attract specific kinds of qualified potential purchasers into their establishments, there to be met face to face and sold. And selling organizations of all kinds use advertising and several kinds of direct marketing approaches both to sell directly and to find qualified prospects who can then be sold face to face.

If you are fortunate enough to be associated with a company that develops large numbers of qualified prospects for you—often as an adjunct of direct-mail marketing and couponed advertising—your job will be made much easier, and your sales production considerably enhanced. Even in that company, and throughout your sales career, you will still need to know a great deal about how to generate your own qualified leads, for that is an indispensable set of career skills for every selling professional. Even if your company generates large numbers of qualified prospects one year, it may not do so the next year. Or you may change jobs, and find yourself in a company that relies upon you to generate qualified prospects. The truth is, if you have not mastered the prospect-getting skills, you are not the complete selling professional and sales generalist you must be to pursue your career in a fast changing business environment. Nor are you properly able to consider striking out on your own, either during your younger years or in a post-retirement occupation, for identifying potential buyers enables you to assess the possibilities—or lack of them—in a projected business move, while finding and reaching them are often essential to business success. Prospecting then is properly seen as an essential entrepreneurial tool throughout a lifetime in selling, whether you work for someone else or for yourself.

It is also true that you will be able to generate some better qualified prospects than any of your home office marketers can generate for you, because you will be generating some of them—the best of them—face to face. That is what referral selling is, after all—the process of generating highly qualified prospects face to face, while simultaneously creating third-party selling material from the referring source.

The best qualified and most receptive prospects you will ever encounter are your own satisfied customers. Even when they are not "your" customers, if they have a history of doing business with your company, they are predisposed to do further business with you. A satisfied customer is a good deal more than someone who has bought goods and services from your company. Such a customer has also "bought" your company, and trusts it to do what it promises to do and to make good, one way or another, on promises it has been unable to keep. When the crucial question of trust has already been solved, it is certainly far easier to sell more of the same, to upgrade, to sell different goods and services, and to introduce new products than it is to an untrusting stranger. A properly untrusting stranger, by the way—buyers are wise to deal with strange or untried sellers at arm's length until those sellers have proven themselves; that is a fact of life in the field.

When you yourself have sold goods and services to a satisfied customer, and especially when sales have been face to face, rather than "service" sales over the telephone, the status of that customer as prospect takes a quantum leap. For from then on you are dealing with someone who has accepted house, product, and you, and the importance of that personal relationship cannot possibly be overestimated. It can be the key to an unending chain of sales to an individual with whom you have an increasingly excellent relationship, to others within the same organization, and to an unbroken succession of business friends and acquaintances over the years. Key buyers and referral sources are indeed the stuff of which successful careers in selling are made. They take a good deal of development—that means time, and time is precious in the field—but they are quite worth the time spent.

Unless you use them as a crutch and fall into the callback trap, of course. As every experienced professional so well knows, it is very comfortable to call on the convinced; they do not really need to be sold, and they will often buy enough—or almost enough—to make the call seem worthwhile. But effective servicing of an account, coupled with constant sale and resale (all of which is right and proper), can all too easily degenerate into profitless continuing callback, wasting precious field time that should far more profitably be spent in effective prospecting and the development of new accounts. It is nice to spend time chatting with an old friend on a snowy or steamy day, but it does not necessarily build a territory or a career.

Satisfied customers will themselves often buy more, especially when they have recently bought from you—very often when they have just bought from you. That is euphoria working in your favor. When you have just sold a customer, he or she is usually "high" after making the "right" decision. You, your company, and your products will never look better than the moment after the close. Which is why your just-sold customer often becomes a highly qualified prospective purchaser immediately after the close of the previous sale. A self-congratulatory customer will, at the moment following the sale, often seriously consider add-on sales, related products, and even quite unrelated product purchases. Your customer will, in the period of euphoria following a buying decision, be very likely to want to help you, and at the same time will want to help some of his or her best business or personal friends (depending on the nature of the product) to be able to make the same sound buying decision.

Referrals.

If handled properly, your just-sold and therefore self-congratulatory customer will provide excellent *referrals*, with the aggregate of your satisfied customers therefore supplying you with a literally endless body of qualified prospects. The keys to securing referred prospects are asking at the right time, it at all possible after you have made a sale; asking for a limited number of referrals at any given time; being careful not to mix the referral request with product recommendation requests; and handling product recommendation requests very gently.

When after the sale you ask for referrals will depend on the specific situation. You are likely to move from the sale just made into an add-on sale try, saving the referral request until after you have tried to make the additional sale, before you gather up your materials in preparation for leaving. But in some instances, you may want to ask for referrals after the initial sale itself, using a question about whether or not one of those referred might be interested in other products as a lead-in for your additional sales attempt. In no instance should you try for a referral with your coat on, your briefcase packed, and ready to go out the door, any more than you should seriously try for an additional sale then. By then, the game is likely to be over, the selling situation gone; you and your customer will both be looking forward to whatever is next in the day.

By asking for a limited number of referrals you are asking for a favor that is very easy to grant, requiring only the recommendation of a couple of friends down the hall, in the same building, across the street, or a few miles away, rather than a serious decision followed by a time-consuming search for addresses and telephone numbers. The right number to ask for is two, as in "Ms. Jones, I'd like a chance to discuss these systems (or products, services, policies, or whatever else it is you are selling) with other people in the industry (or locally, in the city, or around here). Do you know two other people you think it would be worthwhile to talk to?" Note that you have asked for two, rather than one, for a single referral may be easily misconstrued as a recommendation as well as a referral. But only two, rather than "a few," or anything that might be seen as work-creating, and therefore as an unwarranted imposition. And note that you have not asked for any kind of product recommendation, but only for people with whom to discuss specific products.

You will often get two referrals if you ask for them this way. Sometimes you will get more, as you take the two names and then sit, pen poised, obviously waiting to see if more will be volunteered. If no more are volunteered after a moment, it is best to let it go at that. There will be another sale to the same customer another day, as well as service contacts.

When you do get referrals, your customer will also often offer to call those being referred, to tell them that you will be calling. Whether or not that offer is made directly to you then, your customer will often inform friends that you are going to call. If possible, therefore, give your customer a chance to contact his or her friends about you before calling. And bear in mind that busy people may not make the contact immediately, or even on the day they first call each other. If you can hold off calling on referrals for a couple of days, you will have maximized chances that your customer has made an all-important call ahead of you, and that you can call your new prospect for an appointment and get it easily, often with a personal and product recommendation already in place.

Product recommendations are a delicate matter. Think carefully before asking your customer to tell friends how good your products or services are, for a refusal to do so can create an awkward and possibly damaging situation. Putting it a little differently, try not to ask unless you are pretty sure your customer will agree to do so. Some have a second chance to try for referrals from satisfied users; others do not. It depends on whether or not what you have sold requires any kind of installation in which the purchaser is directly involved, as when you have sold an office machine to a small office and install it personally or together with a service representative. For then, if the installation goes well, post-sales opportunities may repeat, with add-on sales and referrals possible from a self-congratulatory customer. Such installations are sometimes quite wrongly seen as nothing but time-consuming chores; they can be that, but they can also be excellent opportunities to create a brand-new sales and referrals situation.

Referrals secured may in some instances be outside your territory or for products that you do not handle. Alert sales organizations therefore often supply incentives for those who generate referrals resulting in sales for others. However, even when organizations fall down on this vital sales-building technique, alert sales professionals find ways to generate leads for each other, in the sure knowledge that swapping prospects so generated will pay everyone handsomely in the long run.

Good referral prospects can also often be generated by satisfied customers who are happy to help you because they think highly of you and your company. Often it happens within the context of a routine service or troubleshooting call. Customers rarely volunteer referrals, though; you must ask, gently, diffidently, and above all consistently.

That is true of family, friends, and even other prospects who have not bought. There are products, such as securities and life insurance, that are sold quite often through the referrals of family and friends. There are prospects who will refer you to others, whether they are still in the buying decision-making process themselves, or have reluctantly deferred purchase until a later date for financial or other business reasons. All will generate good referral prospects; all must be asked to do so.

A reminder: the tricky sales professional is not really much of a professional at all. Claiming business or personal friendships that are merely passing acquaintanceships, or claiming referrals or product recommendations that have not, in fact, been given, is asking for trouble. Somehow the word percolates that there is someone out there selling who cannot be trusted. It does not take much of that to threaten a job and damage a career.

Other Prospect Sources.

Although the prospects generated by current customers can be excellent sales leads, there are many other prospect sources as well. Former customers, if properly cultivated, can be excellent prospects for resale. Every publisher selling periodicals by direct mail knows that; lists of former customers, called *expires,* are second only to current subscriber lists as prospects for other publications. It requires time and attention, usually consisting of a prolonged, systematic effort to rekindle interest and to develop existing proven needs into new desire for what you are selling.

The essence of the matter is the continued existence of those proven needs. When someone has already bought from your company and perhaps directly from you as well, the all-important question of need no longer must be established before the question of buying your products and services can even be addressed. Of course, if the entire nature of a prospect's business has changed, needs may disappear completely, but that is an exceedingly rare situation. It is far more likely that a former customer may have gone over to the competition, or may even have dropped only part of your product line. A resale under those kinds of circumstances is far easier than a new sale to a stranger. That may be true even when relations have been ruptured between your former customer and your company, as over an unpaid bill or an alleged major quality or customer service failure. It is usually far easier to redevelop selling relations with a former customer than to sell a new prospect.

Rekindling interest may be as easy as making sure that all your former customers continue to receive those company promotional and customer-relations mailings you consider relevant, whether through formal company channels or directly through you. Many seasoned professionals regularly mail prospects, and especially former customers, items aimed at stimulating felt need for their products, along with company-generated material. Some also mail items they pick up that seem particularly relevant to the individual or company they are trying to resell, following up periodically with telephone calls. Some take advantage of special promotions and discounts to attempt to rekindle former customer interest, as well as to kindle interest in other prospects.

Buyers of your competition, like former customers—and many of them often are former customers—are also prime prospects, no matter how deeply entrenched your competitors seem to be and how unsuccessful you and others have been in selling to them over the years. That lack of success in selling them, however, often has a great deal to do with continued failure to do so. For the prospect who continues to reject our approaches can easily be seen as rejecting us—not only as businesspeople but as human beings—and nobody likes continued rejection, even seasoned sellers who know how to handle it maturely. The truth is that most of us stop, if rejected often enough and firmly enough. We mask rather effectively what is really happening, of course—we are spending too much time on a lost cause, have to move on to more fruitful prospects, cannot get appointments anyway, but maybe ought to try them again later on sometime. Anyway, if we keep on pushing, we are just going to poison relations and kill any hope of eventually selling them.

Yes, we may indeed. Continually calling and being rebuffed may indeed build up a wall of rejection between you and your prospect. But a continuing set of contacts, such as the contacts you maintain with former customers, coupled with judicious follow-up, may serve your purposes very well indeed. It requires consistent, long-term follow-up, which often in the long term succeeds extraordinarily well. You cannot know which new product announcement, third-party recommendation, or cost-saving tip you mail to a competitive buyer will do the trick; but you can properly assume that sooner or later one of your follow-up calls will result in a face-to-face selling situation.

For the law of life is change. Wants, needs, relationships with competing companies and sales representatives, buying personnel, product lines, pricing arrangements—all these things change, creating new situations that you may take advantage of, if you are properly positioned to do so. Your constant contact with competitive buyers does that positioning for you. It may be a promotion or company change, moving someone who is deeply committed to a competitive product, seller, or company, and removing the block caused by that commitment. It may be that the same kind of product, service, or personal relationship disaster that caused one of your customers some years ago to become a decidedly unfriendly prospect is now occurring with the company to which your customer went. With the shoe now on the other foot, and proper contact having been maintained, the move may be back to you rather than to a third company. It may be a story in a newspaper or told over coffee in a commuter train that morning, about how much better your new product is than a competing product. Do not fall into the negativism trap here, by the way, or at any time when you are handling competitive situations. The right assumption is that your product is always uniquely able to stand on its own merits. Surely you will make sharp competitive comparisons, when they are called for by the situation, but if you let the sale rise or fall on a competitive comparison before you have properly told your unique selling story, you have weighted the decision against yourself. It is one of the oldest basics in selling: sell the positive aspects of what you have to sell, eschewing the negative as much as possible, and never, never, never make a personal attack upon a competing seller, company, or product. That can be construed as dirty pool, and there is nothing better calculated to destroy a growing trust in you, and the selling situation with it.

Lead Creation.

Prospects may also come as leads generated by advertising, direct marketing, or a trade show exhibit. Many companies generate large numbers of leads for their field representatives in these ways, with the quality of the leads ranging all the way from very poor to excellent, depending on such factors as how wide the advertising copy net was cast and the nature and price of the mail-sold products purchased. Because direct-mail leads are buyers of some sort, direct mail on the whole tends to supply somewhat better quality leads than does advertising. But that is more a tendency than an inflexible rule. After all, an advertisement-generated lead for a specific and rather expensive product is likely to be a far better prospect than the mail-order buyer of a $5.00 item, who winds up in your hands as a prospect. And your company may not be very adept at helping you to qualify the prospects sent; you may have little more than a name and address to start with. In that sort of instance, you can only ask, attempt to reach prospects by telephone, attempt to determine the nature of their potential interest and ability to buy as best you can without being face to face, and, when appropriate, try to set up a selling appointment. At worst, you will present to unqualified prospects; at best, you will make some wholly unanticipated sales to people you did not even know existed.

Some of the best company-generated leads you are likely to get will be the names, addresses, and sometimes information about prospects who have seen your company's products and expressed interest at a trade show or some other kind of exhibit. These will often be people who have rather carefully studied your company's sales material and often the products themselves at the exhibit and may have had considerable discussions with your people as well. Such prospects must be reached as soon as possible after receiving company-generated leads.

On the other hand, you may also find yourself receiving all the names of those who registered for a convention or trade show, neatly typed for you on a lead form, without any other information and with no way to determine which of them are superb prospects and which are wholly unqualified. When confronted with that kind of all-too-common situation, you can only try to separate the real prospects from the rest by telephone, once again being ready to waste selling calls on a few unqualified prospects if you must, but not letting the good ones go. The trap here, by the way, as in all mass-lead situations, is that you will let the good ones go. Twenty fruitless telephone calls in a row can sometimes daunt even the hardiest, most experienced "old pro," who should know better—and really does, most of the time. But in the long run it is right to go ahead and make the twenty-first call, and then the forty-first and the fifty-first. Good new prospects can be hard to find, and consistently pursuing home office leads can, in the long run, be an excellent career-building habit.

Consistent prospecting is also a matter of keeping up with some readily available sources of current information. For example, the real estate section of a city or regional newspaper is must reading for many sales professionals; knowing about move-ins in a timely way can make the difference between a substantial sale, and the resulting new customer relationship, and a late and disappointing contact after more alert competitors have sewed up a new firm in town.

A good deal more than move-ins can be derived from such sources. Between the local press and the trade publications in your field, you should be able to get a good deal of vital updating information on promotions and job changes, company developments, and new technology; all can be prospect-creating, if the information is timely, and if you are ready to move in a timely way to take advantage of it. A bit of job-change information can result in a call to a key new executive who is considering—and indeed may have been brought in to accomplish—a set of major changes substantially affecting buying patterns and vendor relationships; that person can become a major new customer for you. The promotion of someone you have cultivated may result in a timely call and sale, rather than a late call and no sale at all. A technological development or move by a company into a new line of business may open up substantial new prospects you may have missed had you not taken the trouble to keep informed.

Prospects are also to be found merely by looking, rather than unobservantly passing by. The tenants' listing in the lobby of an office building may inform you of move-ins even more effectively than the local press, if you take the time to look when you are making a call in the building. Your customers will tell you about new people in the town or area, if you take the time to ask when you are calling on them. There is usually not much sense in spending large amounts of time in cold calling, though; normally it is far better to try to develop information about such "found" prospects and then using the telephone to try to sell a firm appointment.

Some people do enjoy cold calling, though; it can be part of the fun of selling, if it is not carried to wasteful extremes and made a substitute for systematic prospecting and information gathering. Sometimes, between appointments or after a busted appointment, it can be enjoyable and rewarding to turn the handle on the door of a strange office, do your best to find out what you can about the company and its people from the receptionist you then encounter, and even proceed to try to make a cold call upon someone you are not at all sure will turn out to be a qualified buyer. You may sell a later appointment to someone you think may be a qualified buyer; you may even make a totally unexpected sale on the spot, depending on what you are selling and the breaks of the game. All if you have the time, that is, and nothing better to do in that place at that time; cold calling on strangers can be a terrible time waster, and should not be relied on for very much in the way of sales. When you walk into a selling situation without any information at all on your prospect, you are making it harder to sell than it needs to be. Even the telephone call in which you have sold the appointment can yield enough to begin to develop the information you need with which to first qualify and then empathetically sell the prospect; a cold call often does not even take you that far, much less give you an opportunity to develop vitally important prospect information before the selling interview actually takes place.

Basic Information Sources.

There are a wide range of sources from which to derive such prospect information. Your own company files may yield some, if the prospect is a former customer. So may your own prospect files; you cannot remember everything in them, and a new prospect may turn out to be not new at all once you consult your files. Your selling colleagues may be sources of information, if the new prospect is a move-in. And so may your own customers, who may have vital information for you available merely for the asking. Beyond those kinds of sources are a wide variety of published sources of information.

It takes a considerable amount of time and attention to learn how to use published sources or prospect information efficiently. But it is very much worth the effort. Financial and other relevant information on tens of thousands of companies is available, as is biographical information on some millions of Americans. And there are scores of special directories, looseleaf services, books, and newsletters containing information that may provide needed prospect information.

Learning how to use all these sources develops a long-term career-building kind of skill, which makes it possible for you to generate much of the information you need, whatever your selling job and whether you are working for another or on your own. And it is not really very hard to learn what you need to know to use the library effectively, especially if you let the skilled reference librarians you will find there help to the best of their considerable abilities. It is foolish to wander about in a library, trying to figure out how to find the information you need. Even if you ultimately do, all by yourself, you will have wasted a great deal of time and probably settled for far less than is really available. Ask the librarian, if necessary again and again; the more intelligent questions you ask, the better most reference librarians will like it. Learn how to use the wide variety of printed sources you will encounter; also take the time to learn how to find needed information in the other forms in which it is stored, as on microforms and in computer memories. More and more, we are storing information in computer memories now, and calling forth specific pieces of information as needed. That is the shape of the future, a future in which enormous masses of information will be available in computerized forms, and capable of being reached—accessed, as computer people are fond of calling it—through viewing devices in your office and home.

The net of all of the above prospecting and information-gathering activities, assuming consistent and skilled work on your part, is a constant flow of highly qualified prospects, all of whom find their way into your prospect files. To develop files full of prime prospects is to provide yourself with one of the building blocks you need for long-term career success in selling. As so many before us have said, "A good prospect file is like money in the bank." It provides you with resources you can dip into as needed, with a reserve of prospects you can reach for to build a productive day, week, or month. Without it, you are reduced to a great deal of cold calling, overattention to a narrowing group of customers, and constant callbacks on a small and increasingly inhospitable group of prospects. Putting it a little differently, without knowing how to build—and consistently building—a good prospect file, you are very likely to be a former sales representative for a good number of companies, and headed for eventual long-term unemployment. In Chapter 5, we discuss how to organize your prospect and customer files for maximum efficiency. Here we will maintain our focus on the selling process.

INTERVIEW SELLING

Converting a stack of prospect cards into selling appointments requires bringing another group of selling skills into play. For after finding prospects and gathering information about them, you must sell them, and before you can sell them your products you must sell them on the desirability of making a firm appointment to see and discuss your products with you.

The key to successful interview selling is understanding what is happening between you and your prospect. On the telephone, trying to make a firm appointment with your prospect, you are not selling your product—you are selling the interview. All you want to accomplish on the telephone is to sell your prospect on the desirability of talking with you face to face. You will often have to explain something of yourself, your company, and your product so that the prospect can make the interview decision. You might have some questions to ask the prospect to help you determine whether an interview will be worthwhile. But to the extent that you step over the fine line between explaining and selling you will harm your chances of getting a firm appointment with your prospect.

Even for some experienced people that fact can be hard to accept. Once you have a live prospect on the phone, the temptation is to glowingly describe the product, prepare the way for the face-to-face encounter, and go as far as you can to get information and prepare the close. Unfortunately, it just does not work that way. The harder you try to sell your product over the phone the less chance you will have of selling the interview. And being human, the less you succeed in selling interviews, the harder you are likely to try to sell the product over the phone, creating a kind of downward spiral. It is best to reserve product-selling efforts for the face-to-face interview.

The main problem is that when you try to sell your product over the phone you are selling into a partial vacuum. Face to face, you have had a chance to size up the firm, the prospect, and the selling situation. You have asked some questions, given and received both verbal and all-important nonverbal communication, and begun to establish empathy and focus on the prospect's problems. On the phone, all you have is the instrument and a disembodied voice on the other end of the line. You cannot see, feel, empathize; you are just playing cards with the deck stacked against you, and by your own choice. If the situation begins to go bad, your chances of recovery are very slim.

On the other hand, when you sell only the interview, you

are presenting your prospect with a very limited decision—to see you or not. And by setting it up as a firm appointment, both you and the prospect know you are going into a selling situation.

Many companies provide their field forces with prepared telephone-interview selling presentations. If you have one, use it. It has been developed, redeveloped, and honed down fine with the problems and opportunities of your company and its products in mind. It will usually contain a basic presentation and several alternative ways to go as you and your prospect reach choice points in your conversation.

If you do not have such a presentation, it is not too hard to develop one for yourself, as long as you keep your concentration on the goal of the telephone conversation: you are selling the interview, not the product. The opener of one such presentation might go something like this:

> Hello, Mr. Smith. I'm Mary Tate of the Hummus Company. I'm calling this morning to try to set up a meeting with you to discuss how our new line of widgets might be helpful in your production-line operations. Would it be possible to get together tomorrow at ten, or would after lunch be better? [Of course, if you have a referral, it will be "Jack Jones of Jones and Jones suggested that I call you this morning . . ."]

Mr. Smith is likely to want to know a little more about your line of widgets, perhaps about your company, before he can decide whether or not to see you. Answer the questions and then come back to a quick closing question as early as you feel you can. A time-choice close that focuses the prospect's attention on when to see you rather than whether or not to see you will usually work better than a straightforward "Will you see me?" approach. "Will you see me?" courts a straightforward "No!" which ends game, set, and match.

Your prospect will often counter with an early objection, something like, "Oh, yes, I've heard about those widgets. Aren't they pretty expensive?" That is when your resolve to stick to selling the interview gets tested. If you respond quite naturally, "Oh, no, Mr. Smith. Our widgets are not really expensive, when you consider their durability and design excellence," you have just fallen into a trap. Instead, respond with something like, "That's just the kind of question I want to discuss with you face to face, Mr. Smith—costs, savings, durability, design, and how our new widgets can fit into your operations. How would Monday at 10 A.M. be for you?" You have deferred the too-early objection, focused on the interview, and stand a far better chance of selling that interview than if you had fallen into the trap.

Your prospect will often simply stall. Then it is a question of continuing to stress the potential value of the interview, reaching again and again for the close. You probably will not want to try to smoke out the hidden objection under the stall over the phone unless you have been stalled with something like, "Sorry, I don't have time to see you . . . try me next week," again and again.

Quite often, you will have to get through a secretary or administrative assistant before you can get to your prospect. And that person is often responsible for screening just your kind of call.

If you have a good referral, you are likely to get right through. "Hello, I'm Mary Tate of the Hummus Company. Jack Jones of Jones and Jones suggested that I call Mr. Smith this morning. Is he there?" That is pretty straightforward, and "Is he there?" sidesteps the screening function of the person you are talking to. The only decision to be made is whether or not to put you through.

Without a referral, you still may get right through with "Is he there?" If you do not, you may have to explain why you are calling, in much the same words as in your basic telephone presentation. Then your final phrase can be, "Do you make all Mr. Smith's appointments?" In the unlikely event that the screening person does make all appointments, you will try to make one. Much more likely, the answer will be no, and then you will ask to speak with Mr. Smith.

Selling interviews over the phone can be a difficult and

annoying chore for field sales professionals, unless it is done skillfully. But, just as failure at it spirals downward, so does success build success.

THE SELLING SITUATION

Here we deal with you and your prospect or prospects—seller and buyer—in direct encounter and interplay. Now the prospect has been identified and the interview sold—or has been self-identified, as in retail selling—and buyer and seller are in the same place at the same time, soon to be face to face in a selling situation that will or will not result in a sale being made now. Let us stress that *now,* for each selling situation is unique. The sale that is not made in one selling situation should never be seen as merely deferred until another day; it is far more likely that it will have to be made all over again another day, in what is another and different selling situation.

In that sense, every selling situation is new. And that is true in a personal sense, as well. Every sale is, in some ways, the same: the same motives on both sides, the same approaches, sequences, techniques, key words and phrases. Yet every sale is also brand-new, as every game is brand-new, no matter how well the players know the rules. To some people outside your particular game, it can all seem deadeningly stale and boring—but it is not their game. The truth is that most professionals in every game find their work fascinating, and those who sell are no exception. Those who like the game find a great deal of enjoyment in selling, and the best people in any field do it as much for the fun as for any of the other rewards attached to success.

For analytical purposes, it is probably best to distinguish between outside selling and retail selling. Even though the essence of the interplay between buyer and seller is the same, there are some very substantial differences between the two kinds of selling situations.

The most important difference has to do with environment, for in outside selling you come to the buyer and work in the buyer's environment, and in retail selling the buyer comes to you. In outside selling, therefore, you are likely to be dealing with a qualified prospect in an environment very familiar to the prospect and unfamiliar to you, but one in which you will be able to pick up many selling clues. You will also most likely be selling to an individual, rather than a group, and will usually know in advance if it is going to be a group presentation. You will be approaching; often rather formally presenting, perhaps with sales aids, although usually without the product itself to show; handling stalls and objections; and, if all goes well, moving to the close.

In retail selling, however, you will be dealing with self-identified prospects, but will need to qualify them on the spot and while moving into some sort of presentation, which will often feature a direct product demonstration. Your environment will be entirely familiar to you, but not to the prospect. You will therefore have fewer selling clues; you may have to deal with a certain amount of prospect disorientation; you are unlikely, due to the retail environment, to be able to put together anything more than a rather brief presentation; and you can almost count on even that being interrupted. You will also very often be presenting to a group, rather than to an individual, or find yourself presenting to a group after starting to present to an individual. Who said retail selling was easier than outside selling? Prospecting is easier, not selling.

Most sales professionals are involved in outside, rather than retail, selling, and the nature of the selling processes and many of the products involved do make outside selling considerably more complex than retail selling. We will therefore discuss outside selling first, and then more briefly discuss some of the special features of retail selling. We will discuss telephone selling only as an adjunct to face-to-face selling, as when you sell a prospect on an interview; telephone selling is normally so canned as not to need or be willing to pay for the services of sales professionals. For that reason it is also quite unattractive to most professionals.

THE CONTEXT

When you move into someone else's environment, the selling situation starts as soon as you enter that environment. That is not necessarily the prospect's office or other place of business, either. It may be a parking lot, a reception area, the lobby of a large building, or for that matter a restaurant across the street, where your prospect just happens to be having lunch or taking a coffee break.

Times change; social expectations change. The stereotype of the sales professional as a gold-cuff-linked male in an expensive suit driving a big new car is long gone in most places and in most fields. But some axioms do remain. It remains axiomatic that if you drive into your prospect's company parking lot in an automobile that looks as if it is ready to be compacted into scrap, your prospect is highly likely to be idly looking out an office window directly at you, and wondering what kind of person might be willing to drive that kind of wreck. If you arrive in a reception area hot, tired, dusty, and in desperate need of freshening up, the receptionist who announces you—who may have been with the company for 30 years, and may be informally charged with a certain kind of screening—may in tone and telephone manner prejudice your prospect against you before you ever come face to face. And that prejudice is very likely to remain, at least as a question, even though you freshened up after making your disastrous first impression on the receptionist. If you are somehow discourteous to whomever is waiting on the table or the counter in the diner across the street, you may be creating the same kind of first impression; nobody likes a two-faced hypocrite, who is polite to buyers and nasty to those who are powerless. Sales professionals make no mistake about this—the selling situation starts as soon as we enter what even *may* be the prospect's own environment.

That environment can yield very important selling clues to those who take the trouble to cultivate looking and listening reflexes. And reflexes are what are needed, for there is a great deal to ingest and turn to advantage when you have the opportunity to spend a few minutes waiting for a prospect. Some of the questions you may ask yourself—quite reflexively, and without necessarily knowing that you are doing so—are:

- *How does the place look?* Is the office small, dingy, full of tired-looking furniture and peeling plaster, or spacious and prosperous-looking? Is the plant in need of a paint job, with some long-broken windows, or is it modern, efficient, and in good repair? Is the store clean, well-lit, with fresh windows and signs? Many an old-fashioned office is prosperous and forward-looking, but it is much more often true that appearances do not deceive.
- *How's business?* That is a question you are going to ask, one way or another, before you are very far into the selling situation. But it helps to try to size up business a little before you walk into your prospect's office. Do many offices seem untenanted, or is the place bursting with people and action? Is the parking lot crowded? What does the receptionist answer when you ask how business is?
- *How do the people look?* Tight ship or loose rein? Happy or grim? A good deal of time wasting, from what you can see, or a solidly businesslike atmosphere?
- *Are any products or trophies in the reception area?* Companies often use their reception areas as showcases, supplying valuable information on what they consider important by the products they feature and what they are proud of by the trophies they display. That is valuable empathy-developing information for you, and can start your conversation with your prospect. Sometimes it can be direct-selling information as well.
- *Are any promotional materials in sight?* Many companies display their own promotional materials in their

reception areas; valuable information indeed, when you are trying to fit your goods and services to the needs and desires of an unfamiliar firm.

- *What periodicals are in the reception area?* You may find only last year's general interest magazines, but you may also find highly specialized materials reflecting the interests of your prospect—and you are eager to amass as much information as possible about those interests.

Receptionists can also be valuable sources of such information. Even more, they can help supply the "feel" of a new environment, and sometimes valuable clues as to the persona of your prospect. Clearly, if a receptionist obviously does not want to or cannot speak with you, it will not do to force it. Someone working hard to handle a busy phone, receive live callers, and perhaps handle a typing assignment as well may be unable to speak with you, no matter how willing to do so. On the other hand, most people like taking a break, and always respond to a little warmth and news of the outside world. It usually starts with the weather or a balky typewriter, and often very easily turns to work matters, for people love talking about their work; they need only be given the chance to do so. A skilled sales professional can learn a great deal about a prospect in a few minutes with a receptionist. It is always in order to try to secure and remember the receptionist's name—request it if it is not displayed— as you may be calling and coming back personally on other occasions, and remembrance of a name is always appreciated. Basic advice? Certainly. Too basic to be worth mentioning? Certainly not. Even the most experienced of us sometimes find ourselves moving away from sound selling reflexes occasionally. It is always worth reviewing the basics. And equally basic: If you and the receptionist are in the midst of a conversation when a prospect or a prospect's assistant or secretary comes to collect you, break off your conversation apologetically, as you would with anyone else you respected. To end a conversation abruptly is ill-mannered, and will be perceived as such; you will then seem manipulative and insincere, and will have been better off if the conversation had never taken place.

Whether you are collected and taken to the prospect or directed to the prospect's work area, your next contact is likely to be the prospect's assistant or secretary. Either way, you have very little time—important time, not for information gathering, but for communicating warmth, for making contact. You may have spoken with the assistant or secretary over the phone, perhaps when setting up the appointment. If so, contact is easy and necessary, and as simple as a "Thank you." If not, contact is still very easy—as easy as a smile of appreciation and a thank you for having been guided to the right place. Another basic for people who sell in all seasons: if you treat people like people, rather than like inanimate objects, they respond in kind. If you shake hands, get someone's name, take the time to write it down so that you get the spelling right, and say goodbye later with a smile, however the interview worked out, you are very likely to make a friend. That friend may swing an undecided sale for you, for many an assistant or secretary does just that—either way. And that friend can make it very easy—or close to impossible—when you call again for an appointment. It is also well worth bearing in mind that yesterday's competent assistant or secretary may be tomorrow's up-and-coming executive, in this or some other firm, willing to listen to an old friend's selling story, or ready to turn a deaf ear to someone who once treated a lowly assistant or secretary badly.

CHAPTER 4

FACE TO FACE

And now you are face to face with the other player. A whole human being first; also a prospect, buyer, customer. A bundle of contradictions, just as complex as you are, full of concerns, operating on several levels at once, under many and quite diverse pressures. Possessor of a unique personal history, yet sharing many interests and problems with others you meet and work with every day. Ready to hear what you have to say, but simultaneously considering a good many other matters, both business and personal, and highly unlikely to be ready to concentrate on buying the way you are prepared to concentrate on selling. Someone whose attention you will probably have to catch and hold long enough to be able to present coherently, and then someone who must become engaged enough to want to buy. Someone with whom you can achieve empathy and with whom you can move toward a buying decision.

Your prospect is also someone who may be rather outgoing and friendly, or reserved and defensive, decisive or indecisive, attentive or distracted, tired or fresh, sharp or fuzzy—that day, that hour, that moment when you first meet. All are tendencies, all differ with the impact of a wide range of variables, and all require sharp analysis on your part in the selling situation.

For, in essence, you have to control the selling situation, from beginning to end, no matter how the situation was initiated. That is as necessary at the beginning as at the close, in that extraordinarily important first few moments of the interview, in which the whole relationship between you and your prospect is first cast. Those first few moments face to face are so important that they are worth dissecting, move by move.

It is interesting and revealing that the first and by far the most important context-setting move you make is nonverbal, the conveyance of basic attitude toward the prospect with body language. Your set of basic attitudes is first and quite lastingly conveyed by how you move to meet the prospect: relaxed, warm, friendly, intelligent, confident, entirely up to meeting and welcoming a new person and a new situation; or hot, cold, tired, perhaps a little defeated and unsure, quite down, and ready for another rejection. You project who and what you are both by design and quite involuntarily; real attitudes cannot be masked enough to fool the experienced eye, and your real attitudes will in the long run always show and support or defeat you. You project a whole person, to whom others will naturally move as they learn to respect, like, and trust you, and from whom others will withdraw if they perceive falseness and self-defeat.

The second move is also nonverbal; it is a matter of eye contact and close attention to the person you are meeting, who happens to be your prospect, but is first of all a whole human being, just like you. That people who run confidence games look at their victims squarely as a means of cultivating misguided confidence has nothing to do with it; confidence game people are emulating you, not the other way around.

You are then likely to shake hands, because most Americans do. You may run into someone from Great Britain who does not normally shake hands, or someone who, for personal reasons, does not like to shake hands; that poses no problem as long as you come close enough to allow your prospect to do so if desired. Most of us never did any variant of the hearty, bonecrushing "salesman's" handshake and backslap; that is a perennial comedy staple, and quite out of style. Just a firm, quite brief handshake will do.

The rest of the mechanics are straightforward, basic, and worth mentioning only because some who are not sales professionals will be reading this book. If you are carrying a coat, it may already have been taken from you, or the prospect will tell you where to put it. If neither happens after greeting the prospect, look around the room, find a likely place, ask if it is all right to put your coat there, get assent, and do so. The sight of someone who should be a sales professional standing awkwardly holding a coat and not knowing what to do with it is enough to make a sales manager's blood run cold. But it happens.

You will be asked to sit, and will not sit until you are asked. Of course, if some time goes by and you are still not invited, you will surely find some reason to be asked. When you do, try to sit reasonably close to the prospect, in a place that allows you some surface on which to spread sales materials later in the interview. Usually that will be the prospect's desk, and you will probably sit on whatever side of the desk a second chair has been placed. If there is a choice as to which side of the desk to sit on, choose the left side if you are right-handed, the right if you are left-handed. That will allow you to place your briefcase between the desk and your chair so that you can pull materials in and out of it with your best hand, and allow you to use the end of the desk for handling materials, rather than your lap.

During the course of the interview, you are likely to pull a good many materials out of that briefcase. Be sure to leave them out only as long as needed, and then put them away to avoid distracting clutter. As to the briefcase—make sure it is in good condition. A badly scuffed, dirty briefcase can be fairly unobtrusive in a reception area or on the floor of a prospect's office. But the moment you have to put it on your lap, on a table, or on the prospect's desk to get something, it becomes shockingly obtrusive.

You will continue to study the prospect's working environment throughout the interview. It is not a contradiction in terms to give the prospect your complete attention and keep looking at the environment. It merely takes getting used to—and a lot of practice. Mechanically, it is mostly a matter of peripheral vision. Just as you see off to the sides of the road while focusing on the road itself, so you can see a good deal of the office environment around you while focusing on your prospect.

It is important to do so. There are a great many clues in a workplace—products, trophies, photos, books, decor, repair, windows, office placement—and any or all of them can be useful in making the sale. Bear in mind that although each one is a new environment for you, you are in hundreds, even thousands of them. Once you get used to looking for clues, you will find them everywhere, find them more easily as time goes by, and eventually not even have to think about looking for them. Many sales professionals see everything worth seeing with a single, quite automatic glance, and use what they have seen all during the interview. It is simply a matter of training yourself to be observant and getting a good deal of practice.

Beyond the simple mechanics, the key things that are happening in those vitally important early moments of the interview are the beginnings of empathy; you are beginning to be able to put yourself into your prospect's shoes, and are gathering vital information regarding prospect needs and desires that can later lead you to a successful close. You can deliver a presentation carefully calculated to appeal to the wants and needs of the "average" or "typical" prospect, but each prospect is, in some most significant respects, unique; therefore, the early information you gather and later adroitly use is very often the difference between closing or not closing the sale.

The early conversation between you and your prospect, then, is vitally important; it is far from the trivial interchange it so often seems to an unperceptive observer—and often also to the prospect. If it is controlled well, that is. If not, it can indeed consist of little more than useless, situation-deadening trivia, with your prospect becoming restless and you then plunging prematurely into your presentation, with neither the beginnings of empathy nor the vital information you need to take the prospect to the close later on. In that case, you will have fallen into one of the classic early traps, be well on your way to both losing the sale and convincing your prospect that you are someone to be avoided in the future.

It is never really difficult to avoid this kind of trivia trap, as long as you are exercising conscious control over the situation and moving it somewhere, rather than sitting back and letting the situation go. Directionless "friendliness" takes one nowhere. The trivial, friendly opening must quickly be taken in a solid business direction. This is where all your preparation begins to pay off, for your knowledge of the industry, and of specific companies, people, products, and processes, will make you an interesting person to your prospect, and possibly a valuable source of future insight. When it is clear that you know a good deal about matters your prospect needs to know about, you become more than a seller; you become a counselor as well, meaning that your prospect will often rather eagerly open up and discuss problems, needs, and desires with you—just what you need to reach empathetic understanding and develop information. For then you are giving as well as getting, and developing what can be a mutually advantageous and personally satisfactory business relationship—a real two-way street.

Some opportunities also create their own pitfalls. Beware of the prospect who seems to open up and deluge you with problems before you have had much more than a chance to smile and say hello. That is, after all, another classic early trap: the crier, who will, if possible, cry you right out the door, deeply sympathetic over the sad plight of the crier's business—and without a sale.

After not very long, it becomes time to present. When? Oh, when it feels right, when your prospect clearly wants you to do so, or when you feel that enough empathy and information have been generated to make it time. Or, of course, when you are not sure, perhaps having run into some early stalls and objections or seemingly impossible-to-penetrate defensive shell on the part of the prospect. When talking around the main business of the day seems inappropriate, or when you have done pretty much what you wanted to do in the early stages, then it's time to look them right in the eye, speak your piece, and listen just as hard to them as you want them to listen to you.

PRESENTING

Presenting is rather an expensive business. By the time you total up all the costs involved in placing yourself before a qualified prospect—including prospecting time, research time, travel time and costs, other out-of-pocket costs, and presentation materials—you are faced with the sometimes daunting fact that you have spent anywhere from $40–50 to as much as several hundreds of dollars merely to place yourself into a situation in which you can sell effectively. That is a great deal of money spent for the privilege of speaking your piece, and makes it not at all inappropriate to think of your prospect as someone in whom you have already invested a good deal of money. Now it is time to get that investment back, and then some.

The presentation does several things:

- It completely and clearly lays out the major buyer benefits associated with purchase of your products and relates those benefits to the product features being shown.
- It organizes and tells the whole product story, fully and specifically, so that the prospect can fully understand those features you are turning into benefits.
- It relates the early information you have gained on prospect needs and desires to the specific benefits and features of your product.
- It handles, often anticipates, major prospect stalls and objections, including competitive objections.

▪ It provides a sound basis for handling stalls and objections successfully and moving to the close.

Every effective presentation is prepared, one way or another. Nobody really sells entirely "off the cuff," pulling words and concepts out of the air. Anyone who thinks selling happens entirely spontaneously just has not stopped to think through what is really happening. Even if you sell without any kind of consciously prepared presentation, you are working from product descriptions prepared by others—advertisements, brochures, manuals, handbooks, visual materials of several kinds—and developing your thinking around those standard materials.

No matter how creative you are in thought and language, you will still describe benefits and features basically the same way to the same kinds of prospects in the same kinds of situations. Anyone doubting this need only tape his or her own presentations for several weeks. The words, the tone, the appeals are always strikingly similar from situation to situation, and so are the gaps, especially if you have not given sufficient thought to preparing your presentation. It is always startling and often pathetic to watch sellers who have spent hundreds of dollars getting before qualified prospects then muff the selling opportunity by presenting an incomplete, badly put, totally inadequate product features story bereft of the necessary benefits.

On the other hand, watching someone race, letter perfect, through a canned presentation without once making human contact with the prospect is even more painful. Many sales organizations provide fully worded presentations for their sales representatives to memorize and present as is. Some sales management people even provide several long, fully worded presentations at once for their hapless sales representatives to try to memorize and keep memorized, complete with obligatory pauses, head motions, and other body language. That, of course, never works for very long; the pressured representatives memorize in training sessions as best they can, then quite properly jettison the impossible presentation load as soon as they are in the field.

Sometimes sales managements provide their field forces with fully worded, visualized presentations in the forms of slide–audio and motion picture presentations. That kind of presentation has a real place in some highly technical product areas, but little place in most product areas.

Canned presentations were the last generation of sales management's answer to the off-the-cuff approach, and in many situations worked effectively. In this generation, though, given some of the presentation aids available, it is clearly possible to fully prepare effective presentations without losing the crucial ability to sell empathetically.

Most sales managers who insist on fully memorized presentations expect them to be used with some degree of judgment. That means human contact, questioning, listening in the early stages of the interview; pausing to handle a question or objection while going through the canned presentation; moving away from the presentation when the prospect's eyes begin to glaze and breathing becomes too regular. Of course, there are a few sales management people whose incompetence expresses itself in excessive rigidity. They are to be borne if you feel you must and fled from into more rewarding jobs if their demands become onerous.

Use the canned presentation flexibly and add a personal component, even if you are dealing with a motion picture complete with soundtrack. If you are using only a script, usually with some visual materials, take care to analyze it to find places where you will be able to plug in the personal element. For example, you will find some benefits that repeatedly appeal to specific kinds of prospects. You will be looking for that kind of benefit appeal in the early stages of the interview, and often will get verification of your guess that the specific benefit is one of the selling keys for that prospect. Then, when you reach that benefit in the prepared presentation, you can call the prospect's attention to it and drive home how much that benefit can mean. It is as simple as pausing and saying something like "That's the sort of thing you were talking about before, Mr. Smith. These widgets can be used in four different ways, and may solve the setup problem that has been bothering your engineers." Look for a little agreement from Mr. Smith, but do not pause to discuss the whole matter; move on with the presentation.

In a slide–soundtrack or motion picture–soundtrack presentation, it is clearly harder to introduce the personal and empathetic component. But you can still study the presentation and find places for a meaningful look, a nod, and a few words relating what is being shown to the needs and desires earlier discussed with your prospect. And in almost all cases, it is desirable to do that kind of benefit-relating as soon as the presentation is over. It provides an excellent way to start handling objections and to move toward the close.

The most important thing to know about the canned presentation, or about any presentation, for that matter, is that the presentation does not make the sale. You do. No presentation will establish empathy, illuminate prospect needs and desires, handle objections, and use all these things to move to the close. Those are your skills, and they are much of the fun of selling.

Very often, it is possible to develop very effective presentations by combining fully prepared visual and script materials with your own characteristic style and the insights you have gotten from the prospect. It may be as simple as using a company-prepared visual presentation book, with both illustrative visual material and key words and phrases right there on the page before you and the prospect as you are presenting. Or it may be less fully developed, as when you have a whole product line to present, with many alternative ways to go. Then you may be presenting around a single brochure for each product, using the photos and other visual materials in the brochure, the language of the brochure to talk around, and your own language.

The talk-through technique allows you maximum flexibility of expression, and guarantees that you will not leave out anything substantial, or inadvertently mix up the logical order of presentation, or improperly weight presentation elements and so give a distorted benefits picture to the prospect. For most products and in most selling situations, the talk-through is the most effective way to go.

Sometimes you really do go in almost bare-handed as regards presentation materials. It can happen when you are selling for a very small company, or handling several commission lines, or perhaps relying very heavily on samples. It happens less and less, but it still happens.

You cannot very well write a brochure to sell from or develop a talk-through visual presentation. What you can and should do, though, is try to put every significant benefit and feature of each product in writing in the order you think most logical and effective. Figure out where to drop in product samples and any other visual materials you have. Then talk your basic presentation simultaneously into a mirror and a tape recorder. Do it several times before you use it in the field, refining as you go. When you begin to be satisfied with what you have, use it in the field. After each use, jot down some notes on possible refinement. Over a period of time, you will develop a presentation, much as a presentation is developed by any competent home office marketing department team. It may have some deficiencies, but at the very least you will be presenting a complete, clear benefits-and-features product story and moving effectively toward the sale.

Developing a highly professional presentation and group of presentation materials is a job for promotion writers and visual artists, working hand in hand. Although some sales professionals may also be writers, a few may be visual artists, and a very few are both, it is quite unusual to find a field representative developing an excellent presentation. If you are able to do so, fine; but when professionally developed materials are available, they will usually do the job far better—though sometimes with minor modifications suggested by your style and field experience—than you will be able to do yourself.

At the same time, it is vitally important that you know

how to build at least the modestly effective presentation described above. Without the ability to do so, your lifetime career mobility as a sales professional is seriously impaired. For without the ability to build a coherent selling story, you will be unable to sell effectively in situations where you must go it alone, as when you are employed by a very small selling organization, or have gone on your own, either in your own selling organization or in some other kind of small business that requires you to develop a sound selling story.

A good many things can happen in a selling situation; and in the course of a sales career, everything that can happen will happen, usually more than once. There are times when distractions seem to multiply, and other times when it all goes so smoothly that you wonder when and what axe will fall just before the close, frustrating all that has gone before. Some interruptions and distractions will be just that; others will seem so to the neophyte, but will be recognized by the professional as paths to the close. Sometimes smooth sailing will be just that; but often going fluently and uninterruptedly through an entire presentation means only failure to engage the prospect in any way, leaving you with a blank wall where a close should be.

A sound presentation is a story with a beginning, a middle, and an end. For that story to be told well, it must be told more or less in sequence, although not necessarily in exact sequence and entirely whole, as conceived by whoever wrote it. At the same time, a sound presentation is one that helps engage the prospect, who if engaged can be counted on to behave like a lion, rather than a lamb. Someone who is right with you while you are presenting is likely to interrupt, ask difficult questions out of sequence (your sequence, that is), disagree, cut you short, discuss entirely irrelevant matters, and generally behave the same way you would in his or her shoes. To the beginner, and especially a beginner stumbling along trying to remember a completely canned presentation, a really engaged prospect often seems a disaster, rather than someone providing a multitude of closing tools. Of course, the prospect who is far more considerate, and says nothing at all, is quite likely to look a little puzzled after all has been fully recited, and say something like "Thanks, I'll think it over. Good day," or "I'm not entirely sure I understand all that. Would you mind going over that once more? I can give you ten more minutes."

The good professional knows how to stay on the presentation track, while at the same time seeking to engage the prospect. That means being ready for all the interruptions, being poised to handle them well and then to move on. The seller has an immense advantage over the prospect in this: the seller has been there before, a thousand times, and knows what to expect and how to handle it. To control the pace and focus of the situation is to control the whole situation, and much of success or failure in the selling situation—most obviously during the presentation—rests on who controls pace and focus.

Control depends significantly on composure. All of us are familiar with the prospect who plays power games—interrupts to raise purposely misleading questions, attacks your company, accuses you covertly or even overtly of misrepresentation—the kind of person who reflexively attempts to dominate all situations in which he or she is a player. But even that kind of very difficult person can be handled and sold, as long as professionalism is maintained throughout the interview. Professionals do not lose their temper or argue with prospects. They may disagree, even sometimes quite sharply, and express that disagreement, but with composure. Rarely, professionals may even walk away from a particularly disagreeable prospect. Mostly, professionals routinely handle whatever comes up, stay on track, and use seeming interruptions as tools to further the close.

During the presentation, an early question or objection is often encountered, one that you quite routinely expect but want to defer until you have spoken your piece and have laid the foundations for handling it and turning it in the direction of the close. For example, you have just launched your presentation, and the prospect stops you with "Before we go any further, I think you ought to know that we've been buying widgets just like these from Smith and Smith for the last ten years—and we like them fine."

Ah, Smith and Smith, your main competitors, and a set of products you are quite ready to meet head-on when you must. But not now—it's premature. You do have some idea of what you are up against, though, and that can be helpful later. Your response is likely to be something like "Yes, they're a good company. As we go on here, I think you'll see how some of the unique features of our widgets make them especially suitable for you." And on with your presentation, ready to meet Smith and Smith directly later, when it is more appropriate.

Even more often, the prospect has a much-too-early—for you, that is—price question. You are three minutes into your 15-minute presentation, and he or she says, "Excuse me, but how much will the basic system cost me?" That may be an early, casual question that can easily be handled with "Far less than you might imagine," or "I think you'll find them very affordable," then adding to either "particularly with the kind of savings (or whatever other kinds of benefits apply) you will realize from their use. Let me show you how that works as we go along here." And on with the presentation.

The early price question may be just a question, or it may be a crucial question in the mind of the prospect, and one from which the prospect may not so easily be turned. If so, it is still worth trying hard to defer it until later, for if the price question comes up before the product story is told fairly, it may dominate the selling situation, destroy your pace and your focus on the unique benefits of what you have to offer, and kill your sale. If, in the long run, you come to believe that not answering the price question directly will fatally harm your ability to build empathy with your prospect, creating a wall of mistrust between you, then you certainly must answer it—but not until you must.

You may also get an assertion of fact that must be handled with a direct answer. Your prospect may say, "I'm afraid you're barking up the wrong tree here. I believe that your whatsit is incompatible with our whosits." Then it must be a matter of agreement and switch to another product or go on back out the door, or "I think you'll find they are compatible; our engineers have seen to that. Let me show how that works as we go along here." And go back on the presentation track, informed as to a potential problem, and supplied with a closing tool for later.

Interruptions also occur. The prospect who is interrupted five times during the course of a rather brief presentation by secretary, colleagues, and telephone may find it hard to attend properly to you and your selling story. That can destroy a sale; if it is really impossible, you may have to break off and come back to sell another day. More typically, though, you will patiently wait through the interruption, review a bit before going on, and then move back into the presentation. Trying to sell through an interruption does both you and the prospect an injustice.

Only neophytes seriously try to close during the course of their presentations. Occasionally, a prospect will "take the product away from you," cutting the presentation short with questions and comments that so clearly indicate an intent to buy right now that you would be remiss in not closing on the spot. But that is, regrettably, all too rare an occurrence. What does sometimes happen, however, is that a "trial close," that terribly misnamed and entirely right attempt to engage the prospect and simultaneously see how well you are succeeding in doing so, is misunderstood—by seller, prospect, or both—and taken to be a serious closing attempt.

A trial close is only a device—a reflexive question put by the seller—that attempts to get some kind of modest agreement, as when you say, "Doesn't that make sense to you?" or "Don't you agree?" or any other such question as you proceed with your selling story. A blank stare or perhaps the tiniest shrug is a pretty clear indication that you are not getting through; a thoughtful nod or encouraging smile is an indication that you are at least mutually engaged in the selling situation. The trial close is therefore a device aimed at building empathy and agreement—nothing less, but nothing more. To go from the agreement gained in a trial close into a serious attempt to close may destroy whatever empathy you have so far developed, and that is the kind of setback that can cost a sale.

In developing a presentation technique, it is vital to understand that form must in this instance follow function. A demonstration or installation can be achieved in a darkened room and using wholly standard and literally canned (or filmed or cassetted) presentation materials; but a sale can rarely be achieved under those conditions. Marketing managements are sometimes hypnotized by visual and machine-assisted presentation materials, insisting that their sales representatives use them to the exclusion of empathy-building techniques—but not for long, because canned techniques standing alone seldom work for very long. They may work during a new-presentation introduction period, when all else in the selling organization is focused upon them, and while they have the virtue of novelty. And many kinds of visual and audio materials can be extremely useful in selling situations, especially when highly technical products are being sold. But in the long run, no matter how much pressure is applied to a field force by a temporarily wrongheaded marketing management group, skilled sales professionals find ways to use canned materials as adjuncts, rather than as the main motor forces of their selling stories. This is because effective long-term personal selling depends on empathy and mutual problem solving, and that must be done on a person-to-person, situation-by-situation basis, with seller applying products and services to prospect problems, needs, and desires.

That is true even in a group presentation situation, where the need to present to more than one prospect may vitiate the impact of your one-on-one approach, and where you must consider the dynamics of the group in presenting and selling. We are here discussing formally presenting to a group, rather than the kind of informal group presentation retail sellers very often encounter, which we will discuss later.

To a considerable extent, successful group presentation depends on your ability to make and develop one-on-one empathetic selling relationships with one or more of the group's members, while at the same time avoiding the potential trap of falling between contending group members. That means attempting, during the early stages of the interview, to identify the relationships between group members. Sometimes that is very easy: a primary influence in the group self-identifies or is identified by the other group members. When you are presenting to an executive who has brought in several subordinates, your working hypothesis has to be that you are selling primarily to that executive, though you will be watching carefully to see who else in the group may be in a position to seriously influence the buying decision.

On the other hand, you may find yourself presenting to several relatively equal prospects, some of whom are pursuing disagreements that have little to do with you and your product. Then it is a matter of doing your best to get agreement from two or more key prospects, a far more difficult but not at all improbable achievement. It is often tempting to try to play one prospect or group against another in such a situation, forcing the issue by making it turn into a demonstration of power by the most powerful in the group, and making it part of whatever set of internal battles your prospects are involved in. That may force a sale, once in a long while. More often, it will destroy it, and with it your future possibilities with all or some of the group members. People inside an organization may squabble bitterly among themselves, and even let an outsider see them doing it, but they bitterly resent an outsider who attempts to take advantage of their divisions, and they often close ranks against that outsider.

It is often worthwhile in group situations to try to spend more time than you normally would on the early empathy-building stages of the interview, even stalling a bit as you attempt to sort out the structural and power relations between group members, so that you can try to begin to build empathy with the right people in the group before moving into your presentation. That kind of sorting out can be an indispensable adjunct to group selling.

A group presentation is often longer than your normal one-to-one presentation, partly because of the need to sell to more than one group member, but mostly because you may need to repeat yourself a great deal. What is clear to one group member may be absolutely opaque to another. Someone may have missed a basic assumption, been a little shy about saying so, and then demonstrate incomprehension later on, forcing you to review a substantial portion of your presentation. Two group members may have engaged each other in conversation, forcing you to review for them. Several people may listen to your answer to a question during the presentation and start a lively discussion that you find hard to control, or may ask the same question again and again in slightly different ways. The generally correct thing to do is to treat each question or comment with as much close attention as you would if it were coming from the most influential member of the group, answering again questions that have been asked before, re-presenting briefly, as necessary.

Whether fully memorized and using completely canned materials, or done in a talk-through fashion with a minimum of presentation materials—and any of the gradations between—the great enemy of effective presentation is routine. In this, the seller is like an actor in a long run; unless new meanings and depths are found day after day, in the same role or making the same basic presentation, it is highly likely to all turn flat, stale, and boring to you and your prospect. To the neophyte, the great enemy seems to be loss of memory and failure to "get it all in"; but quite the reverse is true. Learning to get most or all of it in is easy; keeping it fresh and therefore effective can be very difficult and challenging.

Keeping it fresh and effective depends to some extent on developing technique and a variety of alternative moves within the framework of the presentation. It depends to a much greater extent on making real contact with the prospect in those vital first few minutes and building that contact and empathy all during the presentation. That is what keeps the presentation—and you, the presenter—fresh, interesting, and effective, both in the short run as regards the specific sale, and in the long run, throughout a career.

Technique itself comes with practice. An exceedingly good presentation is a matter of combining complete familiarity with presentation materials and the language of your selling story with a great deal of product knowledge, and joining all that with the early contact and empathy you have started to build with your prospect in the early stages, before a word of presentation is uttered. Those who can consistently do that, and place themselves before enough qualified prospects, will sell successfully, whatever their other selling weaknesses may be. If they combine the foregoing with the ability to handle stalls and objections, using them to move toward the close, they will sell even more successfully. And if, beyond that, they know how to use all that has gone before to close consistently, they will be top professionals throughout their careers, whatever they sell and to whomever they sell.

STALLS AND OBJECTIONS

Handling stalls and objections well depends on several prior understandings. The first of them is that effective selling is, by the nature of the human interactions involved, a rather untidy process. Prospects ask all kinds of questions and make all kinds of comments out of sequence, irrationally and often irritably. Even worse, some of them do not question or comment at all, leaving you to go through an entire presentation and come to a close that just is not there, because you never really got started on the selling process. Some prospects tease, nit-pick, and—if you let them—provoke you to fury. This is bad for the digestion, even worse for the sale. There are interruptions, distractions, latecomers who force you to re-present; a dozen different things can happen in the course of a selling interview that can cause you to lose your pace and control. Yet that is a great deal of the fun in selling—controlling the pace, the flow of the action, moving into greater and greater empathy with your prospect, through whatever comes, all the way to the close.

Another main understanding is that it is perfectly natural for people to stall and object, no matter how rejecting that may seem to you. It is not realistic to expect prospects to be able to easily understand what you have to say, to trust you, and to make up their minds to buy. There are quite legitimate questions to be answered, reservations to be surmounted, fears as to making a wrong decision to be dealt with, and skepticism to be overcome.

Beyond the entirely understandable, there is also the deep distrust of people who sell carried by so many Americans in this period. That is a fact of life, and there is no use in turning a blind eye to it, as so many in selling tend to do. Nor will it be overcome by piety or time; the technique of gross overstatement used so widely in some print and broadcast advertising will guarantee that. Unfortunately, it is not just a matter of a few unethical mass marketers—far from it; the practice is woven into the fabric of our commercial life. Every time a pharmaceutical maker sincerely advertises a product containing an unnamed wonder ingredient that the overwhelming majority of doctors recommend—which turns out to be plain old aspirin—several somebodies somewhere shake their heads and know that they are seeing or hearing a plain old distortion of the truth so gross as to amount to a lie. Every time a financial firm touts a product that is highly speculative without really saying so, people are once more reminded that skepticism is a healthy thing. Every time people hear inflated claims of the excellence and reliability of some ultimately nonworking appliance, automobile, toy, or other piece of hard goods, in this era of shoddy work and inflated prices, the honest sales professional's work is made harder. No, we don't lie; but most of the people we see are subjected to a barrage of broadcast lies every day, and are conditioned to expect that we will do the same. That creates an extraordinary need to build trust in you, your products, and your company, a need that must be satisfied if the sale is to be made and the relationship built. Formal sales presentations and accompanying materials can be helpful, but what you do with empathy and how you handle stalls and objections on the way to the close are indispensable.

When that is clearly understood, each successfully handled stall or objection can properly be seen as a milestone on the way to the close, and therefore welcomed rather than seen as annoying rejections to be evaded in the hope that they will somehow go away. Certainly, some are to be deferred, and others will go away as you proceed, but when and how to handle a stall or objection is then a matter of timing and judgment, rather than an expression of anxiety on your part.

Some kind of fear is very often at the heart of the matter in stall and objection handling. It can be as simple as the fear that you will not know enough to supply the right answer to a question, or that even the factually correct answer you do have will somehow create unforeseen difficulties. It may be a matter of overconcern about your own products and company, resulting from your own magnification of internal problems. Or—and by far the most common reason here, as it is in closing—it may be a fear of rejection. After all, no matter how good a closing average you have, there are often many "no's" on the way to a "yes," as well as many failures to make a sale at all. It is not very professional to convert failure to sell into a fancied personal rejection, but we would be less than human were that not to happen occasionally.

Yet it is precisely the ability to combine professional distance with empathy that adds up to effective long-term professionalism in selling. Putting it a little differently, we need to be able to see ourselves and others with whom we are involved in a selling situation as players in a game, while playing that game and empathizing with the other players. Once that basic understanding is achieved, and has grown into a set of reflexive responses, handling stalls and objections becomes a simple, rather enjoyable part of the total selling situation and game. And the seller has a great advantage in that he or she handles the same basic stalls and objections every day, and is therefore far more familiar with them than the buyer. Sales professionals expect and are therefore ready for stalls and objections, and know how to use them to move to the close.

It is the way you handle a question, a stall, or an objection that conditions the interaction between you and your prospect, and shapes what can be either an antagonistic confrontation or a confidence-building step on the way to the close. Here are some basics that can easily be forgotten:

▪ *When the prospect talks, listen hard and responsively.* Your attitude toward whatever matters the prospect raises will be conveyed by the way you listen. If you are handling paper or rummaging around in your briefcase, you will not seem to be paying much attention to what the prospect is saying, no matter how hard you are really listening. When the prospect says something, stop what you are doing, relax, and listen attentively. And listen responsively. Do not sit forward in your chair, move restlessly while the prospect is talking, or seem ready to speak as soon as you can. Sit back quietly, hands at rest, and nod or otherwise indicate thoughtful response to whatever is being said. That cannot be just an "act" either. False interest in others shows. The truth is that if you really listen attentively you will often get much of what you need to move to the close, then or later.

▪ *Respond thoughtfully.*   When the prospect is finished talking, you are going to speak. At that point, you are confronting one of the greatest hazards in selling—the glib-seeming response. When you sell, one of the worst potential hazards you face is the stereotype of the "drummer who talks a mile a minute and has the answer to everything before you get the words out of your mouth. Can't trust any of them . . ."

Even when your prospect is asking you a simple question that you have answered completely and correctly hundreds of times in a hundred other situations, be careful to respond thoughtfully. Remember—it may be a simple enough question and answer to you, but it is a new and perhaps important question to your prospect. A quick answer indicates that you do not think much of the question, and perhaps not much of the questioner either. A slower, more thoughtful answer is always more reassuring on both counts. It requires no more than following hard and responsive listening with a pause in which neither of you is talking and you are obviously concentrating on framing your answer, then a carefully considered, moderately toned, clearly put response. That pause need not be more than a second or two and may be preceded by some sort of nonverbal response—a thoughtful look, a nod, anything that is natural and true when you are thinking about and framing a response.

▪ *Respond empathetically.* There is all the difference in the world between a short, sharp "No!" and a thoughtful, friendly, "I can see your point. It may work a little differently here, though." Or "I see what you mean, but I don't believe so." Or even a nonverbal nod, pause, and quiet "No, I don't believe so."

The key to a confidence-building response lies in your ability to separate your regard for and empathy with the prospect from any potential disagreement over what the prospect is saying. It is the basic difference between argument and friendly discussion. You may disagree with a good friend over any number of substantial matters without losing—and often actually deepening—the friendship. You may find that you and your prospect are far apart on many specific business and product questions, yet you will make the sale. Once the prospect has grasped the idea that you are a warm, friendly, helpful, well-informed professional, many seeming obstacles disappear.

You need not agree, though much standard advice to neophyte sellers revolves around getting immediate agreement or seeming agreement followed by going off in one of several turn-the-conversation-to-your-advantage directions. The trouble with blindly following the "seeming agreement" advice is that sellers who do that often run head-on into the "insincere" stereotype. "Sure, they agree with everything you say to disarm you, then twist it around to make it seem as if you really agree with them."

Selling is selling, but as selling has permeated every aspect of American life, prospects have changed a little, often with good cause. People with their buying hats on are a little warier than they were 30 or 40 years ago, when the main reflexes of many now in senior sales management were formed. The advice to agree easily, disarm the prospect, and then move on to handle the hurdle was good advice a generation ago, but today those tactics often run into a wall of skepticism. It is far better to focus on how you listen and respond than to rely on mechanical agreement.

Often, your response will be neither agreement nor disagreement, but a question of your own. You may want to clarify the prospect's question or objection. You may simply want to understand the prospect's comments better, so that you can best frame satisfactory answers. Or you may want to use questions to help the prospect better understand the matters raised. People often frame questions imprecisely. They sometimes ask questions quite different from those they have in mind, questions that can use a little clarification before you give answers that might confuse an already confused situation.

You may want to determine whether re-presenting is called for. Sometimes you will go through much or all of your basic presentation only to find your prospect asking questions and expressing objections that make you feel you may not have communicated on some key points. You will probe then, trying to see where you went wrong. You may very well answer the question or handle the objection by a considerably wider re-presentation than would seem to be called for by the prospect's comments. Often, answering the prospect simply and directly is far from enough; what is called for is going farther back into the benefits story and placing your answer within the context of that story.

For example, you may tell the whole benefits story and immediately find your prospect raising competitive price objections. You thought you had anticipated those objections by stressing quality, durability, and cost effectiveness. Obviously, it did not take. You can restate your conclusions and follow up with proof materials. Or you can restate your conclusions, back up into that part of your presentation, and then come forward to the proof stories.

Answering a question with a question can be a good clarifying technique. Alas, all too often it is not a clarifying technique at all, but rather an argumentative technique. The trouble is that it is very easy to go over from clarifying to arguing. And even when you are quite careful and do not step over that line, your prospect very often does not know it. And what can be very funny on stage can be a disaster in a selling situation. Arguing with questions is a much-used, properly avoided objection-handling technique.

There is also the matter of raising questions in the prospect's mind. Anticipating possible objections is a perfectly valid technique, if used with discretion. And discretion consists of stressing the unique benefits you and your product have to offer without making the mistake of raising potentially damaging questions that might not otherwise have occurred to your prospect.

It can happen rather easily, as when you stress the quality of your products, and mention that they are also "a little more expensive" than those of one or more of your competitors. You have perhaps quite properly anticipated a possible price objection on the part of your prospect by stressing quality; but you have also raised the price question, which your prospect might not have seen or raised, and you may have created wholly unnecessary problems for yourself by so doing. Or you may decide to meet a competitor head-on, and sell directly against it right from the start, as so many mass advertisers do. But in so doing you may cause your prospect to seriously consider your competitor—which might otherwise not have happened—and perhaps seriously harm your own possible sale. When price, competition, or any other kind of objection is raised by your prospect, you will handle it, in your own way and in your own time. But when you cause the objection to be raised by something you say or do, you have made a possibly costly error—one that can be easily avoided, with care.

Stalls and objections are easy to identify and deal with—in a book. For in a book we separate them and deal with them individually for study purposes. But in life they come in groups, inextricably intertwined. People often have complex reasons for making buying decisions, and seldom say exactly what they mean in selling situations; indeed, they often do not know precisely what they mean or why they buy. That is up to us to figure out in the course of selling to them.

COMMON STALLS AND OBJECTIONS

Here are some of the most common stalls and objections. They may come early, before the presentation. They may come during the presentation, or after the presentation. They do come, one way or another, at one time or another, throughout a career in selling. There are relatively few of them, though to the beginner, who has not yet had a chance to get used to them, they may seem legion. To the seasoned professional, they are all a little different, because each situation and each prospect is a little different, but at the same time they resolve themselves into a few basic hurdles to handle on the way to the close.

The three most common kinds of objections encountered in the field have to do with price, competition, and your own product. The price objection cuts across most other potential hurdles. Competitive objections, need, and product questions are all often put in terms of price. Many hidden objections add up to price, as do many outright stalls and evasions.

There is no easy answer to the price objection—but there is one essential way to handle it from the start. That way is to see your product as a unique benefits story and to tell that story fully and well. If prospect needs and desires are well enough stimulated by your benefits story, price will often play a minor role in the buying decision. That is why price is one major objection you will try hard to defer, no matter how sharply it seems to be raised early in the interview. Occasionally you will have to put price forward early, but even then you should try to proceed immediately with the presentation to show how well your prices are justified by the benefits attached to product purchase. No matter how straightforwardly and sincerely the prospect raises the question of price as the key to the buying decision, if you let in the question of price too early, you run the risk of price dominating the entire discussion and pushing aside your benefits story before it can be told. Then the odds become great that you will lose the sale.

Many sales professionals have whole lines to sell, with a number of models, styles, and price options. Therefore, when you move into a selling situation, it is often a little difficult to decide precisely which product to present. In those situations, part of what you are doing in the early stages of the interview is trying to develop information that will help you decide which product or products to present.

When that is the case, and you run into strong price objection, early or late in the interview, it is often tempting to move with the objection and step down to a lower-priced product. That is usually a mistake. You have partially or fully presented a benefits story, and at that point can expect your step down to result in a discussion that turns almost exclusively on price, rather than on the benefits connected with the lower-priced product. You may even find that the lower price is acceptable, but that some key benefits available with the purchase of the higher-priced product are make-or-break for the prospect. Then you are trapped, and you probably can't close the sale either way. You may also find, after stepping down, that price is not really the main issue at all, and that the sale swings on other factors. Then you still have not presented a full benefits story for any product, are in a discussion that hinges on price, and are quite unable to recover.

If you should run into a strong price objection very early in the interview, before you have presented any benefits story, it is possible to step down without significant penalty as long as you can move into a full benefits story without having the new story aborted by another price objection. But if you are committed and presenting, it is far better to present and re-present on the benefits of the higher-priced product than to let yourself fall into the price objection trap.

You may have some price flexibility. If so, do not let it get away from you early in the interview in response to a price objection. Hold it for the close. It may be an especially important tool where price is a central question to the prospect. Even in closing, though, use price flexibility very carefully. Any sale that depends on price concessions is intrinsically weaker than a sale that closes on customer benefits. Benefits can be stated, restated, and worked with at the close. Price flexibility, once used, again turns the sale on too narrow a ground, and makes the close fragile and easy to lose if the price is not good enough or if the objections turn out to be more than price-related.

Competitive objections can appear at any point in the selling interview. They are almost always best deferred as long as possible, and then dealt with as necessary, rather than anticipated and prematurely discussed. Usually, you will run into competitive objections in a selling situation when you are trying to replace entrenched competition. And the normal reaction of many sellers and sales managers, therefore, is to go head-on into competition, right from the start, making highly comparative presentations and closing on comparative matters.

That is usually a mistake. Replacing competition seldom rests on comparing features and benefits, if for no other reason than that entrenched competition is indeed entrenched. The prospect is accustomed to the competition; there is an existing set of working relationships with the competitive company and selling staff. And remember, the prospect has bought the competition and is satisfied that good judgment was shown in the purchase.

A competitive presentation is best handled like any other presentation, but with more sensitivity to inevitable competitive comparisons as you handle objections and move to the close. That means presenting your products as a unique benefits story, not with competitive comparisons from the start. Competitors need not even be mentioned until, and unless, the prospect brings them up.

When competitive objections are raised, however, you had best have done your homework. You need to know the nuts and bolts of your competitor's products as well as you do your own. You need to know strengths and weaknesses, prices, applications, main selling approaches, and the main competitive arguments used against you and your products. Your company will usually be very helpful in this area; so will your multiple contacts with prospects who buy competitive products.

You will always get far more mileage out of stressing and restressing your own benefits than in attacking the weaknesses of competitors. Do not worry about the prospect not knowing competitive weaknesses. Just as your customers know many of the weaknesses of your product, so competitive customers know the weaknesses of what they are buying.

Product objections can arise around anything you sell. A prospect may say something like: "I don't think this is for us. It won't do the job we want done," or "No, it looks a little too fragile to me. And I'm not too sure the styling would suit us." There are a good many entirely honest, straightforward product objections. They are expressed in terms of product deficiencies, but they are always to be answered in terms of benefits. You will normally answer the honest product objection with re-presentation of features and translation of those features into user benefits. You will often follow with proof stories that tell of customers satisfied in just the areas in which your prospect has doubts. Those doubts, once put to rest, can often become the levers you will use to close the sale. If you can prove to the prospect's satisfaction that your product is not fragile, but very strong and durable, and if that is an area of major prospect concern, then you have probably also found a major buying motive.

Product objections are often comparative. People often buy whatever they think is the best choice available, and rarely wait for the "ideal" product to come along. If the prospect feels that your product "won't do the job," there is probably some thought that a competitive product will. Your astute questioning will often be able to uncover the hidden competitive objection, and enable you to deal with it.

Occasionally, there are expressed reservations or even open hostility toward your company: "We bought a gross of widgets from your company two years ago, and none of them worked right. Tried to get credit, and had to go through a lot of red tape to get it."

That is not too hard to straighten out. You will try to find out what went wrong, and let the prospect know that your company has a wonderful customer service department, especially since the new complaint processing system was installed. You will also have several happy customers the prospect can call to prove how well your company handles complaints these days. Your prospect has gotten what was probably a very minor complaint, which has become magnified over the years, off his or her chest. You have responded soothingly, and you can both get down to business.

More often, it is a matter of vaguely remembered problems with your company, or bad word-of-mouth in the industry, or even competitive badmouthing. Then you must empathize, present, and re-present your benefits story, and let the hidden objection either be forgotten or eventually surface. If the objection is a tough one, it may be at the root of the stall you have had a hard time handling, and may give you a good deal of trouble at the close. But it may be the kind of hidden objection that is overcome by the warmly empathetic relationship you and your prospect develop during the interview. Convinced of the potential benefits, but unsure about the company, the prospect buys your honesty and the kind of guarantees that that honesty brings.

Once in a great while, the problem is not a matter of price, competition, product, or company, but of the relationship between you and your prospect. Sales professionals very, very rarely trigger adverse personal reactions with anything they say or do. Your chances of generating that kind of reaction are remote. But your chances of running into someone "who got up on the wrong side of the bed this morning" are far from remote. Your chances of selling to people who are under severe personal and business pressures of many kinds are quite good. Your chances of running into people with ego problems, who are personally abusive to those around them, are excellent.

No sales professional should take personal abuse—and those who refuse to take abuse get the respect of all those they meet. That does not mean meeting abuse with abuse, emotion with emotion. It means developing and keeping a friendly, businesslike approach in every selling situation. If possible, a descent to personalities is to be ignored, while you get on with your business. If it cannot be ignored, then it is time to leave. Do not argue or get emotional—just leave.

It is also possible to run into prejudice, which by its very nature is unreasonable, irrational, and destructive. Women can run into sexual prejudice. Blacks can run into racial prejudice. People have all kinds of language, ethnic, age, and appearance prejudices.

You are there to sell, not to try to change the social attitudes of your prospects. You are there to sell, not to lose your composure. And you do not have to take any abuse at all. Do what you are there for, ignore covert prejudice, and do whatever is necessary to keep your self-respect in the face of overt prejudice. If that means terminating the interview, do so. Most of the time, it will mean selling right on through, by your very composure and professionalism effectively removing the problems caused by prejudice. Prejudice springs from ignorance, and your prospect's working contact with you and other targets of prejudice will do more to bring about attitude change than all the arguing in the world.

Many objections are unspoken. They are often called *hidden objections*—but they're hidden only to the unprofessional eye. When you have presented fully, clearly, and well, answered some questions, turned some objections into closing tools and seeming product weaknesses into product strengths, and the prospect is still cold, you know it. You know that somewhere along the way you missed some vital clue or clues, missed some unspoken central objection. You will probe, re-present, and try to smoke out what it is you have missed so far. It might be anything, or a combination of factors. It may be as simple as general uneasiness, resulting from an inadequate grasp of the benefits picture. It may be unspoken competitive objection. Or it may be that you have misassessed the rightness of the prospect; you may be talking to someone who cannot make the buying decision.

The unspoken objection is often part of a stall—"I won't buy now, but I won't tell you the real reason why." The key to smoking it out usually lies in the first few minutes of the interview, before you have even begun to present. If you have handled the empathy-building stage of the interview well, most of what might have been unspoken objections will be spoken. And if you have built empathy well, those objections that remain unspoken will become spoken for the asking.

There is some debate among sales trainers and managers about whether or not to come right out and ask for the unspoken objection. Those who are for it in essence say, "Why not? If you are deep into the interview and still have not smoked out the hidden objection that is holding up the close, you have little to lose by asking for unspoken objections, even 'putting words in the prospect's mouth' to try to smoke out the objection." Those who oppose it in essence say, "Don't do it. You may raise objections that were never in the prospect's mind. Even if you don't, you'll lose control of the interview."

Unnecessary debate—it misses the point. If you have no real empathy, and have not smoked out the real objection, it does not matter whether you ask or not. You will not get what you want, and you will not make the sale. Conversely, if you have real empathy, there will be very few unspoken objections, and your prospect will be glad to tell you what the problem is if you ask. The truth is that the prospect often has no more idea of what the hidden objection is than you do, and needs to figure it out with you before it can be dealt with.

Note that unless you have made a prospecting or early information-gathering error, and are trying to sell something entirely inappropriate to your prospect, "I don't need it" is never to be taken as literally true. It always means something else, like "I'll keep the one I have. You haven't convinced me yours is worth the money," or simply "I'm not convinced." The main tactic then is re-presentation and careful questioning to determine the real set of hidden objections. "I don't need it" may hide any kind of objection or stall.

Stalls are scarcely diabolical plots aimed at frustrating your best efforts—though they often seem so. There is nothing quite so frustrating as the prospect who goes all the way with you to the close, and then responds with some variation of "No, not right now. I'll think it over. Don't call us—we'll call you," or "I'm just not convinced it will do the job. Maybe I ought to think it over a little while longer."

Here are some major reasons for stalls:

▪ *Unwillingness to make a buying decision.*   Most people dislike making decisions, especially buying decisions. No matter how well everything else has gone, there is often that final hurdle to surmount. That is much of what closing is about, and why closing merits very special treatment in any book on selling. The stall is almost always directed at avoiding the buying decision, often at forestalling any attempt on your part to close. It is sometimes a conscious maneuver on the part of the prospect, but much more often quite unconscious.

▪ *Inability to make a buying decision.*   Sometimes you are talking to someone who cannot make a buying decision at all, as when an assistant is "screening" products for a superior who will make the buying decision. If you find that to be true, you will have to make an on-the-spot, sometimes difficult, decision as to whether or not to press for an immediate interview with that superior. It is often preferable to come back another day to present to the real prospect rather than spinning your wheels and perhaps being eliminated by the unqualified assistant.

On other occasions, you may find yourself with a thoroughly qualified prospect, but one who finds the size of the buying decision larger than anticipated. When that happens, you may not really know whether you are being put off by the "I have to talk to my partner (or company president) about this" stall, or whether it is simply fact. In the vast majority of instances, it is just a stall, and it is worth trying to move through to the close. Very often, your prospect will be unwilling to admit inability to make a buying decision, feeling that this somehow diminishes his or her standing in your eyes. Then you may get all kinds of stalls and evasions, and will have to try to reach through to the hidden objection, which is simply pride.

  • *Lack of conviction.* Sometimes the stall just means "Sell me some more. I'm not convinced." Then the prospect is not really saying no, will not say yes, but wants you to somehow do it all again, without literally redoing the whole selling interview.

When you perceive that kind of motive for the stall, you will want to re-present on strengths, use agreed-upon strengths to move to the close. You will "review" whatever seemed most important to the prospect, get agreement again and again, question to try to find hidden objections, and try to build further upon the confidence in you, your company, and your products that has been developing throughout the interview. Often it is a matter of giving the prospect a little more time to get used to an idea and move to the buying decision. Re-presenting on strengths supplies that time in the most constructive possible way.

CLOSING

And now to the close, to which all that has gone before is prologue. All the attitude building, preparation, prospecting, approaching, presenting, and objection handling add up to one thing: success or failure, sale or no sale, home run or strikeout. None who are sales professionals make any mistake about that—in every selling situation, you either close the sale or you don't. Whatever the reasons and no matter how well you may have positioned yourself to come back and try again another day, no sale is only no sale. Even if you have done everything superbly, you still have not made the sale. Conversely, you may not have done nearly as well as you would have liked during the course of the interview, and still made the sale—and that is ultimately what matters most. However sales professionals work, whatever they do on the way to and at the close, they all share the ability to close successfully, day after day, year after year, all during their selling careers. For without that ability, there is no career in selling.

There is no simple formula that unlocks the secret of successful closing. Nor is there a bag of tricks, a single set of words of art, or a preset number of serious closing tries that works best. All that is pure nonsense, and has nothing at all to do with you, the selling process, or that part of the process that is closing.

There are keys to successful closing, though; and there are techniques that many have found useful at the close. The techniques are quite simple, easy to learn, and, in the right hands, rather effective. But they are the least portion of the matter. What is far more important is your attitude going into and throughout the selling process and how you have conducted the selling interview throughout. The truth is, if you have seen yourself and the selling situation properly, and moved empathetically throughout the selling situation, the close will be there when you and the prospect are ready for it, and there will come a time in the interview when you will close the sale. The truth is also that if you have not been able to move the whole situation properly throughout the interview, no closing technique or combination of techniques will do. It will not matter whether you try to close one time or ten times. The harder you try, the weaker your position will be, and the farther away your prospect. There is no successful hard sell, soft sell, or any sell at all if you have not moved toward agreement throughout the interview.

You cannot very well build confidence in yourself, your company, or your products without really having that confidence yourself. And, as we have previously discussed, there is no way to fake it; your real attitudes permeate every step of the selling process.

We all dislike being rejected by others and dislike repeated rejections most of all. Yet if we develop real fear of rejection, we generate a downward spiral in which rejection feeds fear, fear develops hesitancy that is communicated to prospects, and failure builds on failure. Fear of rejection often turns into a self-fulfilling prophecy, in selling and throughout every aspect of our lives. Fear of rejection feeds fear of failure. In a culture that values success as much as it values anything, the will to win and its flip side, the fear of failure, are extremely powerful motivators. The will to win and fear of failure exist side by side. Although the will to win is stressed and is held consciously as a major goal, the fear of failure is the dark, hidden side that exists in every powerful, competitive winner. In a very real sense, then, fears of rejection and failure are perfectly normal—everyone has them. And like any other fears, they are not to be suppressed and overridden. That leads only to stiffness, rigidity in personal and business matters, and unnecessary and counterproductive personal pain.

In selling, fears of rejection and failure can best be handled by the kind of professional excellence, in every aspect of selling, that guarantees success. In a way, that sounds absurd—you handle your fear of losing by winning. But it is not at all absurd when you consider how a sound sales professional wins. The winning sales professional is much like a star scorer in any sport. When the puck goes into the net, the ball through the basket or between the goal posts, it is not a fluke. When you see a superb athlete working, you know the skills and the moves are there. Yes, success builds on success, scoring on scoring, close on close. But the really skilled sales professional knows that whatever the product, the company, the competition, the advantages and disadvantages, there are going to be a lot of successful closes. The reasons are internal, not external. You sell or fail to sell mainly for those internal reasons.

Winning attitudes and fears show up most clearly in closing. It is in closing that direct success and direct rejection come. And, because you cannot expect to hit 1.000 or even .500 consistently, there are usually more rejections and failures than there are successes. A lot more. Even when you make a sale, it may be after several rejections or seeming rejections on the way to the close. In selling, you often seem to be fighting uphill against a wall of rejection or failure, even when you are an outstanding selling success.

The strong closer is simply someone who makes contact with the prospect, builds confidence all the way, and confidently asks for the order again and again when it feels right. The weak closer usually has problems in developing empathy. He or she compounds these problems by sliding away from, rather than handling, stalls and objections for fear of rejection, and then is afraid to try to close. For the strong closer, there are many right times to close. For the weak closer, no time is the right time.

There is really no magic time to close. Nor is there a magic number of times to close. Those who say you must close at least five (or four, six, or ten) times are simply wrong. That is incompetently rendered advice, and not an act of either leadership or friendship, for it misinterprets the nature of the selling process and leads up a blind alley to frustration and failure.

Once developed, you keep the habit of listening, seeing, putting yourself in the prospect's shoes, and continually sizing up where you and your prospect are in the selling situation. Once you learn how to read, you do not forget how to do it. When you have been handling the interview well, you will see and correctly read the closing indicators. No matter which of you is talking, you and your prospect will continue to communicate in many ways, and the prospect's state of mind will be crystal clear to you in most situations.

Even when you run into a prospect who habitually masks reactions, you will see signs that will tell you what you need to know.

Watch most for attitudes expressed nonverbally and in tone of voice. Look at the prospect's body set. Is the prospect sitting back, uninterested, covertly glancing at some papers, or is he or she leaning forward a little, following your comments, fully engaged? Make real eye contact. Eyes go pretty blank and expressionless when you are not getting through. They involuntarily respond when you are. Eyes tend to narrow a little when the prospect concentrates, blink when you make a particularly telling point, and visibly focus and become more alert-looking when you have complete attention.

Watch the prospect carefully. Boredom is often accompanied by a head that is immobile or sags a little, legs that cross and uncross nervously, fingers that imperceptibly and unconsciously tap or play with a pen or paperweight. As real interest develops, the body becomes more focused and still, leans forward. Hands often open and move a little in tune with your gestures; the head nods imperceptibly in agreement. Not the full, studied nod that is used by many as a defensive tic—the imperceptible nod that means real agreement.

Tone tells you a great deal. Personal warmth usually means you have gotten through at least partially; studied coldness usually means you have not even made contact, no matter how long you have been in the room. Of course, sometimes a cool, dry style can merely be a good defensive stance, so that coolness alone does not mean rejection. Tone is best considered in terms of how questions are asked or answered. "Did you say these widgets will last ten years on average?" can be a strong closing indicator or an expression of complete incredulity. You are not about to try to close someone who has just come very close to calling you a liar; you will re-present on strengths.

Some specific questions are prime closing indicators, if their tone is right. A price question late in the interview, with your prospect starting to write down the figures you supply is often a message to ask for the order right now. Late-interview questions on delivery time, service contracts, customer relations policies, and other post-sales matters very often mean you should close now.

Assuming sale is often described as a closing technique. In that context, it simply means getting to what you think is a right time to close, assuming that the customer is with you, and moving right past the buying decision. When you assume sale, you shift focus to such matters as choice of options, delivery, installation dates, and other minor considerations, and away from the possible barrier created by focusing on the buying decision itself. It is usually done with the order form, or some such device aimed at focusing attention on post-buying decision mechanics. And when well done, it is an excellent closing technique, the technique most favored by sales professionals.

It is the most favored and widely used technique for an excellent reason: it is far, far more than a closing technique. In fact, the "assume the sale" attitude permeates the entire selling process; it is an attitude that favorably affects every step of the process, every aspect of the developing relationship of confidence between you and your prospect.

When you move into a selling situation, you will assume that you are there to close a sale. Not to meet someone or to present your products, but to close a sale. Every move you make will spring from that assumption. And it is not a matter of whether you will close the sale, but only of when. That means understanding that every step toward prospect confidence is a step toward the close, that every "yes" develops further yeses, every "no" breeds more nos.

You will be looking for verbal and nonverbal yeses, avoiding negatives. You will try very hard not to ask questions that can be answered with a simple "no." You will want affirmation on a minor matter rather than triggering a "no." For example, early on you are unlikely to ask: "Do our widgets look right for your operation?" You are much more likely to ask: "How might these widgets fit into your operation?" It is really the same question, but not one the prospect can simply answer "no." That is why you will look for the "how, which, when" kinds of questions, rather than the "yes or no" questions. It is also the reason for avoiding the "why" kinds of questions if possible. The answers to "why" questions often take you so far off the track that you do not reach the affirmation you are looking for at all.

In a very real sense, "assuming sale" describes much of what you are trying to do, and can be your most powerful tool throughout the selling process. It is natural to move from a well-handled question or objection into a close. You have told the benefits story, built a good deal of agreement, answered some questions, and handled some objections. At this point, you have a pretty good idea as to where you and your prospect stand, and you think it is time to start asking the prospect to buy now.

For example, you have just successfully handled a major price objection late in the interview. Your prospect seems satisfied, interested, untroubled by any other pressing questions at the moment. However you choose to ask for it, what better time to ask for the order? If the prospect is not ready to buy, nothing has been lost. You have sized up the situation well enough to bet that "no" will really mean "not yet" or "sell me a little more—I'm not quite convinced." On the other hand, if you have guessed wrong about the prospect's state of mind, it is time to learn about the error. If it gets too late, you will run out of re-presenting time.

People are used to being asked to buy. Your prospect would not be talking to you if he or she were not considering buying what you have to sell. It is only when the closing attempt is entirely inappropriate, when you and the prospect just have not gotten together, that resentment can arise.

When they do buy, it is likely to be when they have developed real confidence in you, your company, and your products. The well-handled objection converts what the prospect thought might be a substantial weakness into a strength—sometimes a substantial strength. That develops confidence, and provides a closing opportunity.

It is important to distinguish between removing an objection and developing confidence. It is one thing to point out successfully that your price is competitive. That removes a price objection, and is desirable. But it is far more important to make the competitive price point and then move forward to advantage, the kind of advantage gained from combining competitive price and longer wear. "Ms. Jones, we estimate that our combination of competitive pricing and far greater durability will save you between 20% and 25% of the money you now spend for widgets over a 10-year period. Given your widget consumption, that should come to between $80,000 and $100,000, or $8,000 to $10,000 per year. Would you like delivery March 1, or would April 1 be better for your planning purposes?" Converting the well-handled objection into a close is a natural, sound way of moving to success in the selling situation.

Beware the *trap close*. It happens every day in automobile agencies. Seller has some price leeway, prospect has a price objection. It is late in the interview. Seller feels that giving way on price without pinning the prospect down is a waste of what may be the only closing tool left. Seller finally says: "Well, I just don't know. I guess I can try knocking $500 off this price, but I don't know if I can make it stick. Let's write it up on that basis, and give it a try." Prospect agrees, and they write it up. Of course, the order goes through, being well within the price leeway the seller has.

"Aha! Trapped the prospect. That is one good way to do it. Nothing tricky or sneaky about it—all's fair in love, war, and selling."

That's what you think. In this suspicious age, the prospect is much more likely to have snapped to mental attention when the seller tried out this hoary old chestnut and said something like: "Wait a minute. Why don't you go right on back to the office over there and see if you can sell the car at this price. If you can, let's talk about it some more. If you can't, tell me so. And if no one here can settle the price, I'll just take a walk for myself. Saw some nice cars a little way down the street." And then the seller has lost whatever confidence the prospect had been building up all during the sales process. The odds are that any price concession then will not be enough. Previously handled prospect reservations and objections will suddenly resurface. The prospect will want more time to think the whole thing over. No sale.

That is called the trap close. Sometimes it is described as the boomerang close. Occasionally, it is dressed in new jargon to hide its true nature. And it is the kind of thing that sometimes gives selling a bad name. Don't use it. For every "successful" use, you will have many of the worst kinds of failures, the kinds of failures that alienate prospects and create the kind of bad word of mouth that ruins sales careers. Your integrity and credibility are crucial success factors, and that kind of shoddy trickery destroys them.

A closing technique is just a way of asking for the order. It is valuable to have several good ways of doing it, if only because you are very likely to ask for the order several times in the course of the interview, and it sounds and feels forced to ask the prospect to buy now again and again in exactly the same way.

One prime technique is to assume sale. Your assumption of eventual sale has been your central attitude all during the selling process. Now, at the close, you want to make it easy for the prospect to hurdle the final barrier—the buying decision itself. The easiest way to do that is to avoid forcing the prospect to say, "Okay, I'll buy it." The decision is made just as surely if it is a silent one, but it is easier to make.

It is often done with the order form. At some point during the interview, seller has the order out, ready to be filled in. Often, the form is placed at the end of the presentation materials, so that it is naturally out and open at the end of the presentation and stays there during the rest of the interview. Then, at an appropriate closing time, pen poised, seller says, "Ms. O'Brien, how do you spell your name?" gets an answer, and proceeds to fill out the form, quietly and completely, as they continue to talk. Then the seller places the order form before the prospect with the place to sign clearly indicated, and waits.

The filled-in order form sometimes generates a startled "Wait a minute. I'm not ready for that yet." Fine, then it is time to re-present and tell the benefits story a little more. The order form still stays right there, waiting for a signature, is often picked up, studied, and signed as the discussion proceeds.

The assumptive technique sometimes works best with simple silence. You have filled out the order form, have it before the prospect ready to be signed, and have stopped talking. The prospect says nothing, is thinking it over. The silence lengthens, deepens, acquires a weight between you. Somehow, you both know that whoever breaks that silence first is at a great disadvantage. What can happen is that the prospect ultimately picks up the pen and signs the contract.

Silence does have a great weight, especially in a room with two people who have been talking for some time. It develops decision-making tension, seems to stretch out, and can fool your sense of time completely. Twenty seconds can seem like a minute, a minute like ten. Use silence as a closing tool if you have the strength to keep quiet. If you are too nervous for it, leave the technique to others; you have plenty of other ways to go.

You can also close on smaller alternatives. This approach is often called a "choice" close or "closing on a small choice," and can provide another good way of helping the prospect avoid the overt, spoken buying decision. In a way, it is like assuming sale, and can often be done with the order form and silence techniques. Choices can be in any post-sale area—options, colors, delivery dates, styles—anything that assumes the sale has been made, the buying decision is behind the prospect, and there are only some minor choices still to be made.

"Good. Would you like delivery March 1, or would April 1 be better?"

"Fine. Would you like it in black or red?"

"Excellent. Do you want it with or without the case?"

You can also close on a special offer basis.

"We have two dozen of these punch presses left, and are
selling them at 25% off their list price. When they're
gone, that's it. We're discontinuing this model."
"We're bringing out this book at $18.95 list until Christ-
mas. After December 25, the list price goes up to
$22.95."
"We have a special introductory price . . ."
"For a limited time only, we're offering . . ."

There is nothing wrong with a bargain-basis closing. It
can move a wavering prospect to make a buying decision
now and act as an effective closing tool. The technique has to
be used carefully, though. For the sake of your credibility
and that of your company, be sure that what you say is true.
The "limited offer" that turns out to be standard is seen by
prospects as a trap close, and resented. It guarantees that
you will run into price objections early and often in the
future, finding them terribly difficult to handle successfully.

If you sell one punch press at 25% off and ten others at
30% off, the odds are pretty good that the prospect who
bought at 25% off will feel "taken," even if the 25% discount
made the press a superb buy. You will create needless
difficulty for yourself by offering varying discount arrangements, and once again will guarantee very serious price
objection and credibility problems in the future.

Watch out for the bargain-basis variant known as the *get
on board* or *standing room only* technique. It goes something
like: "We only have five of these left . . . don't know when we
can get any more at this price, or any more at all for that
matter . . . have to have your decision right now." In a circus
sideshow, it starts "Hurry, hurry, hurry. . . ." Whether it is a
con game or not, it is very likely to be looked upon as one by
your prospects. Don't do it. Leave it at a bargain-basis offer,
and do not try to ram the sale through with these kinds of
pressure tactics. Prospects resent it, it hardly ever works,

and even when it does work it creates ill feeling that costs a lot more than the sale can possibly be worth.

Almost anyone can close "on approval," because that is hardly even selling at all. All that such a *trial sale* does is place your merchandise in the hands of the prospect. It bypasses a real buying decision, and all too often defers it to your very great disadvantage. The worst part of it is that when you sell on approval, the real buying decision is almost invariably made in your absence. You have no real ability to influence the decision from a distance and are not in a face-to-face selling situation with your prospect when the decision is made.

In some kinds of mail sales, especially on low-priced items, selling with "money-back guarantees," "on approval," and on a "trial basis" works very well. It is also a standard arrangement between manufacturer and retailer in a few industries, such as book publishing. But for the kinds of goods sold by most sales professionals face to face with qualified prospects, "maybe" sales like these are not worth doing. It is almost always far better to stick with it, go for a real close, than to settle for a trial sale.

One closing tool that is sometimes neglected is simply asking for the order. At the right time, there is nothing wrong with doing just that. It is often just a matter of saying, "Good. Will you please put your name here?" Note: "put" your name, not "sign" your name; people often have a well-developed aversion to signing anything, but will "put" their names on pieces of paper quite readily.

In some situations, direct asking can be better than either the assumptive or the choice closes. There are a good many direct, businesslike, sometimes rather sophisticated people around who do not like being asked for the order indirectly. They do not want any part of what they think of as selling tricks. They want to make an open, hard, and fast decision and get on with their business. When you are selling to that kind of person, you will know it, and may want simply to ask for the order.

AFTER THE CLOSE

The selling situation is not over after the close. It does not end until you are out the door. What has changed is your relationship with the prospect. That prospect is now a customer, and a new set of obligations and opportunities opens up for you.

Here is the situation. You have closed the sale. There is a signed contract on the table between you and your customer. You have some post-sale details to cover and some selling opportunities as well. You certainly will not want to try to "sell up" at that point. The buying decision has been made, the order signed, and that's it. On another day, you will raise questions relating to more expensive versions of what was just bought; you do not want to upset the sale now.

But that does not mean you will avoid all additional selling now. You know that right after the close there is often a period of euphoria, which, if handled properly, can result in an expanded sale. Most dictionaries define *euphoria* as a blissful feeling, a feeling of great happiness. That is exactly the situation you often find yourself in just after the close. You are happy that you have made the sale; the prospect is happy over the decision, often over having made any decision at all. As long as you do not try to sell something new and large or introduce a whole new set of buying decisions, you can sell some more.

You may want to try for an increased quantity. You may have been talking during the interview about one dozen or two dozen widgets, and have wound up with an order for one dozen. For now the prospect is a customer and may look upon adding another dozen widgets as just a sensible supply economy, when ten minutes before it was twice as large a buying decision. And you may be able to make it a little easier to buy, with quantity discounts that look better now than they did before.

You may want to sell *options*. The outstanding instance of option selling in America is the automobile agency, which closes a car sale and then proceeds to load on additional sales as *options*. It is by no means limited to the automobile industry. All kinds of products, from copying machines to computers, have options, which are really additional sales made after the close.

You may also want to sell replaceables. When you buy a ballpoint pen, you may buy several replacement cartridges. When you buy a copying machine, you have to buy supplies to feed it. After the close is the best possible time to add a substantial replaceables sale to the sale you have just made.

The sale and customer relationship can often be badly damaged when the post-sale mechanics are badly handled. Even if you feel your prospect becoming a little restless after the close and before you have risen to leave, it is worthwhile to spend the small amount of time necessary to guarantee sound post-sale handling of the order.

Be sure that you really know what delivery times to expect on whatever you have just sold. Be doubly sure that your customer knows approximately when to expect delivery, that you will keep close watch over the delivery situation, and will keep your customer informed as to any changes in anticipated delivery dates. Many a promising new customer relationship has foundered on the delivery date question, with euphoria giving way to annoyance and then bitter anger as promised delivery dates go by, a far-off home office makes pledges that are not kept, and the seller is nowhere to be found.

Beware of extra charges. Absurdly enough, a $1,000 sale can be ruined by an unanticipated $5.00 charge. When there are any extra charges at all, be very sure to call your customer's attention to them, whether or not they are plainly printed on the order form for all to see. That means everything—taxes that must be added, normal shipping charges, extra charges for requested rush deliveries—anything, no matter how small the amount, how trivial the extra charge seems. Beware the customer who will cheerfully buy at full price, but somehow feels "taken" by an unstated 50-cent charge.

Whether you install whatever was sold or your company

arranges for installation by others, by all means make sure that what you sold is properly installed, that customer and staff know how to use and maintain it, and that guarantee and repair policies are clearly understood by all. Sound installation and explanation build the customer relationship, paving the way for future sales as well as guaranteeing that current sales stick.

Checking on installation and use is often best done personally. But even when your schedule, as in a far-flung travel territory, precludes a personal appearance just after installation, you are still as near as the telephone. The call to "see that everything's okay" is always much appreciated; failure to make that call has ruined many a customer relationship that could have been saved with a little attention at the right time. Be sure that your customers understand service charges, if any. When you state service charges clearly right at the start of a customer relationship, you are guaranteeing against unpleasant, disruptive surprises. If there is a service contract of some sort, sell it, and make sure it is completely understood, including any extra charges or service exclusions in special situations. You certainly do not want to be identified in the customer's mind with hidden service charges.

Service calls are sales opportunities, and should be treated as such. Every time you service an account, you build up credits and make the customer relationship just a little firmer. A service call may provide an opportunity for making an appointment for a product presentation, turn up a referral from a grateful customer, provide a quick add-on sale.

The party's over—almost. You have done it all and are about to put that signed, option-added, expanded order in your briefcase. Then you are going to rise, shake hands with your happy customer, and leave the premises after smiling at assistants and receptionists.

Once you put that order in your briefcase and rise, it is over. Making an additional sale or getting a key referral after turning dramatically away from the office door to reconfront the customer sounds wonderful. It makes a great training session or sales meeting story. Trouble is, it hardly ever happens—which is why it makes such a good story. It is far better to keep the order on the table, cover it with your hand, pick it up preparatory to putting it away, or just look away from it.

Then ask for referrals. "There is one more thing before I go, Ms. Jones. I'd like to get these widgets the widest possible distribution, feeling as I do about their unusual value for people like yourself. Do you have two business friends I might see about them?"

Word it yourself, in whatever fashion best suits your personal style and the situation. But do ask for referrals, at precisely that time and generally in that way. That technique alone can supply you with a literally endless supply of qualified prospects.

RETAIL SELLING

Mostly, selling is selling. If you are successful at selling business services, the odds are good that you will be successful at selling automobiles. If you are good at selling retail furniture, you will probably be good at selling wholesale groceries. The main face-to-face success factors are the same, whether selling inside or outside, and whether selling tangibles or intangibles. In retail selling, the successful seller makes contact with the prospect, questions, listens responsively, empathizes, learns what needs and desires to satisfy, presents, answers, handles objections, and closes.

There are some special aspects worth noting, though. In outside selling, a great deal of time and attention must be devoted to getting to qualified prospects. You need to organize, prospect, sell interviews, make cold calls—all the time-consuming necessities connected with coming face to face with substantial numbers of qualified prospects.

But retail selling starts with the prospect coming through your front door. A great deal of time, concentration, and cash is spent to get that prospect through the front door, starting with site location and including advertising, promotion, and astute business building, but ultimately the retail prospect comes to the retail seller, rather than the seller to the prospect as in outside selling.

That means the prospect is coming into your totally familiar daily environment, just the reverse of the outside selling situation. The prospect is in new surroundings and needs to ingest the unfamiliar place and its contents. It also means that you often have an excellent opportunity to observe the prospect while letting that process of adjustment proceed.

Prospects come into retail establishments looking to buy. Very occasionally, someone comes in to keep warm for a few minutes on a cold day or spend a few minutes pleasantly browsing, but that is not the main reason most people come in. And even the casual browser, as all bookstore owners know, can be a fertile source of impulse buys. But because they need a little time for adjustment and do not want to be harassed by over-eager sellers, they often adopt the "I'm just looking" attitude when approached.

There is nothing wrong with letting them look before making a real first approach, but let them know you are aware of their presence, if only by a smile and nod while you are taking care of another customer.

Here is a typical situation. A prospect comes through the front door of your appliance store. You are on your feet checking stock a little way back in the store. Your habit of close observation comes into immediate play. In less time than it takes to tell, you mentally register: "Woman, probably mid-forties, casually dressed as people are around town on an ordinary workday, but expensive coat and handbag."

She stops just inside the entrance, blinks, adjusts to the light. It is a sunny day; people need a moment to get used to the dimmer lighting inside the store. She scans the store, sees you, half nods, keeps looking. You nod, smile, make no move toward her. She is in motion, anyway, is looking at some dishwashers a little to the left of the door. She spends a few more moments looking at the dishwashers, studying one medium-priced machine rather carefully, then moving on to another higher-priced machine, then back to the medium-priced machine. You keep on "checking stock," actually watching as carefully and unobtrusively as you can manage.

Finally, she looks up, seems a little puzzled—still not looking at you. But that's your cue. You stop checking stock, make eye contact across the store, focus absolutely full attention, and move to greet her. "Good morning. Can I help you?" At that point, you are fully into the selling situation. From the moment you start moving across the store to greet her, nothing exists for you but the prospect. If you were interrupted in your move across the floor by another customer, you would have said something like "Excuse me, I'll be right over," and kept on going. At the moment you made eye contact, you were committed. The process of empathetic selling had begun.

What you say in greeting is not very important; when and how you say it is. If your approach is easy, open, and natural, rather than bright, artificial, and false, your prospect will respond favorably, whether you are selling outside or inside.

It is easy to assault and thereby insult and alienate your potential customer. The overly aggressive move to the front door with an effusive "Hello. What can I do for you today?" while someone is blinking and getting used to the difference in light can be unsettling and offensive to the prospect. The "merchandise" approach, in which seller accosts unwary customer by flashing a piece of merchandise and extolling its virtues, is great for a circus sideshow, but wildly inappropriate for selling in America in this part of the twentieth century. For just as in outside selling, retail prospects are very, very wary of being "taken," and respond with aversion to what they think are pressure tactics. And remember: they have a very easy answer to pressure tactics—they can simply walk back out through the front door.

When you see a group of people come in together, one of the earliest questions you have to ask yourself is: "Are they buying as a group, or as two or more individuals?" When a couple comes in, starts looking at merchandise together, and within a very few seconds one wanders off and idly strolls the aisles while the other focuses on some merchandise, you are most likely going to be selling to the focuser. On the other hand, beware the stroller. He or she may come back after the presentation and damage the sale.

When two or more people come in and start discussing the merits of some specific merchandise together, you are probably in an informal group sales situation. Then there are some special things to consider during the selling process.

▪ *Identify the primary buyer.*   You want to come as close as you can to knowing who the primary buyer in the group is before you get very far into the presentation. That is accomplished by closely watching who seems to be dominating the conversation, leading the group, before you even approach. You may even want to hold off that approach as long as possible to try to understand the group dynamics as well as you can before going face to face. After the approach, skillful questioning will often make the primary buyer apparent.

▪ *Include all group members in your presentation.* While you are selling to that primary buyer, it pays not to ignore the other group members, perhaps by keeping good eye contact with all group members and moving your eyes to meet each member as you proceed with the presentation.

▪ *Let the group members argue among themselves.* Groups, and especially family groups, are capable of arguing about anything. Sometimes the arguments seem trivial, and the outsider is tempted to comment offhandedly and move on with business. Don't do it. Squabbles often mask much deeper disagreements. It is very easy to get sucked into a family argument and lose the sale. And even if you make the sale, you may not see that family group again.

▪ *Don't use group members against each other.*   Along similar lines, avoid the temptation to use group members against each other when handling objections. It may seem very easy to look appealingly at a husband while a wife objects to a product feature, or at a wife when a husband has doubts about service policies. Again, don't do it. Faced with those tactics, groups will often unite against you.

▪ *Handle all group questions and objections, even if redundant.* In a busy retail establishment, it is very easy for a prospect to be distracted. The environment is unfamiliar, people are moving about, other products suddenly attract and distract. You may be focusing on the primary buyer, and be suddenly confronted by a question you have fully answered some time ago from another group member. When that happens, it is best to answer it all over again, without reference to the previous answer. It is a chance to represent, and it guarantees that you will not be floored by a late ill-informed objection from any member of the group.

▪ *Treat children as part of the group.* It is always be-nice-to-and-patient-with-children week in retail selling. If you possibly can, treat them as adults and include them in the presentation. In doing so, you will often find that children can exert a good deal of positive influence on the buying decision. If you do not, they can distract the prospect, cut short the interview, and ruin the sale.

All too often in retail selling, interruptions occur. The phone rings and must be answered, a deliverer has a question, another customer breaks in with question or comment—your conversation is broken and the selling situation invaded. It will happen. When it does, all you can do is try to keep the interruption brief and keep focusing on the prospect. You can often return a telephone call later, rather than handling it while selling, hold off the deliverer's question or refer it to someone else, do the same with the interrupting customer.

If you must turn away from your prospect, do it with a smile, and make it clear that you are handling the interruption so that you can focus more fully on the prospect when you return. That is particularly effective when you decide to try to handle more than one customer at a time. It is not usually a good idea to try to do so, but occasionally you find yourself somehow boxed into doing it. When you must, the difference between a smiling temporary interruption and an abrupt, harassed breakoff is often the difference between returning to make the sale and finding the prospect long gone when you do return after the interruption.

When your retail establishment has had a quiet day in the middle of a quiet week in a very quiet month, it is very easy to start making weak sales. There are two major kinds, with many variations on the main themes:

▪ *Inconsistent bargains.*   Price concessions are a standard, entirely acceptable way of moving stock that you want moved at less-than usual profit margins. In a bargain sale, a store offers stock at a discounted percentage or at firm below-list prices, and can often generate business by doing so. The trouble starts when the bargains are not uniform, when sellers in individual selling situations show prospects that their prices are anything but firm. Then everything turns on price, very detrimental words get around about your price policies, and you are in trouble. Your good customers feel cheated for having bought at full price, and your prospects want to talk about price rather than hear your product benefits story.

▪ *Money-back guarantees.*   Anybody who offers money-back guarantees is looked on with considerable suspicion in the marketplace. The people you want as customers are unlikely to come in because they regard that kind of "guarantee" as just a come-on, which it usually is. Those who do buy on that basis are merely gullible.

But what often happens is that a seller will say something like "Look, Mr. Smith, why don't you try it? We've been in business a long time, and I can't remember us turning anybody down who was dissatisfied with this product and wanted to return it with full credit. It's nothing I can offer you formally, and I know you'll understand that. But just between us, why don't you try it?"

The temptation for a weak seller and weak closer to try that one is obvious. Many succumb, at one time or another. Don't do it. A combination of dissatisfied buyer and outraged employer can play havoc with your job and career.

In retail selling, as in outside selling, it is strong, consistent empathetic selling that builds a successful sales career.

CHAPTER 5

MANAGING YOUR TIME AND WORK

Managing time and work well is a matter of developing sturdy techniques, based on sound work habits, into lifelong reflexes that will see us through all kinds of situations and jobs, in and out of selling. We are whole people, after all; a fragmented and erratic approach to the personal side of life will inevitably be reflected to great disadvantage on the working side.

A life in selling really requires a great deal of self-management, and backup piled upon backup. For the truth is that without astute and consistent work planning and execution, even the best face-to-face selling skills in the world will not suffice to build selling success and your career. And that excellent self-management is increasingly necessary; prospects and customers, faced with extremely difficult personal and business lives, are all too often pressed and somewhat demoralized by the blizzard of paper, telephone calls, and people in which they find themselves, so we must be better organized than ever before to maximize our field effectiveness.

Sales professionals can all too easily be pressed and demoralized, too, if they let control over their working lives slip away from them. It can happen in a score of ways on any day—a couple of missed appointments, a fire to put out way over on the other side of a territory, a mislaid prospect file, a flood of telephone calls because of a widespread service problem, a maladjusted carburetor, an unanticipated dinner engagement and consequent inadequate preparation for the next day, an insistent home office call about some long-delayed and entirely insignificant report—and all these only begin to tickle the negative possibilities. On top of these kinds of very real external problems, there are the sour apple who manages, over time-wasting morning coffee, to sour your day, too; the argument at home over the time you are spending on paperwork and planning; the complaint from your children last time you set out on the road; the missed quota; the unpaid bills; and myriad other negative emotional possibilities. All of which—the concrete and the emotional—can harm your concentration, your ability to plan and execute, and your sales success, thereby making matters that much worse. Sales professionals depend upon attitude, skill, and consistency; the out-of-control tailspin is the greatest of all short-term hazards, and can grow into a career breaker, if you let it.

That, in the largest sense, is what organization is for: to help you to concentrate, plan, execute well, and build success on success, whatever the negative factors might be in work and life. Efficiency builds sales and makes money; that is a prime result of the proper organization and management of time and work. Beyond that is the control that excellent self-management gives you, which builds your professional career—and that is the most important result of all.

It starts with some basic understandings of what it takes—in time, attention, and skill—to manage a selling career. No, it does not start with organizational forms, complete with neat time charts and boxes to fill in; it starts with understanding, the most important of which stems from analysis of what we must do, and how and when we must do it.

One of the greatest enemies of selling effectiveness is the concept of *prime selling time*. Not only when carried to absurdity, as it so often is by the least effective (and often the laziest) of us; that is easy to see. When a field representative solemnly assures you that the best possible time to sell them is between 10:00 and 11:30 A.M., and between 2:30 (when "they" get back from lunch) and 4:00 P.M., you know that you are looking at either an amateur or someone who thinks you are an amateur. And it is absurd; people will buy what you are selling at any time they are willing to make a firm appointment and place themselves in what they know will be a selling situation. That is axiomatic; all sales professionals know that, whether admitting it to others or not.

But even some professionals fall for the prime selling time concept in a different and quite damaging way. What grows is the seemingly self-serving notion that some times really can be better than others for selling, and that so much other work is connected with selling that some time has to be spent during the working day doing the nuts and bolts kinds of things: prospect file updating, telephone service calls, call reports, pre-heat letters, and a wide-ranging miscellany of time-consuming trivia. That can mean a good deal of office time, whether in the company office, the office at home, or a motel while on the road. Usually, it means starting the actual selling day "just a little later" and ending it "just a little earlier." Except that just a half hour spent on this sort of thing every day, when you should be on the way to your first—and very early, if possible—appointment of the day, can be very, very expensive in the long run. And just a half hour at the end of the day can be equally expensive; so can a half hour spent each morning having coffee with a group of failing time wasters from your office. The fact is that prime selling time is any time your qualified prospects are at work—or elsewhere—and are willing to talk to you in a selling situation. And every possible hour of that prime selling time should be spent setting up selling interviews, getting to those interviews, selling, taking care of existing customers, and refueling self and vehicle as necessary, and the less time you have to spend on getting to them and refueling, the better it is. The paperwork and all that is for another time, when your prospects and customers are not willing to be sold. They are just as likely as you are to be working in nonprime times—just not ready to be sold.

Time, work, and career building are all aspects of a single professional life; all are a single seamless web and all must be managed together, within the context of a satisfying personal life. The controlled weaving together of all these elements adds up to successful self-management; and all depend on constant evaluation and reevaluation, setting and resetting, of personal and professional goals.

In the area of time management, for example, it is always very tempting to start by pointing out that there are only 168 hours in a week, to proceed by setting forth a series of mechanisms that will in the aggregate help us to use our time most effectively, and then to embellish lovingly what is essentially a series of simple techniques with scores of checklists, charts, graphs, and other visual materials designed to help drive home the simple points made. Useful, certainly, but by itself utterly misleading. For without a deep understanding of your own personal and professional goals, and of the work within which you are to a considerable extent encased, these simple techniques will take you nowhere, no matter how effectively and attractively presented. In this instance, one picture is not worth a thousand words; quite the opposite. A few well-chosen words, reflecting your own hard analysis and illuminating the nature of your goals and environment, are likely to be worth a thousand graphs, checklists, charts, and cartoons.

Our main long-term goals are least likely to change as our careers develop. To put it a little differently, jobs, tasks, environments, and career goals may change, but we will continue attempting to keep our home situations stable, maintain our physical and emotional health, build our skills and careers, make our organizations successful, and provide for our later years, no matter how much else changes.

Except for relatively brief periods, as in the early years of selling, or in such unstable periods as those of marital breakup, most of us will insist on trying to develop and grow healthy home situations, no matter what the demands of our work. That is not new; however, the extent and bedrock nature of that insistence is new, and reflects the expectations and emphases developed by two generations of concentration upon such matters as mental health and sound interpersonal relations. It is even quite likely to be true of the "liberated single," who is very often, underneath the appurtenances of life style, just a rather traditional American man or woman who demonstrates the need for stability by attempting to build long-term relationships out of some very unlikely material and situations.

For sales professionals, that bedrock insistence often seems in sharp contradiction with professional needs and job demands. For the truth is that most of us do not work even nearly the hours we seem to work. You may work a 35-hour week—in the field—but aside from holidays you are highly unlikely to have devoted as few as 35 hours a week to the practice of your profession in all your working life. There is always work to do at home, much of it vital to job success. There are always networks to be cultivated for career-building purposes, on the job and also, most significantly, on your "own" time. There are professional publications to read and assess, and professional organizations that quite properly require a good deal of attention. All these on personal time.

Personal time? Nonsense. That is the conceptual error that creates the seeming contradiction between the very real 50–80 hours a week you spend pursuing your career and your bedrock insistence on a sound personal life. To think of the time spent during the "normal" business day as paid work time, and the rest of your professional time as a set of unpaid and deeply resented encroachments upon your personal life, is purely and simply to set yourself up for a life of continual personal resentment and abrasion at home, and for a foredoomed lifelong attempt to somehow cut your out-of-the-field professional time demands as close as possible to zero.

THE DEMANDS OF PROFESSIONAL LIFE

It just does not work that way. It never did. A sales professional can no more avoid "after-hours" professional responsibilities than can a lawyer, who must keep up with current professional developments and develop and sustain client relationships for much of each working week, far beyond the time actually spent in office, court, or library. Or a doctor, who must keep up with professional developments and association activities, even though a direct working week may be as long as 60–80 hours, sometimes even more. Or a manager, who may leave a clean desk at the office after spending a seven-hour day there, but then goes home with a briefcase full of planning and paperwork, and spends large amounts of commuting, evening, and weekend time on work and career-related matters.

Putting it that way, there is no reason to expect that your professional life should be less busy than the lives of other kinds of professionals. Real adjustments must be made between professional and home matters, but they need only be adjustments, rather than the kinds of seemingly unmanageable contradictions that stem from misunderstanding the nature of a professional life. You do not simply sell time, on an hourly, weekly, or yearly basis; you pursue an entire career, with field time and current compensation only part of that career. With that understanding clearly in mind, expectations can be realistic; so can be moves aimed at improving total effectiveness, saving valuable time, and increasing control over both professional and personal life.

In any event, sales professionals should expect to spend a good deal of valuable working time at home, on the road, and in some cases while commuting to and from offices. The nature of the work and the need to pursue a career makes it so. Your after-hours work is vital and normal, and to be planned for, no matter how effective your selling style may be.

Once the professional practice of selling is seen this way, the seeming and real contradictions between business and home life come into focus. The real contradictions remain; they are the same time choices caused by the practice of any work requiring long hours and close attention. However, the seeming contradictions—and these are the ones that cause so much trouble at home—disappear. They are replaced by recognition of the need to organize effectively that part of the work that is properly done out of the field, so that it may be done well and within time bounds you have consciously set, rather than expanding to fill and thereby destroy your own personal life and the lives of others with whom you live.

That requires most of all the will to do so, which can only come from shared understandings. It does not matter how efficiently you may have set up an office at home if those you live with expect your almost undivided attention at home. For example, a woman in selling whose family expects her to come home to cook, clean, nurse, and in general watch and ward for them during all the rest of her waking hours is a woman whose career and home life are probably in disastrous conflict. Not because she is spending too much or too little time with either business or personal life, but because her family does not understand that her profession demands that she continue to practice it at home as well as in the office.

Similarly, a man or woman who is heavily and continually criticized at home for "not spending enough time with the family" may indeed be a compulsive and self-destroying person; or may be simply a working professional trying to practice that part of his or her trade that must be practiced at home, under terribly adverse conditions. There are work compulsives, of course; but there is also widespread misunderstanding of when and where the profession of selling is practiced. Someone who works 60 or 70 hours a week, and sometimes even more, including many hours at home, may be a "work compulsive," who is in the process of destroying home and family; he or she is far more likely to be a quite normal, considerably overworked sales professional, trying to pursue a difficult profession in the twin maelstroms of home and field.

And there is the key. You have to be able to think, plan, and organize somewhere, whenever you want to. It is a must; it is indispensable to the practice of the profession. It cannot be done during a day in the field; it must be done before or after hours, and elsewhere. Usually that means at home. Usually—but not always. Some who travel a lot accomplish a great deal of "office" work on the road, and some who commute accomplish much while traveling to and from work.

AN OFFICE AT HOME

In the long run, however, most sales professionals need an office at home. Nothing else will do. A real office, as carefully organized and equipped as any other professional office. For most of those living in their own homes, that is not terribly hard to accomplish, with a little investment and foresight in home selection. For those necessarily living in crowded city or suburban apartments or condominiums, that is often much harder to accomplish—harder, but not less necessary.

A real office at home is a separate space, preferably a separate room, as isolated as possible. It is a dedicated space; offices at home have nothing to do with kitchen or dining room tables co-opted for work while families either continue their normal activities and thereby make it impossible to work properly, or tiptoe about resentfully, making it impossible to have a normal family life.

Beyond the basic understanding that selling is also practiced at home, and that an office at home must be private and dedicated to its working functions, offices will vary as widely as do working styles, mechanical skills, needs, and available technology. For some, an office at home may be a very small room, containing little more than a desk, a filing cabinet, good lighting, and a telephone. Some will add such machines as calculators, typewriters, dictating machines, and personal computers, or will be tied into substantial computer systems through terminals at home. Some, where such possibilities exist, may choose to set up working quarters in separate structures, much as an artist sets up a studio in a barn or other outbuilding. Whatever the home office setup is, the physical rules are basically the same at home as at any other office: an adequate table or desk; such other surfaces as are needed; letter- or legal-size files; good-to-excellent lighting (a must); decent heat and ventilation; high-quality machines that work consistently; a comfortable rolling chair; adequate book space; and a reasonable set of office supplies.

Your office-at-home telephone requires a good deal of careful control. For without close control and careful handling, your business calls at home can significantly damage your personal life. It is not difficult to prevent an uncontrolled flow of business calls into your home, calls that must be answered by you or other members of your family at times that may be very, very inconvenient. That is where a separate line, that rings only in your home office, and an answering machine are so valuable. Together they can completely insulate your family from your business calls, and make it possible for you to take calls only when you wish, stacking the rest and returning them at your own convenience.

Get a machine that can be set to ring only once; better yet, look for one that can be set not to ring at all. And get one with a monitoring device, so that you can listen to incoming calls, if you wish, and decide whether or not to pick up before the caller finishes putting a message on your machine. Don't worry about people who are uneasy about talking to answering machines; they are fewer and fewer, especially in the business world. You may also want to get a machine with a remote device, so that you can call from outside for messages, without bothering your family or depending on family members to be home when you call for messages.

Telephone control is one very significant aspect of what must be a lifelong drive to control the seemingly uncontrollable, to work effectively in what can all too easily become a maelstrom of ringing telephones and demanding people, an avalanche of problems, and a storm of paper. Effective telephone control succeeds in significantly limiting and organizing your exposure to others.

Note that many modern companies—even in difficult

times—clearly recognize the stake they have in making it as easy as possible for sales professionals to pursue job-connected matters in a well-equipped office at home. Such pieces of equipment as computer terminals tied in to large, main-frame computers and distributed data bases, minicomputers, dictating equipment, answering machines, typewriters, office supplies, and even some items of standard office furniture are routinely supplied by some companies. Others will supply these kinds of goods and services if you take the trouble to ask, and press the point. Still others will do so only if you have made it part of the whole body of items negotiated when you took the job. These items should not be regarded as fringe benefits, by the way; they are essential working tools for professionals who are doing their jobs properly, and should be supplied as readily to offices at home as they are to offices on company premises.

Those working at home cannot always tightly schedule and ration time spent on business matters. On the other hand, it is quite possible to set aside recognized periods in which others can expect you to be working at business matters, and to stay generally within the patterns established. Your work at home then becomes expected and mostly predictable. Without that kind of predictability, someone working at home is always cast in the role of a villain who can be relied upon only to frustrate family plans, and any work you have accomplished at home seems to have been done at the expense of others and against strong family resistance.

These may easily be seen as trivial matters; taken one by one, they may be. But in the aggregate, proper understanding and handling of professional work needs and of work at home is a central matter in terms of both relationships with others and satisfaction of our own lifetime goals and expectations.

When seen clearly, such matters as long-term work time commitment and bedrock insistence on a healthy family life are most fruitfully perceived as processes, whether or not so stated. There are milestones along each of the intertwined ways in which our strategies work themselves out: shorter-term goals achieved or not, desires reached or not, battles won or not. That much of your professional life will be pursued at home must be a shared long-term understanding with those you love, whatever the changing physical and time arrangements are over the years.

Similarly, and intertwined, is the question of focus. Or, to put it a little differently, the question of at least seemingly unbalanced focus.

A standard, and only sometimes useful, bit of folk-wisdom is that if you spend most of your time at home focusing on work-related matters, and perhaps spend an unnecessarily large part of your time traveling, you are conveying a clear signal that something is very wrong with your personal relationships, and that you may be getting ready for a change of partners. Perhaps, perhaps not. It is at least equally likely—in the early years, anyway, before one-sided focus really can destroy relationships—that you are in the process of being caught by a set of job and professional needs, in a set of games you may not know how to play terribly well. After all, winning objective after objective does not bring you any nearer to the end of the professional game; only time does that. While the game is being played—and that is for a whole career—it can expand to fill every bit of time in your life, if you let it.

Except for that other bedrock personal goal, so sharply demanded by the people of our time and place: insistence on trying to find and build long-term personal relationships. For we are, in the long run, desolate if we are unable to do so, and almost equally distressed if we are unable to do so in our work. All of which sets a considerably amended set of contexts within which we pursue our careers in this last portion of the twentieth century, and helps explain our focus on such matters as interpersonal relations, time management, and several kinds of people-handling matters.

The current focus upon time management is quite appropriate, seen in this set of contexts. For without excellent personal organization and priority setting within a clearly understood body of long-term goals, all of life can very easily become a maelstrom, and few, if any, long-term personal or business goals can be consistently pursued.

The main thing is to keep those goals firmly in mind, continually assessing and reassessing them in light of events. Beyond that central and indispensable activity, there are a few simple time-, people-, and task-handling techniques that can make life relatively easier and can enhance efficiency considerably, if they are developed into habit. None of them have to do with time alone, for all are inextricably inter-twined with tasks, people, tactics, and strategies; as is usually true in life, time saving and efficiency are means rather than ends in themselves. All are simple enough, as sophistication is simple; all taken together add up to cultivation of a set of excellent working reflexes, which begin to make it possible to consistently translate long-term goals into the stuff of everyday life and work.

ORGANIZING YOURSELF

The most important working reflex of all is to develop the habit of continually putting to oneself two related self-management questions, and of having the answers to those questions before you constantly, written down in the form of ever-changing lists of tasks and priorities. The questions are: "What do I want to get done?" and "What needs to be done?"; and "When?" is implied in each.

These are the essential self-organizing questions. Note that they do not lead to exploration of a wide range of alternatives; that is part of longer-term decision making and planning. In contrast, effective day-to-day self-management requires limitation of alternatives and development of current action from proven skills and strengths. A list of possible actions, rather than a list of specific actions to be performed, is likely to be quite useless, a waste of time to prepare, and a worthless self-organizing tool. A good deal of effective thinking must precede preparation of a list of things to do; it is the process of preparing the list that is the key act of self-organization.

Very few of us need to be convinced that listing is a necessary device. It is axiomatic that no one can remember more than a modest fraction of all that needs to be done in business and personal life; it is equally axiomatic that five undone things bouncing about unlisted inside your head feel like 50 undone things. Indeed, the best way to convince someone of the value of listing is to go through the process. Almost always, that person's "I always seem to have so much to do" results in a far shorter list than he or she had imagined. The listing process also often turns up vital matters that had not been on that person's mental list.

Listing always seems simple enough. You take a sheet of paper, a notebook, or a personal computer, for that matter, and write what needs to be accomplished. You include everything from "Get haircut," to "Explore job change," to "Do major prospect list analysis." Then, as things get done or proceed toward accomplishment, entries are crossed off or updated; as new items develop, they in turn are listed. The result is an all-inclusive, undifferentiated list; it takes the least possible time to prepare and update, and you do not have to spend half your time listing, updating, excising, adding, and thinking about lists. Simplicity itself—but not nearly enough.

For listing is a key act of personal planning, and many of the matters with which you deal routinely are not intrinsically simple and easy to accomplish. Oh, you can and should keep the trivia of the day and week before you at all times on a running list; given the complicated lives most of us lead, to do otherwise can be maddening. But if all you do is keep an undifferentiated list, you are quite likely to find yourself dealing superbly well with trivial matters and perhaps filling your life with nobly handled trivialities, while missing the main matters with which you should be dealing, except as they are forced upon you by outside events. "Get haircut" is easy; "Do major prospect list analysis" is a lot harder and more time-consuming, and the kind of indispensable forward planning that is all too often deferred or even abandoned, as far less important day-to-day events crowd it out.

The main thing to understand about listing is that it is only the basic and indispensable start of effective planning. Certainly you will start with a relatively undifferentiated mass of items, but you will need to develop several special-purpose lists adapted to your particular needs. Once these are in being, you may quite routinely update and study several lists simultaneously—perhaps as you sit down on a Sunday night to plan your coming week's work—rather than making a single list and then transferring items out to special-purpose lists. As you proceed through each day, you are quite likely to enter items on several running lists, although some people prefer to keep an undifferentiated list and transfer items once a day to special-purpose lists. For many kinds of items, such as interview appointments and timed customer and prospect calls, you will use such calendar devices as appointment books and desk diaries, which you will carry with you routinely, and use both in the field and in home or company offices. For these purposes, lists kept on personal computers are difficult to use. It is a physical problem; you need to be able to carry lists into many different kinds of places and situations, and plain old paper and print are better for that than computer screens. That may change in coming decades; later on we may all find ourselves carrying small computer devices hooked into remote memories. But that kind of change will be measured in decades, not in years; for now, lists are best done in paper and print. You will develop a series of lists and listing tools that suit your personal preferences and needs, so lists and listing devices will vary considerably. But whatever the mechanical devices used, well-organized sales professionals are likely to find themselves using five general kinds of lists, with considerable overlap among them: prospect files, customer lists, day-by-day item lists, major project lists, and datebook lists.

Prospect and Customer Files.

How you hold and update your prospect file will to a considerable extent depend on your company's practice and your own approach to organization. If your company has a standard way of keeping prospect files, it may supply company-generated prospects in a standard way into its own standard system, and you will feed your prospects into that system. If there is no company form, you will need to develop your own, which will probably consist of large cards or a loose-leaf notebook. Whatever form you choose, it must be one that allows you to capture a fairly substantial and growing body of information about your prospects in one easily reached place, so that it may be seen easily during a telephone call or in an automobile you have just parked in a company parking lot prior to a selling appointment. In many instances, your prospect card will also function as a customer card; keeping your prospect and customer cards in the same basic form can save paperwork, if the products you handle and your company paperwork arrangements make that solution possible.

Whatever the form of your files, they must be capable of being reached easily and being used effectively over the phone and in the field. That means keeping them entirely up to date at all times, and making sure that they carry all the relevant facts you need to help you sell the prospect. You will often want to refresh yourself on a prospect before a contact of any kind, and that makes it necessary to keep at least the following information about each of your prospects in the file.

• The full name, address, and telephone number of each prospect. Where individuals within a firm have separate telephone numbers, they should be included.

• As much basic personal information as you have or can develop about the prospect, such as current business title and business interests, schools, prior jobs, family, hobbies, and whatever else that can help provide some basis for empathy.

▪ As much relevant material as can be developed about those around your prospect, such as others who may participate in buying decisions and such support people as assistants, secretaries, telephone operators, and receptionists.

▪ How the prospect was developed and when, complete with prospect source, date of first contact, and any other relevant information.

▪ What has happened so far—a record of every prospect contact, whether face to face or by telephone or mail, and the result of the contact.

Many people who sell seem to spend a great deal of time—or so it seems to them—shuffling prospect cards. They are usually alphabetized, and often further sorted and alphabetized within sorted groups. Many are taken out of the main file when appointments are made, and put in a chronological file, which acts as a "pop-up" file for appointments, and makes use of the cards as an alerting device. When the appointment has been completed, the card will then either be put in place in a chronological file for callback of some sort or put back in the prospect file, to wait for another day and another try at selling the prospect.

Many travelers take all or substantial portions of their prospect files on the road with them. If you do that, you may want to seriously consider making a duplicate set of prospect files and leaving it at home. It is a good deal of extra work to either maintain two sets of prospect files, or periodically photocopy your card file, but the thought of losing prospect files or any substantial portion of them is enough to make a sales representative's blood run cold. The truth is that loss of your only set of prospect files, "safely" locked into the trunk of your subsequently stolen car, may effectively put you out of business for quite a long time, and cost you far more than the car itself. You can insure a car, but you will have a very hard time insuring prospect files for any more than the slightest fraction of their real worth. Because for you, as for all sales professionals, that real worth is enormous.

But prospect files can be reconstituted, if necessary. What is really most important is the development of the prospecting skills needed to create them, and the consistent application of those skills throughout a selling career.

A second kind of basic business list that must be carried in usable form by selling people on the move is the customer list. In earlier times, that list would be carried as a looseleaf notebook or set of cards, one or more pages or cards to a customer, with updating done by hand. Today, it is far more likely to be carried in the form of a mammoth, computer-generated printout on accordion-folded paper, impossible to add to a bulging briefcase and arriving in updated form monthly or weekly. Indeed, field representatives sometimes feel as if those printouts arrive every other day, for the sole purpose of straining already overstrained storage space in home offices, closets, and basements. But not so—if used well, as reference material, those printouts can save a good deal of laborious hand entry into your own records.

But computer printouts are no substitute for a customer file that is a current selling file, rather than a reference file. You should still have every customer on a looseleaf page or card, with the same kinds of information you carry in your prospect file, for customers are, in most instances, also your best prospects. And it still takes some hand entry; for example, when a customer buys a relatively small item from your company by mail, you will want to note that on your customer-as-prospect file, for the mail sale is very often the key to a much larger personally achieved field sale.

There is good reason to carry prospect files and customer-as-prospect files in the same form, if possible, whether as cards or looseleaf pages, as you will probably want to mix them in your chronological files, with both kinds of prospects popping up on the same day and in the same geographical areas or zones for further selling efforts.

Lists and Calendars.

The third kind of basic list is the day-by-day, rather undifferentiated, item list, which will contain mostly trivia, but will also include recent additions not yet added to other special-purpose lists. That list is probably best carried separately and constantly, as on a pad or looseleaf memo book. For selling people, who move about a good deal, such lists should be pocket-sized, and therefore easy to carry and use in most situations. When something occurs to you in an elevator or train, on a street or in a restaurant, during "working" hours or at other times, it is important to be able to jot it down, to capture and set the thought. That is true whether what occurs is a task to be listed or some other thought you will want to pursue later; you will therefore want to be able to use a single memo device that allows you to add to a running list or make other notes.

This is a raw list; some of the items you add will be crossed off on reflection. Others will prove to duplicate items already on this or other lists. No harm. That will become apparent when you stop to consider the items you have added, which you certainly should make every attempt to do daily. A caution: Do not triumphantly excise items as soon as you think they have been accomplished; all too often you have accomplished only part of an item, or must verify later to make sure that something has, in fact, been accomplished. Premature excision can cause you to lose items; that is a bother at least, and sometimes can cause real problems.

Some people carry these kinds of raw lists in their pocket appointment books. That is attractive, but the sheer mass of trivia often causes unnecessary duplication, with many items carried over and rewritten day after day, until accomplished. On balance, it seems more efficient to carry the raw list separately, making or updating diary entries only if timing elements are involved, either from the start or at various stages of accomplishment. For example, "Get haircut" will be part of a raw running list until it is either done or you make an appointment to get it done. If done, it is removed from your list. If an appointment has been set, it leaves the running list and is put in place in your appointment book, at the time indicated. Similarly, "Call prospect on June 30" may first go on your undifferentiated running list and then, at the end of the day, be put on a prospect card and that card placed in the chronologically organized portion of your prospect file.

Effective planning demands that major personal projects be listed separately, not just in those raw and calendar lists through which they enter and are worked out within your planning system. No matter how active you may be—or how overworked you may feel—it should be possible to place every one of your substantial projects on the fourth kind of list, which is a single ever-developing major planning list, with key elements and project status always in clear view.

And that project list must be viewed and reviewed continually and critically, for that major planning list is one of the key differences between the career builder and the time server. It is a device through which you can place business, personal, and career-building tasks and goals side by side, all in one place, continually evaluating progress, making connections that work for you, and setting and resetting your view of the context within which you are functioning.

A project list will certainly include "Do complete prospect file review," as well as "Open up widget market," and "Start next year's sales forecast." It will also include such skill-building items as "Develop better computer literacy. Explore possible sources." And such career-development items as "Become more active in Sales Executives' Club this year"; "Cultivate Mary, Joe, Tom re field training assignments"; and "Explore and consolidate sales recruiter contacts—weak here." This is a comprehensive, personal, and very private project list, and should be for your own eyes only.

Your project list should be all in one place, and if possible on one sheet of paper, to help you to reach and hold most easily a complete view of your personal situation and priorities. At the same time, it needs to contain outlines of the main tasks to be done to help make projects move along. That can usually be accomplished with a combination of your own abbreviations and appended materials as necessary. This is a list that provides an overview, but it is also a working list, and you must have enough detail to be able to note progress and revise as you go.

As a working list, your project list will indicate priorities, often by the order in which you place projects and also by your appended comments. Similarly, you will probably use such marks as asterisks and underlining to call attention to priority matters. Priorities change; so will those marks and comments.

You will need to provide yourself with a fresh copy of this list periodically, as your neat, clean copy gradually turns into a mass of hand-scribbled additions, updates, and excisions. How frequently you will need to do so will depend largely upon how actively you pursue your projects. Planning tools like lists are meant to be worked with; if any of your lists are as clean at the end of the week as at the beginning, your progress in the areas covered by those lists has probably been negligible.

The fifth kind of general list is the calendar, which may occur in such various forms as pocket-sized appointment books, day- or week-at-a-glance desk diaries, loose-leaf memo books, pop-up files or ticklers, and desk and wall calendars. Whatever form or forms you use, you will want to provide ample space for note taking and changes, because the most efficient way to handle timed matters is to attempt to put them all together in one place. For example, a single page of a day-by-day appointment book, with one page for each day, may contain business appointments, personal appointments, timed calls to make, personal and business trivia, and personal and business events, such as professional meetings, birthdays, trade shows, anniversaries, and due dates of several kinds.

With that kind of information in hand, all in one place, it becomes possible to do what should be done and to avoid the kind of surprise and dismay that so often occurs when you forget things important to others—and sometimes to you, too. That argues strongly for keeping a fair-sized day-by-day book, with enough space to hold all those items and the accompanying inevitable mass of changes. You may also keep more complex tools, as dictated by preferences and job needs; some people buy and use quite elaborate planning board devices; others use computers to help them master their timing needs, and expand such uses to include personal and business planning materials. Most of us, though, will find the appointment book enough, if we use it well and consistently.

That appointment book should travel with you, from home to field to office and back again. With you, and not in your luggage, by the way; its loss would be a small disaster. It is as much a part of your personal equipment as a watch or eyeglasses, and is far more important than either, for watches and eyeglasses can be easily replaced.

MONITORING PROGRESS

The appointment book technique makes some extraordinarily important self-analysis possible, for it enables you to consistently track how and with whom you spend your time. And keeping track of your time on a regular basis is one of the most valuable planning-related activities in which any sales professional can engage; it can help you convert or partially convert a seeming maelstrom into a set of manageable sequences in business and personal life.

Let us stress the central importance of consistency here. As elsewhere, consistency is essential when you seek to turn well-reasoned approaches into good reflexes, and repeated actions into habits. It really does not do to carefully log your time once in a while; to make a few remedial moves to attempt to make better use of your time; and then slowly to sink once again into a sea of trivia, time-consuming chores, and callbacks that seem to take up all available time. That is all too often the norm. Repeated, it is disheartening and can become demoralizing.

Some counselors on time management may be contributing to the problem rather than to the solution. The difficulty lies in the complexity of the self-analytical material and techniques offered, and the special attention that must be paid to them. If, to manage your time effectively, you must develop and learn how to use new and complex tools, replete with forms and flow charts, the odds are that you will not do so, continue to do so, make it all over into habit, and then do what every good professional does—make it look easy. If complex materials are needed, then the odds are that you will read a book, take a course, or both, and apply what you have learned once, if at all. The application will seem to help, though you will not be sure whether that is because the techniques are helping or because you are momentarily paying close attention to time management matters. But it will not help enough for you to make the extra effort needed over a long period of time to develop it all into habit. It is usually too special, too complex, too time-consuming.

It is far more to the point to use a time-oriented tool already at your disposal for other purposes: your appointment book. If you develop the habit of noting in it precisely how you spend your time, day after day, throughout a career, you will be able to begin exercising as much control of your time as is possible in your specific circumstances, whatever your job, company, and personal contexts.

That means using your book as both planner and time log, not only in field and office, but also at home, while traveling, and perhaps while commuting. Your whole time situation can come into proper focus when you record all your time expenditures; to record only what you do during your field working day is to miss much of your professional life.

It is impractical to suggest logging every minute of every day of the year, but it is entirely practical—indeed vital—to suggest doing exactly that at stated periods throughout the year. You can very easily pick one week in each quarter of each year for close time logging, note those weeks in your book at the beginning of each year, and then proceed in very orderly fashion to do just that, as the prescribed date pops up. That, too, is a good habit. Scheduled, it is anticipated and easy.

For most of the year, your book will serve as a basic time log, if you get one that devotes at least a full page to each day, and breaks up the day hour by hour. During close time-logging periods, you may need a little more space than that, adding additional space and entries as necessary, or even keeping your time log separately. But do try to keep your time log in your diary, if at all possible, even during such periods, however you must compress your notes to do so.

No matter how long and consistently you record your time expenditures, you are likely to find each successive time log reevaluation rewarding and surprising. Very few of us really know how we spend our time, and most of us, when asked, will respond with substantially inaccurate estimates. When closely analyzed, far too many days turn out to have included little time spent with qualified prospects in real selling situations; likewise, far too many hours spent "lining up prospects" and "cementing customer relations" turn out to have been wasted trying to reheat old leads over the telephone and stuck deep in a set of callback traps. All of us waste travel time at one time or another zigzagging about a territory to make unanticipated selling and servicing calls. All of us sag at one time or another, and find ourselves spending time with colleagues or customers who are chronic time wasters. But close and consistent analysis of how we spend our time can make those kinds of instances exceptional rather than usual. With analysis, patterns become apparent, and success patterns can be reached for, held, and turned into reflexes.

With long-term goals in order, and a full personal and business project list before you, thoughtful time log analysis can yield excellent—though not necessarily unpredictable—results. Most of us find ourselves wasting enormous amounts of time on trivial matters; spending far too little time on projects; barely touching some of our most important long-term strategic goals, particularly in career- and skills-building areas; and tending to fill our personal lives with the same kind of trivial business matters that occupy so much of our workdays. No matter that much of the trivia is generated by our own companies, prospects, customers, and families; our job is to manage our time and work so as to minimize waste and maximize both effectiveness and the satisfactions to be gained from living rewarding personal lives.

That takes a great deal of thought and attention, and often necessitates sharp limitation of some kinds of time demands placed upon us by our situations and by others. All the personal planning, replanning, listing, relisting, logging, and analysis we have been discussing takes valuable time—a good deal of it—and it is in the long run only worthwhile if it can be made to pay. That requires a good deal of action, some of it not always acceptable at first to those around you, as you move to control the seemingly uncontrollable in your life and work.

CONTROLLING TIME WASTERS

"I'm just spinning my wheels . . ."

"Spent all day running around putting out fires; I feel like a dog chasing his tail."

"Went out for a cup of coffee with Anne this morning, and she chewed my ear off for an hour about how awful it all is . . ."

"Awful nice guy, but every time I go in there I lose half a day. Don't want to offend him . . . and you know, they're big customers. . . ."

Controlling the uncontrollable is first of all a lifelong dedication to the elimination of time-wasting attitudes, actions, and people. Yes, there are times when you cannot seem to make a firm selling appointment to save your soul, no matter how well the same basic telephone technique has worked for years. And times when you call in from one end of your territory and find that there is a real emergency that must be handled today, requiring that you drive 50 miles out and then 50 miles back to resume—if you can—your busted selling day. But these are exceptional kinds of things; when they happen often, you may either not be taking enough care to avoid time-wasting traps or are welcoming them. Or a little bit of both, of course.

Unproductively spent field time is the great enemy of the sales professional. As a stoutly resisted exception, it is a normal—and merely sometimes frustrating—part of the game. As a set of unfolding patterns, it is a career breaker.

Unnecessary moving about through failure to control your territory is one of the greatest of all time wasters. In these days of high travel costs, it is also a very expensive time waster. Much of it is avoidable, though, with proper zoning and telephone use.

Zoning is quite simply a matter of breaking up your selling area into bite-size pieces, and trying your very best to spend usable chunks of time in one piece at a time, rather than racing around between the various pieces. If you are on the road for some days, it also means organizing your moves so that you move from piece to piece in as efficient a fashion as possible. It is as simple as keeping a map of your territory with you at all times, setting up your chronological customer-as-prospect and prospect files to conform with the zones you have set up on that map, and making every effort to schedule appointments of all kinds in a single zone on a given day. Then, aside from real emergencies, you will not find yourself spending needless and expensive hours traveling that should better be spent selling. Caution: It is always tempting to make a promising out-of-zone selling call, particularly when you do not yet have a firm set of appointments for the only day all week your prospect is willing to meet with you. But it is usually a mistake, although it may occasionally eventuate in a sale. Most likely, it will only result in a broken-up and inefficiently spent day. Nobody sells them all, prospects cancel scheduled appointments, and appointments made later, many miles away, may be even more promising. It is best to keep to your zoned plans, if at all possible, rather than running off to seek pie in the wrong part of the sky on the wrong day.

There are also a great many friendly people out there, and especially friendly, long-term customers. Some of them will like you so much that they will do their best to ruin your career, by encouraging you to waste inordinate amounts of your time and theirs in fruitless conversation. Beware of the too-friendly time-wasting customer; remember, anyone who has a great deal of rather pointlessly spent time to spend with you is likely to be a time server and time waster on a larger scale as well. Those who treasure time wasters as valued business contacts are quite likely to find their friends gone one day when they come to call. Looking at it that way, it is appropriate to see a time waster as someone likely to be in trouble, and to view the situation as one in which you should without delay cultivate others in the firm if you want to safeguard the account.

There is also the callback trap, always the refuge of the slumping field representative. When someone calls again and again on the same few prospects and customers, trying to warm up potential sales that have long since ceased to have any immediacy and current possibility, that someone has fallen into the callback trap. Certainly, some sales require several selling calls, for all kinds of reasons. There can be several buyers and buying decisions involved, inter-rupted and therefore unconsummated selling interviews that have to be entirely redone, more information to be secured from a home office, and even some stalls that somehow cannot be broken through on the way to the close. But when your appointment book shows call after call on the same prospect over a period of weeks or even months, you may truly just be "spinning your wheels," and deep in a set of callback traps. And that is one of the worst time-wasting patterns of all, often requiring a deep look at your whole prospect file and set of selling attitudes—sometimes even a look at whether or not you are in the right selling job. No, not a look at whether or not selling is the right career—that is hardly ever the problem, though it is perfectly natural to have it cross your mind when you are in the middle of a long slump, deep in a set of time-wasting callback traps, and perhaps long since ready for a job change.

All quite controllable, if the effort is consistently made. As are some of our time-wasting colleagues, who might like us to coffee with them every morning, for "just a few minutes." That few minutes, of course, becomes anywhere from 15 to 45 minutes, and the time wasted thereby may be anywhere from a little over an hour a week to nearly four hours a week. Or putting it a little differently, the convivial coffee-ers in your office may be wasting as much as 200 hours a year having coffee with each other for "just a few minutes" every morning. That is well over a month of good selling time wasted every year—lost, never to return. The direct costs to those who so waste time may be some thousands of dollars a year; the indirect costs, in terms of career building, can be much higher.

Goal setting, developing a sound office at home, listing, self-evaluating, zoning, prospect and customer record handling, avoiding the standard time-wasting traps—all these begin to add up to astute self-management of time and work. Now add consistent control of the mass of paper that often seems about to drown us. We get computerized customer lists, sales leads, customer complaints, home office requests, memos, contest bulletins, questionnaires, in-house newsletters, brochures, technical manuals, and miscellaneous product and promotion information; and we reach out for a mass of professional and general information aimed at helping us to effectively pursue and build our sales and careers. We are expected to produce considerable quantities of call reports, expense statements, memos, letters, prospect information, and a wide miscellany of forms and reports aimed at helping sales management and marketing people do their jobs as effectively as possible. We need to ingest and produce it all on the fly, so to speak. Sales professionals spend as much time as possible selling; all the rest of it gets done in other than selling time, and in a wide variety of "offices," including company offices, home offices, motel rooms, commuter trains, airplanes, restaurants, and traffic jams at raised drawbridges. But all that paper must be handled, and handled well.

That calls for selectivity and consistency. Selectivity first. If you are not selective about what you read, what you put aside to use as reference material, and what you quite ruthlessly discard, you will spend a whole lifetime in selling and in the business world hopelessly trying to catch up with all you think you should read, and hopelessly behind in handling all the business matters you should very definitely be handling.

Selectivity means scanning newspapers, professional journals, manuals, brochures, newsletter articles, and other broadcast printed materials, rather than attempting to read literally everything in sight. You will follow general matters as a responsible and interested citizen and as you like, but scan the business, industry and company news for matters of direct interest and significance to you, and ruthlessly jettison the rest. You will read as much as you feel appropriate of company-generated materials, but scan whatever you can, putting much aside for use as reference material. You will be likely to use computer-generated reports mainly as reference materials, after a quick scan and study of any summaries provided.

Consistency means promptly disposing of anything that can be disposed of easily and quickly. To let your desk disappear under a mountain of unanswered memos and letters is, to put it very gently, counterproductive, in that it will only result in more memos and letters, with small and routine matters becoming problems that grow large as time goes by. To let undone call reports and expense accounts pile up is only to guarantee that you will do them at difficult and inconvenient times after you receive requesting, and then demanding, letters and calls urging you to do so.

Selling people are always people in motion, and often people on the road, whether in travel territories or holding regional, national, or international selling responsibilities. For sales professionals, effective time and work management often depends on finding and setting personal styles that enable them to handle a wide variety of paper and planning tasks while on the road. For if you hold a great deal of your reading, planning, and office work until you return home, you will find yourself trying to catch up with a mass of tasks and materials that grows faster than you can handle it.

USING TRAVEL TIME

For many of us, time spent "on the road" is dead time, aside from actual field work and the most routine paper-handling tasks. Yet the truth is that travel time offers multiple and high-quality time-expansion possibilities, if we take care to develop good working reflexes. In the short run, effective use of travel time can help you avoid drowning in a mass of paper. In the long run—if you put your mind to it—it can be a real career builder, for long, potentially very lonely evenings can turn into evenings full of plans; notes to a wide network of career-building contacts, including and far beyond your current colleagues, customers, and prospects; and other self-development activities.

Not at all incidentally, this is also the best possible way to prevent the kinds of problems that can and so often do beset people who travel a good deal. Loneliness and disorientation can trigger very difficult personal problems, and empty conviviality with strangers in a motel bar is far more likely to create problems than solve them. Most women who travel do not even have that motel bar to go to; and when you feel trapped in a motel room on the edge of a strange town, you can become very lonely indeed. Which is one of the kinds of things that make closet alcoholics, by the way. There is nothing quite like waking up at 4 A.M. in a motel with no facilities open, with a television set that presents only a blank, buzzing face when turned on, and without a working radio. Or the first, jaggedly disorienting time you find yourself walking down a windowless corridor in a hotel or motel and realize that you do not have the slightest idea of what city you are in, or for that matter what time of day or day of the week it is. Travel—if you let it—often becomes little more than an endless series of motels, restaurants, appointment-setting telephone calls, sales interviews, and roads; also boredom, loneliness, drink, sometimes casual and entirely unrewarding sexual partners, and the condition of disconnection from time and place technically known as anomie, which can signal the onset of very serious emotional problems.

Not much fun, and a lot of hazards. But it is all controllable, and capable of being turned into growing time. The best solution to travel problems is work—sound, fruitful, consistent career-building work, with travel time viewed as opportunity time rather than dead time.

Clearly, attitude is the key in this area. But astute traveling also requires some selectivity, preparation, and skill. Selectivity starts with the travel decisions themselves. The right cost-and-time-efficient question is always "Is this trip necessary?" There is no magic or virtue at all in making a quarterly trip to a set of remote locations because you did so last year and the year before, or because that was "what was done" by your predecessors. There is no reason to reflexively exhibit at a convention or trade show because "we've always been there," or because it is important to "show the flag." Do people expect you, and look forward to your coming? Perhaps, and that may be reason enough to go, even though the trip is not directly cost-effective. But is satisfying their expectations enough reason to make the trip and spend thousands of dollars in out-of-pocket expenses and wasted time? Have you taken a zero-based look at the trip, by costing it out and trying to make a reasonable cost–benefits estimate?

Selectivity extends to the details in travel plans. When you are in an area, it is always very tempting to make every possible customer relations call, without stopping to reflect on the time costs involved. It is possible to spend a day making such calls, sell very little, if anything at all, and bed down in a motel, convinced that you have somehow spent a fruitful day. More than likely, it has not been so; what was missing was only the heart of the matter: selling effectively to qualified prospects in selling situations.

Most sales professionals work very hard when they travel. Days start early, traveling times are often long, and the end of the selling day is often only the beginning of a trip to somewhere else, so that the next day can be started fresh and rested. Working harder is seldom needed advice; on the other hand, living smarter on the road is very often possible. That means planning your itinerary so that you will not routinely court exhaustion because of too-long driving distances; staying away from nightcaps that can turn into long, sleepless nights; eating decently and regularly, rather than gulping junk foods at odd hours; and in general taking care of yourself at least as well on the road as you do at home. You have to be able to develop a deliberate, effective personal pace on the road, containing the kind of self-regenerating reflexes that will last a whole career. By all means locate and use recreational places; a swim, run, or tennis game at the end of a long day in the field can mean a great deal to mind and body. Cultivate some friends, if your road is a repeated swing through familiar territory. Real human contact can make a great deal of difference. Work and self-development are the keys; recreation and friends can help a great deal, too.

People who travel long distances, such as those handling national accounts, face some very special hazards, for jet leg is dangerous, both physically and to the successful consummation of selling plans. Most of us in recent years have come to understand—intellectually, at least—the physical aspects of jet lag, but very few really act upon that knowledge. Many are still capable of working all day in field or office, jumping aboard a flight to a time zone several hours west, and coming off the plane to keep an appointment that may go on into dinner and even later. Then, after having effectively stayed up all night working, they compound their error by dropping into bed for only a couple of hours of sleep, before starting to work again, perhaps handling delicate and demanding matters.

Some personal and work problems accompany that kind of pattern. First, it is extraordinarily hard on the body. To work all day and all night, spending many hours in transit while doing so, places enormous short-term strain on some pretty important and sometimes fragile organs, including heart and nervous system. To wake in what, for us, is the middle of the night, because of time zone differences and the way our bodies are attuned, creates enormous additional strains. It is perfectly clear by now that it is exceedingly short-sighted and dangerous to work our travel in this way; yet many of us continue to do it, figuring that "the next guy" will be the one who has the heart attack. Well, it may not be the next guy.

And a perfectly obvious set of working problems are created, too. You stack the deck against yourself when you go to work exhausted. Exhausted people tend to sell impatiently and to antagonize those they are there to persuade. And exhausted people fighting jet lag and working full days in a quite different time zone stay exhausted.

It is far better for the body and for work objectives if you take exhaustion and jet lag into account in planning long-distance trips. If you must travel at night, arrive quietly, go to your lodging, stay up until you are quite tired—but relaxed—and to go sleep. You may wake up rather early the next morning, but you will be well on your way to conquering jet lag, and will not be exhausted. If you must work the night of the day you travel, by all means travel early on that day if you can, so that you may arrive, acclimate, and perhaps fit in a nap before you have to go to work in what, for you, is the middle of the night.

The converse is also true. If you are flying from west to east any considerable distance, your problem will arise the next morning. You will not have been able to go to sleep until the middle of the night in your arrival time zone, and should not attempt to schedule anything until the afternoon of the first full day in the new zone; otherwise you will find yourself fighting to stay awake all that day, rather than being in top condition for whatever has to be done. If you stay on, bear in mind that you will still be attuned to a different time zone; try not to schedule very early morning appointments until your body has had a few days to acclimatize.

If working effectiveness is to be maximized and working opportunities used, considerable care must be paid to other early timing-related questions as well. When and how closely to schedule planes and other transport; how closely to schedule appointments on the same day; and whether or not to travel to dinner at that wonderful French restaurant just 40 miles down the coast after a five-hour flight—these are all matters to consider carefully.

Travelers' Tools.

Proper physical preparation for "office" work is far more important when traveling than when working at your office or home. Small working tools that can be taken for granted in a familiar environment can become vital omissions on the road. Some basic working tools are apparent and part of the working equipment of almost all business travelers; but some equally basic tools are often overlooked. On the road, you should have:

- A properly flexible, small wardrobe, as washable as possible.
- Adequate writing instruments, and paper to write on. If you normally use a typewriter, then by all means take along a small electric portable, with paper and carbon sets, so that you can send your originals and keep the carbons as safety copies.
- A small calculator, with a paper tape. Some may prefer the kind of hand-held calculator that is easily carried in pocket or bag, and without the tape attachment, but serious work is much easier with the tape, which can be removed and attached to the work done.

- A cassette recorder, for dictating notes and communications. Some of the very small models are quite attractive, but will take only 15- or 30-minute tapes. On balance, it is desirable to carry the smallest sturdy recorder you can find that will take 60- or, at most, 90-minute tapes. Beware of tapes taking over 60 minutes of material—that is, more than 30 minutes a side; these tapes are more fragile and have much less chance of standing up to the rigors of travel. Caution: Do not take your tapes through airport detecting machines, which can scramble the information you record on magnetic tapes; instead, take them out of your carrying case and have the attendant pass them around to you. Note that many companies now have order-processing dictating equipment in their offices that can be used by remote entry over telephone lines. Your orders and some or all of your communications from the road can be sent directly in that fashion, if your company is so equipped.
- A small, high-intensity lamp and bulb, so that you can convert almost any dimly lit hotel room into a workplace. Many otherwise completely acceptable rooms are designed as bedrooms rather than as offices and are therefore inadequately lit for working purposes. Bear in mind that without adequate light you cannot work effectively; also that your eyes age faster than the rest of you, and need much care.
- Two three-socket conversion plugs, so that you can convert a single socket into three sockets, and thereby accommodate the equipment you are carrying. If you are going abroad to where electrical systems are different, then you also need appropriate conversion units.
- A heavy 12-foot extension cord, which should be long enough to reach from an available plug to that part of the room where you are using your equipment.
- An extra pair of reading glasses, if you use them, as emergency spares. These should be obvious, but are often omitted.

- Your working lists of all kinds, which should always travel with you.
- A small quantity of precisely the same office tools and supplies you normally use: a small stapler, a staple remover, paper clips, rubber bands, small scissors, and the like.

It will help a great deal to outline your needs to hotel-keepers wherever you are going. It is often as simple as specifying "a room suitable for working in, with table, chair, and good light." People who do not do that risk arriving at hotels and motels that might have been able to accommodate modest working needs if they had been informed earlier, but are now fully booked and cannot. On the other hand, a hotel may ignore your careful specifications; if so, it is still sometimes possible to get a proper working place on arrival, if you ask, rather than taking the luck of the draw in a randomly assigned room. Hotelkeepers can and should be pushed as necessary in these areas; most will try to be helpful without pushing, but some will not, and you cannot know which is which until you try. By all means, force the situation a bit if you must; it will be worth it in terms of being able to take better advantage of work opportunities on the road.

Using Travel Time.

Reading for information and insight is prime work to do while traveling. The road can be a real opportunity for reflective reading of periodicals and of some of the longer and deeper works you might otherwise have difficulty finding sufficient time for. The same holds for some of the longer reports and memos that we all too often put aside. Better take along some light reading, too, if only as a kind of security blanket; the world can be a lonely place in that airport motel at 4 A.M., far away from home.

Not all travel time expansion opportunities depend on long evenings away from home. Many sales professionals work out of offices, especially those working in major metropolitan areas. When it takes an hour—or sometimes even two—to commute to work, and you are not doing the driving, you find yourself with two or more hours every day that are not otherwise committed, in which a great deal can be accomplished. That woman or man who obviously works hard to and from work every day, rather than playing cards or sleeping, is not necessarily a compulsive worker. What the card players and sleepers—when they wake up—see every day may be a very effective professional, using what might otherwise be dead and boring time to read, write, and think in what can very easily be made into a totally private environment, with no ringing telephones, happy and noisy children, or traffic to fight. As many have found over the years, you can get an enormous amount of work done during commuting hours, if you see your career commitment needs properly.

To work successfully while commuting, all you need is a supply of relevant materials to carry back and forth; a hard flat surface to write upon, such as a briefcase; and basic writing (or dictating) materials. And a seat. All is lost here if you have to stand on the way, which makes unremitting agitation for adequate commuting facilities far more than a matter of comfort. If you cannot sit and work, you are being robbed of productive work opportunities for from two to four hours a day, and that is a few hundred to a thousand hours a year, depending on the length of the commute and the away-from-office travel time. Not a small amount, and the work many can accomplish while commuting is not a small matter.

Successful management of time and work makes it possible to identify and reach for selling and career-building opportunities; it is well within the competence of, and very much a career "must" for, sales professionals.

CHAPTER 6

EFFECTIVE COMMUNICATION

Sales professionals must be particularly sensitive to the need to communicate with others clearly and persuasively. They, more than most other professionals in the business world, spend a great deal of each working day reaching for understanding with others and then moving from understanding to persuasion. Therefore, anything that continually hinders clarity of expression must be excised, and anything in an existing personal style that customarily helps move forward the twin processes of understanding and persuasion is to be encouraged. Effective communication and persuasion mean clear speaking; clear nonverbal communication that enhances, rather than detracts from, clear speaking; and clear writing. Clear and mutually enhancing speaking and nonverbal communication are basic to both successful selling and career building. Clear writing is basic to career building and in conducting business affairs, and is useful in selling as well.

Because of the very nature of the selling process, most communication with customers and prospects is one-to-one, and at root informal, no matter how well-prepared the set of presentations we deliver. Beyond prepared presentations is selling; people in selling who cannot understand this usually find themselves in other lines of work. That is also true when selling to small groups, and when using the telephone. All of which means that sales professionals are not actors or politicians, able to operate from a distance and use techniques that convey personalities that are not their own. In a very real sense, we usually convey to others what we are, warts and all. And if what we are is any great distance from what we would like to seem to be, then we have problems—especially in selling and career building.

In this sense, *effective communication* is more fact than aim; in a mixture of verbal and nonverbal ways, which add up to a great deal more than the sum of their parts, what we are comes through to others, whether we like it or not. And what we are is not very much changed by cosmetic work on speech, body language, appearance, or close attention to manipulative techniques. People who are arrogant or very defensive can do a good deal of work on speech, body language, and appearance, and still not be able to soften the kind of closed coldness that makes it impossible for them to empathize (thereby find buying motives) and sell. Nor will sharpening personal communications skills help very much when basic attitudes are worsening—the sour and personally defeated will not sell and build their careers well, no matter how much they are exposed to training in verbal and nonverbal communication.

That said, however, there are some ways we can help ourselves to communicate and persuade more effectively. Each of us develops a unique personal style, a characteristic mode of expression that reflects both basic attitudes and communicating and persuading skills; that develops and changes as our personalities and skills develop and change; and that sums up the whole face we present to the world. As long as they are not loaded down with self-defeating attitudes, these personal styles can be sharpened in many ways. Clear thinking and lucid expression can, to a considerable extent, be learned. Body language can be consciously molded and remolded, and made into a set of good habits. Appearance can be adjusted rather easily.

SPEAKING

First—and most important for sales professionals—are speaking skills. People who develop the lifelong habit of speaking in a clear, relaxed, and thoughtful fashion go a long way toward selling and career-building success. In the informal set of contexts that characterizes most selling and other business situations, that basic speaking—and thinking—approach is the one most likely to wear well in the long run.

This style starts with an old childhood admonition: Think before you speak. Yes, it is as simple and basic as that; developing and maintaining the habit of thinking before you speak is the most important single key to effective spoken communication. For the habits of speaking before you have quite collected your thoughts, of filling silences with words, and of responding too quickly in conversation can be lifelong impediments to career success, and especially so for sales professionals. These are habits that cause you to speak unclearly, no matter how well you are physically able to form and speak words and sentences; unclarity of thought brings unclarity of expression.

There are physical speech flaws that come with unthinking talk, too. Unthinking speakers tend to talk too fast, in a higher pitch than they need to, and louder than they should. They often compound the error with body language pressure and succeed in conveying that they do not really know what they are talking about, and are trying hard to make sales any way they can.

Like so many other bad habits, this is fairly easy to change once you know what is wrong and what you want to do about it. All you really need to do is to listen hard and responsively when in conversation. That listening process alone will cause you to take a mental "deep breath" before saying anything. And if you are starting a conversation, take that mental deep breath before opening your mouth. One key thing to remember is that hardly anyone you are likely to meet, in or out of selling, will be offended by your habit of fairly slow-starting, very thoughtful speech. Quite the contrary. Thoughtful, careful speakers are highly prized in our culture. You will be listened to, and respected, and will communicate and sell even more effectively.

A second lifelong effective speaking habit to cultivate is that of relaxation—and we mean that quite literally. Relax your whole body while you speak. It will do you, your speaking style, and the entire communicating situation a world of good. There is nothing quite like relaxation to provide the basis for clarity, empathy, and persuasion. If you are tense, you will communicate that tension, and will often cause others to develop tension. Tension builds walls, which is exactly the opposite of what you want. If your voice communicates real warmth, ease, and relaxation, you are quite likely to be met similarly by others. Relaxation does good physical things for your speech, too. A relaxed speaker usually speaks more effectively than a tense one. The voice is deeper and more resonant; the words are often much more clearly spoken. There is more variety in the voice, with a much wider range of volume and better breath control. The total result is far more effective communication.

A third key effective speech habit is that of speaking rather slowly. That is something easy to advise and sometimes very hard to do. Use the mirror, time yourself, and press family and friends into service as volunteer listeners. Those who speak quickly are often startled at how much better they sound and how much more clearly they communicate when the slow their speech down even a little. Forming words fully helps slow speech, but the main thing is to consciously speak slowly. At first, it sounds to you (never to others—they appreciate and respect slower speech) as if you are dragging out words and sentences. In a short time, the slower, clearer, more effective speech will become a valuable new habit.

A fourth very basic habit to cultivate is that of speaking clearly. Many people do not. Relaxation and slow, thoughtful speech help clarity a great deal but, by themselves, are often not enough to achieve the clarity you want.

Often we develop unclear speech habits simply because those around us speak unclearly. Sometimes it is the effect of a regional speech pattern, as when New Englanders leave off the "r's" at the ends of syllables and words, and the words "order" and "Harvard" come out "awduh" and "Havahd." That is fine in New England, but may require some minor speech adjustments when talking to Midwesterners, who pronounce a very hard "r" in the same circumstances.

More often, though, it is a certain laziness and sloppiness that creeps into our language over the years. After all, we are understood perfectly well by friends and family, aren't we? True, but in selling we are often speaking to people with a much wider set of backgrounds than those normally close to us, and we have to make ourselves understood by people from all over the country.

It is usually fairly easy once you know what to look for. Practicing before a mirror can be very useful. Listening to a taped recording of your voice or watching and hearing a video recording of yourself can help even more. When you talk quickly and carelessly into the mirror you will see common sentences come out startlingly unclearly. When you talk slowly, carefully, and clearly into the mirror, opening your mouth and forming the words, you will see yourself looking the same, taking what seems to be just about the same time (time it, the difference is insignificant) to say the words, but speaking a great deal more effectively.

Do not worry about regional, national, ethnic, or any other "special" accents and influences in your speech, except for such minor adjustments as indicated above. You need not and probably should not try to change the speech patterns of a lifetime in your search for effective speech. When you try to change your normal patterns and rhythms, without the trained eye and ear of the professional performer, you may very well achieve only affected, stilted, phony sounding speech, which is far more disagreeable and, for that matter, far more noticeable than any regional accent you may be trying to change. Speak slowly and clearly, form your words fully, and you will be understood and respected.

Sometimes, as when the New Englander we mentioned earlier relocates in the Midwest, or when a Southerner relocates in the North, people want to make long-term changes in their regional speech patterns. Usually, it simply happens. When you talk with people every day, listen responsively, and are in the business of communicating your thoughts to others, your speech patterns are likely to change to meet the normal patterns around you.

If you want to move the processes of change along a little faster, you need only to listen to the vowels and word endings a little harder. A great deal of regional and other special speech is a matter of how the vowels are pronounced and how the word endings are handled. We are a collection of regions and a nation of immigrants, with languages from all over the world still being fused into the American language, but the language is indeed in the process of fusing, and it is easier and easier to move your speech into the main patterns of the region you are in.

Speaking Problems.

Your voice is an instrument of considerable range and variety. It can be used to create music, to speak poetry, in a theater or on a platform. It can be used to communicate clearly, sharply, and persuasively; and misused so that it will stand in the way of selling and career-building success. One major hazard lies in the area of pitch. A voice that is pitched high, coming out of a tense, tight throat, often offends the ear of the listener. It is described as "grating," "shrill," "unpleasant," and often causes listeners to want to escape. Sometimes it is associated with a high, aggrieved whine that seems to multiply its offensiveness.

Like most other such problems, the trouble can be cured once you know what the problem is. But often you do not even know the problem exists. You talk a certain way all your life, are understood and accepted by friends and family, and have no reason to believe there is anything wrong with the way you speak. That is literally true—there is nothing "wrong" with the way you speak. It is just that other people may find it somewhat unacceptable. That is not much of a problem, unless you are in a profession that requires good personal communication, like selling. Then a high, tense whine can be a major disability.

To improve your voice, you need a little help from family, friends, and co-workers. Especially co-workers, who are less accustomed to your speech patterns than family and friends. Normally, people will not tell you if they think there is something disagreeable about your voice, or for that matter any other aspect of your personality. But they will do so if you ask for purposes of self-improvement. Your manager and other sales professionals can tell you about any pitch control problems and can help you practice your way out of them.

The answers are very often in areas already discussed. Relaxation and responsive listening loosen the throat, which results in a lower, softer pitch. Slowing too-rapid speech and using clear word formation often seem to bring down the voice a whole octave, softening hard, rasping edges in your speech.

Those are the normal solutions to problems of too-loud speech, as well. Too-soft speech, which is rarer, is usually a question of self-confidence, and cures itself as the deeper question of self-confidence is solved. Too-loud speech sometimes has a simple physical basis. You can be a little hard of hearing and not know it. Family and friends tend to accept us as we are, do not think about the fact that we talk louder than they do, or perhaps discount it as some kind of personality need.

Once again, it is not much of a problem unless you are in a communications-related profession like selling. And once again, co-workers can be very helpful. If you do have a hearing problem and need some sort of mechanical aid, it is far better to have and use the aid than to go without it—better for your career and a great deal better for you personally. The chief reaction of people who have not known they needed hearing assistance who have then secured some help is: "This is great. I didn't know what I was missing."

Many of us have speech habits that get in the way of effective communication. Usually, we are not aware that we have them and are often surprised and somewhat embarrassed to discover them. Here are some of the most common verbal "tics."

"Like, y'know." "Like I was driving to the store last night and like this other driver like cut me off and like we nearly had like a real bad accident." "You know, I really think he was nearly sold, but you know it didn't work out quite right" and "you know I'm going back in there next time though and you know I'm really going to sell him then." Except that it usually comes out "y'know" rather than "you know."

Not many sales professionals talk that way, but millions of other Americans do, and no one is immune to the development of that kind of bad speech habit. Words and phrases such as "like" and "y'know" seem to fill in the pauses in speech. They seem to impart a certain rhythm and structure. If you have the slightest tendency to develop a case of the "likes" and "y'knows," fight it hard. These examples are not just "bad speech" in academic terms; they are the enemies of clarity and effective selling.

The a . . . "A . . ., Ms. Jones, I a . . . want to a . . . show you our a . . . new line of a . . . green a . . . widgets from a . . . Afghanistan. They're a . . . some of the best a . . . widgets we've a . . . ever a . . . shown." This is a disastrous habit, and the most common one in the world. It is also something that is almost impossible to hear yourself doing. You literally do not hear the "a . . ." and are enormously surprised to learn that you are doing it. This one calls for a tape recorder. If you have any thought that you are an "a . . .-er," tape yourself talking and listen carefully. If you have any tendency in that direction, cure it.

Throat-clearing. We often develop the habit of literally or figuratively clearing our throats before we speak. That can take the form of compulsive throat clearing before launching into conversation, or, more often, it can take the form of a meaningless word or phrase repeated again and again. For example, you may habitually respond, "Well, Ms. Jones," when the word "well" has nothing to do with anything you are discussing. Or you may preface with a "Yes," even when you are really about to say "no." It happens often, and is worth guarding against.

Throat clearing is both a verbal and physical tic. There are other physical tics as well. Most of us develop some in the course of life and career, and can fix them fairly easily—once recognized—unless they reflect deeper tensions that must be analyzed and handled in more basic ways. These kinds of tics are all the little unconscious, repeated physical moves that can so distract others while face to face with you. They can range from head scratching to finger tapping, and often involve the hands. For example, there is the kind of tic that involves playing with something while in a selling situation. You may continually handle your glasses, pen, presentation materials, tie, handbag, or order form, without realizing you are doing so. You may also be a nose rubber, head scratcher, or chin scraper. Or you may fold and unfold your hands a dozen times during a conversation, shift about in your chair, or even be an arm folder or finger tapper. All indicate tension, all impede communication and persuasion, and all are normally rather easily fixable, with proper attention.

BODY LANGUAGE

Effective face-to-face communication and persuasion depend as much upon nonverbal as upon verbal communication. In practice, verbal and nonverbal are intimately intertwined, part of the same set of processes, each occurring side by side whether we like it or not. We communicate with our whole bodies, and it is our bodies that usually convey the subtle emotional signals that are so important in any kind of persuasion.

Each of us has spent a lifetime developing a style of personal expression, a combination of words and body language that serves to communicate and persuade. As with speech, it is best not to try to make large changes in that basic style when dealing with matters of body language, but rather to shape natural style to career-building and selling needs. For example, if you move a little too quickly, slow down a little. Speed makes people nervous; moving a little more slowly makes for easier, more empathetic communication and relationships.

It is also appropriate to do your best to adopt a reasonably relaxed body set. When you are listening responsively, you will probably lean forward just a little, perhaps cock your head, sometimes smile appreciatively, often nod when a telling point is made. All these movements can and should happen quite naturally if you are really listening and responding. If you are tense and force your responses, people will usually know it, realize that you are faking warmth and response, and they will close up tight. It is always your natural style that works best—with modest improvements and avoiding basic errors—but still your own open and natural style.

Some sales professionals are a little afraid of using their own natural expressive styles. This fear usually predates going into selling and indicates a rather defensive attitude toward the world and the people in it. Their usually unspoken thought is that by avoiding body language as much as possible, they will preserve their privacy, keep up their defenses against the world and others, be able to stick to business, and avoid personalities. But it does not quite work that way. Quite the contrary: carefully controlled people reflect tension, tightness, and the presence of a wall between themselves and others. The personal attitudes projected are often tension, coldness, arrogance, even distaste for others. The physical results are often tightness of face and body, constricted motion, voice tension, and inability to relax and listen responsively.

Body language has a great deal to do with success or failure in selling. The only way you can avoid using body language in selling is to avoid face-to-face selling situations. And anyone who needs to do that needs to find a different line of work. Far better to learn to relax, use and improve on your own personal expressive style, and move ahead.

By all means talk with your hands—or any other part of your anatomy, for that matter—if that is part of your natural style. "Don't talk with your hands" is nonsensical advice. Of course it is all right to talk with your hands, your shoulders, and the angle of your head, as it is all right to talk with your lips, tongue, and the air that flows from your diaphragm to be shaped into words.

One of the most common problems faced in speech is that of the "stiff upper lip." Try talking with your upper lip held purposely as stiff as you can. Difficult, isn't it? You come out like Humphrey Bogart playing one of his early gangster roles. If you have a stiff-upper-lip problem, you will want to cure it, to achieve more mobile, effective speech.

Similarly, the main problem in body language is not "Don't talk with your hands." Quite the opposite. It is the problem of stiffness, inability to loosen up and get the tremendous expressive advantages that flow from free and fluid use of your body along with free and fluid use of your voice. Do talk with your hands, if that is your style. If you study yourself as you talk, and find your gestures so broad, sharp, and strong that they rivet the prospect's attention on your hands rather than on what you are trying to communicate, then you must moderate your gestures. That is very easy. Once you are aware of the problem, you will be able to turn the sweeping gesture into a shorter, equally communicative, less distracting motion. The sharp, hard, cutting gesture can be turned into an equally useful, much less distracting aid in making your point.

And do talk with your whole body. Just sensitize yourself to what you are doing. Study yourself in the mirror as if you were a stranger. See the main natural things you do, and moderate them, rather than try to force yourself into rigid, uncommunicative patterns of "acceptable" behavior.

HANDLING THE TELEPHONE

On the telephone we are unable to use body language, so effective communication and persuasion become far more difficult than they are face to face. Most sales professionals know this very well; that is why they so much prefer face-to-face selling, and strongly resist the temptation to sell products by telephone as long as face-to-face selling is possible. That is not merely habit, as some who favor telephone selling might suppose; rather, it reflects an understanding of the role that nonverbal communication can and normally does play in the selling process. It would be nice to be able to sell by telephone—no more traffic to fight, no day-destroying broken appointments, just a string of sales interviews adroitly conducted by telephone. The trouble is that field selling is much more effective when conducted face to face. That is why telephone selling—and some kinds of telephone selling can be quite cost-effective—is usually done not by sales professionals but by rather modestly paid people, using fully canned presentations, complete with alternative ways to handle the most common stalls and objections encountered.

Sales professionals do communicate by telephone a good deal, though. We sell appointments, handle customer relations matters, talk to our home offices, sales managers, and colleagues, and do a wide variety of other things on the telephone. It all adds up to a good deal of time spent relying solely on our voices for effective communication, using an instrument that is inherently not capable of handling a full range of communication. That places a premium on such purely verbal matters as roundness of tone, low and pleasant-sounding pitch, moderation of volume, relatively slow delivery, careful pronunciation, and control of regional and ethnic accents. On the telephone, you must first of all be understood, clearly and completely, and there is no way to check nonverbal response to see if you are being understood, much less being persuasive.

Telephone conversations must therefore go more slowly—often much more slowly—than you would like, to become effective communications. Even when conducted very carefully, you still cannot be as sure as you can be face to face that understanding—and, if desired, persuasion—are actually taking place. It is not at all unusual for agreements reached over the telephone to become, in practice, partial or even total disagreements, with both parties to the conversation thinking the other at least rather stupid and at worst unforgivably dishonest.

Because of the frustrating nature of the human contact possible by telephone, many of us talk too long, wasting valuable time trying to develop some kind of rapport, and simultaneously causing those with whom we are speaking to dearly wish the conversation had never started. We also sometimes talk far too brusquely, quite antagonizing others, and behaving in what is perceived by others as an insulting fashion. No, sales professionals are rarely insulting, by telephone or face to face; but they can be inept on the telephone, and seem to be insulting. Unfortunately, whatever the reason, unskilled telephone behavior conveys lack of control and arrogance to others. Handling the telephone badly is a sales-losing and career-harming reflex; it is also discourteous, and the old axiom is still right: Those who give no respect deserve no respect.

Professional telephone handling includes getting the mechanics right. The telephone instrument should be placed to the left of those who write with their right hands, and vice versa, with the wire coming from that side, rather than trailing over your desk from the wrong side and impeding your prime reading and writing area. Writing materials and appointment book should be next to your writing hand, rather than requiring a reach every time you want to write during a telephone conversation. The telephone instrument should be easily reached, held a few inches away from your mouth, and you should speak into it naturally and easily, rather than raising your voice. If you find it comfortable, by all means get a shoulder cradle that lets you operate hands-free, or a desk microphone that lets you speak and listen without using a receiver, if you find one that works well enough. Such advice is simple and basic, certainly. But it is honored only in theory by many people who pay less attention to organizing the mechanics of personal telephone handling than they do to buying a tennis racket, even though they spend hundreds of hours each year on the telephone. Good telephone handling focuses on using the telephone primarily for what it does best, and doing your best to sell face to face. But when we do get on the telephone, we want to do our best to handle it well.

WRITING

The same is true of writing. For, while most face-to-face sales professionals do not in the normal course of events need to be polished professional writers, they do find themselves putting a surprising number of words on paper—and on tapes and discs, as well—in the course of even a couple of months in the field. There are letters to customers and prospects, memos to management and regional and home office people, letters to professional and personal acquaintances and friends, and sometimes even a personally written piece of sales material, although that is rare. Whenever possible, field people should rely upon trained promotion people for written sales material, as promotion writing is very much a writer's special task. It is the sort of thing that, like selling, looks easy from the outside, but in fact requires a good deal of training and focus to come out well. Proposal writing is also a special skill, and those whose selling responsibilities include a good deal of such work will be well advised to seek the necessary special training, from their companies and from published work on this special skill.

From the point of view of career building, good writing skills are a considerable asset, especially for those who want to make the move into management. Managers write a great deal, and need to be good at clearly and persuasively putting their words into written form. Assessment of the suitability of prospects for a move into management always includes a close look at their writing skills.

Good business writing is just that—a skill. It requires a proper set of attitudes, careful preparation, organization, work, rework, attention to detail, and practice. It does not require a great deal of talent, and it most emphatically does not require long-winded multisyllabic language full of professional jargon. In this, good business writing is like good business speech—it is clear, easy-flowing, relaxed, and friendly. The best possible approach a sales professional can take to writing is to think before writing, organize those thoughts into a coherent whole, and then write the way you speak. No, not the way *other* people write, or the way you might think you should write—the way you speak. Then, after getting it on paper, rework it for clarity and friendliness, again and again as necessary, until you have it the way you want it. Then type it or have it typed and do a final proofreading and editing, if necessary typing it again. Worry about such matters as grammar and word agreement during rework and editing, not during the basic writing. The key to the whole process is to let it flow, get it down, and then spend whatever time you need to fix it up in final form. Conversely, the main enemy is fear—of being misunderstood, of being laughed at, of somehow saying less and being less persuasive than you know you can be face to face, of exposing ignorance, of not being able to "fix it all up" with body language as you do face to face or as you do with extra words on the telephone. A good writer learns to relax and let a personal style—an individual and authentic voice—emerge in writing, just as a good face-to-face selling professional does in the field. For both, the main enemy is "freezing up"; for both, the best approach is turning learned skills into lifelong reflexes.

Effective business writing is aimed at the audience it addresses. Your letter confirming an appointment with a prospect is likely to be written differently than your letter to a complaining customer, and both are likely to be written differently than a letter to the marketing management of your company. But whatever your audience, it is usually a good idea to keep your writing free of jargon and shop-talk terms. A letter or memo that cannot be understood does not accomplish the writer's purpose and wastes everyone's time. When you are uncertain about the audience, aim for a general lay level. There are times, however, when the shorthand of shop talk is appropriate. Reserve shop talk for internal memos, when you are absolutely sure of your audience and its understanding of the subject.

The purpose and audience of your communication will guide you in setting the tone. How do you wish to come across to your readers? Are you handling a complaint or making a pitch? Do you want your voice to seem authoritative, friendly, or sympathetic?

Consider your relationship to the reader (is it formal or informal?) as well as any biases the reader may have toward you or your subject. Choose words that will communicate the right attitude. It is not always easy, especially if the subject is a delicate one. Since you cannot see the reader, you cannot judge any reaction to your words by watching facial expressions, and change your tone accordingly. Sometimes factors beyond your control or knowledge—such as political or personal sensitivities, or differing interpretations of the meaning of certain words—will make a reader "hear" the wrong tone.

Your best approach is to try to place yourself in the reader's position and anticipate how that person is likely to react to what you say in print. For example, a customer with a complaint may want empathy and assurance that a problem is being resolved. Notice the difference in tone between the two letters in Figure 1.

FIGURE 1

a.

Dear Mr. Raymond:

Pursuant to your letter of June 30, we have shipped you one wide-angle lens #A58, which you ordered from our catalog. We are sorry for the delay, and thank you for bringing it to our attention.

b.

Dear Mr. Raymond:

The wide-angle lens #A58 you ordered from our catalog has been shipped to you by Parcel Post.

The delay in filling your order was due to a clerical oversight. We customarily process orders within one week of receiving them.

I hope you have not been inconvenienced. Thank you for doing business with us, and please consider us again for your future optical needs.

Both are perfectly correct, but the first is wooden and brusque, while the second communicates understanding and personal attention. The recipient of the second letter is much more likely to place repeat business with the company.

Above all, remember that writing is communication between human beings. Too many of us think business writing must be formal, dry, and riddled with ornate prose, rather than clear and friendly. Where it is appropriate, stay in touch with your audience through the use of personal pronouns such as "I," "you," and "we." Imagine you are having a conversation with the reader. Face to face, you would never say, "ABC company wishes to extend its appreciation for your introduction of our new widget line to your customers." Instead, you would say something more like "Thank you for joining in the introduction of our new widget line, for which we all have high hopes." Set a warm, human tone that will help you accomplish your purposes.

It is also important to be aware of timing. If you are setting your own deadline, consider whether purpose or content hinge on a time factor. Then you should plan your writing schedule to meet the deadline, with time to spare. Be sure to build into your schedule time to conduct necessary research or obtain information from other sources. Do not count on wrapping up your communication at the last minute, because—as in Murphy's Law—something is bound to go wrong. An emergency will sidetrack your attention or your typist will get sick. You also will need time for revising and editing. Few good writers ever stop with their first, or even second, draft. Even one-page letters and memos need a once-over for corrections and polish.

Your writing environment is also extremely important. Wherever you write—whether in office, home, airplane, or hotel room—make your working area as comfortable as possible. Have all your notes and reference materials at hand. It is annoying, as well as counterproductive, to stop writing to search for a piece of information. Most offices are reasonably well set up for writing work, but sales professionals, who often write elsewhere, must carefully create the proper environment. Otherwise the task is not as productive as it could be—and far more frustrating than it should be.

At home, do your writing away from main family activity areas, especially where a television set or radio is on. If you have not yet set up a full office at home, at least shut yourself in a bedroom or study and request that you not be disturbed. Writing at the kitchen or dining room table or in a living room easy chair invites interruption. It is best to work at a desk or table, with a chair of the right height for your working surface. A chair that is too low or too high causes muscle strain. Metal folding chairs are unsuitable for long periods of writing work. If you do a lot of work at home—and sales professionals should expect to do just that—it would be wise to invest in a good-quality office chair; the added comfort will be well worth it. Otherwise, try your kitchen or dining room chairs, adding a cushion if necessary. Above all, you need adequate light to avoid straining your eyes; overhead lights are not enough. Compact, high-intensity desk lamps are inexpensive and portable, and some models have clip-on features for attachments to furniture.

The same comfort considerations should be given to your hotel or motel accommodations. Ask for a room with a desk or table and chair and try them out as soon as you check in. If the furniture does not feel comfortable or the lighting is not good, request another room. You will get far more accomplished, with less fatigue, in an adequate work area.

You can also make productive use of flying time by carrying on writing work. The small meal trays are not well suited to be writing surfaces, however, because they usually force you to lean forward to write. Use an attaché case in your lap as a writing surface; or if you carry a soft portfolio, include in it a clipboard or hard notebook binder. If you plan to work throughout a long flight, minimize mental and muscle fatigue by taking an occasional walk down the aisle.

Effective writing also requires good writing habits. That means disciplining yourself to write, whether or not you "feel" like it and in spite of minor distractions. If professional writers wrote only when they "felt" like it, newspapers, magazines, and books would never get published.

WRITING EFFECTIVE LETTERS

A good business letter, whether it accepts, rejects, tells, or sells, has warmth and a human touch. It is direct, polite, and sincere, and tells the recipient what he or she needs to know. Above all, letters should have a pleasant tone, even if you want to complain about something. Angry letters do not accomplish nearly as much as firm, reasoned ones.

Before you write a letter, think first of what you would say to the recipient if you were communicating in person. Would you ever really say, "I am sending forthwith . . ." or "re your letter of August 18 . . ."? We hope not. Certainly you should avoid such cumbersome, overly formal phrases in your writing. A pleasant tone is not conveyed by awkward, stilted phrases.

The use of personal pronouns, such as *I*, *we*, and *you*,

helps set a pleasant tone in letters. Avoid using harsh negatives and commands. Instead of saying, "we cannot fill your order," say "we are unable to fill your order." Do not tell the recipient that he or she "must" or "has to" do something. Instead of "You must sign the enclosed form letter before we can issue the title," say: "We need your signature on the enclosed form before we can issue the title." For an informal tone, use contractions, which are more conversational.

Letters should come right to the point. Give the pertinent information and sign off, not abruptly, but without digression or padding. One significant exception to that rule, though, is a letter replying to a complaint, in which you are trying to soothe someone, and in which you may not want to come to the point quite so quickly.

Whatever their subjects or purposes, all letters have in common a salutation and a closing. Each must be chosen to suit the tone you have adopted—formal or informal—and the relationship between you and your reader. The most common salutation is "Dear _____" followed by a comma (informal) or a colon (formal, and most commonly used for business purposes).

> Dear Mary,
> Dear Mr. Jones,
> Dear Ms. Randall:

Very formal salutations are "Dear Sir" and "Dear Madam"; reserve those for persons of very high rank or eminence. You may wish to use "Dear Sir or Madam," "Dear Sirs or Mesdames," or "Dear Ladies and Gentlemen," when you are uncertain who will receive your letter. Although none of these choices is terribly attractive, they are preferable to "To Whom It May Concern," which has a legalistic, antiquated sound to it.

What if you are uncertain of the gender of the recipient? Say you are writing a formal letter to a Leslie Smith, but you do not know if the person is male or female. Do not use "Sir/Madam" or "Dear Mr./Ms. Smith." Above all, don't guess. Instead, write out the full name:

Dear Leslie Smith:

It may sound a little cumbersome, but it is far better than risking an insulting error. If you do not know the marital status of a woman, use *Ms.* The neutral title has lost its militant image and is now widely used and accepted. Many businesswomen prefer it, regardless of marital status.

Closings are simpler. The choice is simply between informal and formal. The best all-purpose closings are "Sincerely" and "Sincerely yours." Some good informal closings include:

Cordially	Regards
Best wishes	Warmly

Some more formal closings are:

Respectfully	Respectfully yours
Yours truly	Very truly yours
Very cordially yours	Very sincerely yours

Avoid being cute or clever in closings. In general, avoid extremes, like the too-casual "Yours" or the somewhat archaic "Respectfully submitted."

As all sales professionals know, mistakes do happen. If you are on the receiving end of a valid complaint, own up to it with a polite apology. See example a in Figure 2.

If the complainer is in error, or if you cannot comply with the request, be polite but firm. See example b in Figure 2.

Whatever kinds of letters you routinely have to write, you will benefit from developing your own standard "form" letters. Examine your own files for a certain period, isolate the various types of letters, and analyze the contents, retaining what you think—on reflection—worked well, and replacing what did not. You will save yourself a good deal of rethinking for those parts of your letters that are relatively routine. A caution, however: avoid form letters when you are dealing with a single person or company over a long period of time. They would surely be insulted by such letters.

FIGURE 2

---

a.

Dear Mr. Southwell:

Since we received your letter about the improper printing of the last issue of *Bird News*, our vice president of production has met with our press foreman to determine what the problem was.

Apparently, a press person loaded the paper feeder incorrectly. The error was spotted, and the bad copies were pulled out of production. Evidently a few slipped through—we think it could not have been more than 30 copies.

This was a human error, and all personnel have been alerted to be much more careful in the future. We apologize for the mistake and wish to assure you that all precautions will be taken in the future to deliver a product of which we can all be proud.

b.

Dear Mr. Calder:

We have doublechecked our records and find that our last billing was correct. Your last payment was received on March 17, and your account shows that $54.29 is still owed us.

Perhaps your payment envelope was misplaced or lost in the mail. If so, you may still avoid a finance charge by remitting the above amount by the next billing date.

SOME WRITING CAUTIONS

Bear in mind that jargon—nonwords and often meaningless gibberish—is a bane to clarity and conciseness. In government agencies and businesses large and small across the nation, people are "solutioning" problems, "dollarizing" new production processes, getting "oriented" to situations, and "throughputting" suggestions. Although some corporate publications have taken up a "ban the jargon" standard, and many seminars and books tackle the subject, jargon still thrives.

We are guilty of using jargon when we turn nouns into

verbs, create nonwords, and otherwise mangle the English language. A favorite in the business lexicon is *escalate*. Used properly, it means "to increase in extent, scope, or volume." Used as jargon, it means taking an issue to a higher authority, as when someone dislikes a decision and announces, "I'm going to escalate this to the vice president." Not surprisingly, lawyers are among the worst jargon offenders. Legal mumbo jumbo renders inscrutable many contracts, laws, regulations, and applications.

Jargon and obfuscation have long been problems in the bureaucratic ranks of the federal government—so much so that an internal campaign was launched in 1979 to fight them. Members of the Document Design Center, a division of the private, nonprofit American Institute of Research, have been instructing government employees how to write in plain English. Alas, thousands of confusing regulations and application forms still are churned out every year. Ironically, the campaign has created some new jargon: "good paper" and "bad paper," which describe the clarity of government writing.

Much jargon comes from plain laziness. It is faster to say "dollarize this" than to say "estimate how much it will cost to do this." Some jargon comes from ignorance: *solution* is a noun, *solve* a verb. Problems are solved, not solutioned. A quick check with a dictionary would save many a writer the embarrassment of an improperly used or nonexistent word; like the sales executive who reported that sales of a certain product were "denigrating." (He meant declining.)

Some jargon users sincerely believe that jargon makes them sound impressive—quite the opposite. At worst, jargon will reduce your writing to gibberish, and make you appear uneducated; at best, it is annoying clutter. If some jargon has crept into your draft, excise it. Do you really mean "electronic mail" instead of "electronic document distribution"? Are you "offering" suggestions instead of "inputting" them?

An active voice, rather than a passive voice, will contribute to your clarity and conciseness. In an active voice, the subject of a sentence performs an activity or takes action. In a passive voice, the subject receives action. A passive voice, which is used far too often in business communications, weakens sentences and dilutes their meanings. Because it can provide an anonymous cloak, it is a favorite of writers who wish to blunt their words or evade responsibility for a statement.

See how much stronger the following sentences are when written in an active voice.

Passive: Replacement of existing copiers with newer, faster models is being planned for the next fiscal year.

Active: We plan to replace all copiers with newer, faster models next fiscal year.

Passive: It is recommended that our prices be increased by 10%.

Active: I recommend a 10% price increase.

Note that the active voice sentences are shorter, more concise, and more powerful, and have more impact on the reader. If you find that your writing is largely passive, rewrite your sentences in the active voice during editing.

It is also important to establish a smooth pace and pleasant cadence for the written word, just as for the spoken word. Sentences that are short and choppy give the reader an unsettled, stop-and-go feeling. Long sentences, which must be reread and deciphered, leave the reader feeling exhausted and confused.

Here is a single sentence published in the U.S. Department of Agriculture's October 1981 telephone book. Fill your lungs and try to get through it in one breath:

> To ensure that the information on all USDA employees on file within O&F is current, it is essential that all employees promptly notify their designated agency contact of all changes to any of the information contained in the alphabetical listing section of the directory, i.e., name, room number, building location, and telephone

> number, so the contacts can transmit this information to the AMLS and Telephone Directory Section of the Production and Distribution Division which maintains the data base for this information from which the alphabetical listing section of the USDA Telephone Directory is prepared as well as periodic updates of the telephone directory information on USA employees which are transmitted to the GSA Locater Service here in Washington, D.C.

Do you know what that says? There are 135 words in this sentence, counting the abbreviations as single words.

These two possible revisions are more understandable and save the reader considerable time in reading and re-reading.

> Please submit promptly all changes of name, address, and telephone number to your agency contact in order to keep federal directories up to date. (One sentence, 24 words.)

> Please help keep federal directories up to date. Submit promptly all changes of name, address, and telephone number to your agency contact. (Two sentences, 8 and 14 words, respectively.)

For your readers' sakes, keep your sentences of a manageable length. If your sentences *average* 17 to 20 words in length, you are in the right ball park. Some sentences will be shorter and some longer, of course. You should vary the lengths to avoid monotony. Calculate the lengths of a few sentences you have written. If they *all* run longer than 20 words, break several of them into shorter sentences. Your information should be evenly paced throughout your document, too. Do not drop too much on the reader at once, but do not skip over something too lightly either.

Give your material a test by reading it aloud. Do any parts of it sound jerky, as though you are missing a transition? Can you combine two choppy sentences into a single sentence? Does your material look pleasing to the eye? Is information neatly packaged in manageable paragraphs? If it is a long memo, have you used headings and subheadings to break up chunks of type? Most often, editing involves dealing with several types of problems at once. Be ruthless in chopping out unnecessary words and jargon, and in changing sentences from passive into active ones.

Take considerable care to desex your writing. It is acceptable to use *him or her*, *his or hers*, and *he or she*, but do so infrequently, because they are clumsy. Similarly, avoid *he/she, his/hers, s/he and (s)he*. In those rare instances when you want to use masculine pronouns to represent everyone, be sure to announce that choice in the beginning of your text. In most cases, though, it is best to try to write around gender.

Find neutral substitutes for words that traditionally have been masculine, such as *chairman, mailman, stockboy, manpower, manhours,* and *salesman*. Here are a few examples of neutral nouns:

Chairman	chair
mailman	mail carrier
stockboy	stock clerk
manpower	workforce
manhours	workhours
salesman	sales representative

It is best not to substitute *-person* or *-woman* in masculine words, such as *chairperson* or *chairwoman*, although you may do so in a pinch.

Along similar lines, avoid describing women by their personal appearance, unless it is essential to what you are saying and you are treating men the same way.

If you said this about a woman, "Senator James, an attractive redhead . . . ," would you say this about a man, "Senator Harris, balding and broad-shouldered . . . ?" Personal appearance rarely has anything to do with a person's professional ability or standing, and such descriptions have no place in business writing.

Clear and persuasive speaking, body language, telephone handling, and writing are essential career-building skills for sales professionals, and are well worth the time and attention it takes to learn to do them well. With them, professionalism is enormously enhanced, and you are more readily able to move anywhere and handle almost any kind of work in the world of selling—which is pretty much what professionalism is all about.

CHAPTER 7

APPEARANCES THAT COUNT

Matters of dress, grooming, and equipment are matters of personal "packaging"; as such, they are important, though not nearly as important as what we are and how we convey what we are to others. And we project what we are with speech and body language far more than we do with appearance. That successful sales professionals are always people who look as if they had just stepped out of a Fifth Avenue show window is a myth; many seasoned and very successful people in selling look about as fashionable as an average middle- to upper-grade civil service employee anywhere in the country.

That said, appearance does still deserve careful attention, for while excellent appearance can help sales results and career development only a little, poor appearance can cause sales and careers a great deal of harm.

A good—meaning rather conservative, classically styled, and fairly expensive—personal appearance can help others to accept you as a working professional, in the field and in your company. Conversely, an appearance that is too far from current behavioral or stylistic norms can jar, and set up unnecessary barriers between yourself and others. In exteme instances, when grooming and dress are very far from current styles, it is even possible to severely harm sales and career possibilities. These are only matters of current style, of course, and have nothing at all to do with professional skills. Yet they can be important, if current norms are bent too far. The main thing to understand about dress and grooming is not so much that you can do yourself a great deal of good by dressing and looking good, but that you can do yourself a great deal of harm with a poor appearance. That means keeping up with current standards, looking clean, cool, and alert at all times, and in all climates and conditions; and it means dressing comfortably and classically, and not worrying too much about how you look to others.

Although such matters as how to dress are enormously overrated as selling and career-building factors, it is possible to make situations—and particularly new situations, with new people—far more difficult than they need be by conveying wrong signals about yourself with manner and dress. Most experienced people have trained themselves to pick up useful clues from a quick first look. Such minor grooming matters as uncombed hair, scuffed shoes, or not quite fully cleaned fingernails can easily be seen as evidences of a general carelessness that may show up in other, more serious ways. The person who seems unwilling to tend to such small matters may not care enough about much more important matters; such a little thing can tip a buying or hiring decision the wrong way. Similarly, those who dress quite inexpensively are all too often seen as people who may not quite be making it financially; that can jar others enough to make them somewhat uneasy about them as buyers, as employers, and as co-networkers over a period of years. We want those we do business with, and our associates, protégés, friends, and allies, to "look good"; it makes us look good, and it makes our company look good.

Similarly, the sales professional who dresses too trendily or too sexily, or who uses too much cologne, perfume, hair tonic, lipstick, or whatever else is not *in* this year, tends to jar others. Among business professionals, the least questioned and most accepted image is still basically that created by Gregory Peck in *The Man in the Grey Flannel Suit*, in the period following World War II. This image, however, is no longer solely a white, Anglo-Saxon, Protestant male image, but now encompasses female, black, Hispanic, Jewish, East Asian, Native American, and a score of other national and ethnic images, as well. But all of them share this: they are still conservatively and traditionally dressed and groomed, and in every verbal and nonverbal way convey that they carry upper-middle-class status. This is not upper-class economic status and the social attitudes assumed to go with "old money," which are thought by so many others to be rather nastily condescending. The main American business image of this period continues to be that of the small-town boy—or girl—who made good, and now occupies one of the big houses on the right side of the tracks.

PLANNING A BUSINESS WARDROBE

What constitutes effective business dress varies somewhat regionally and by industry. A southeastern regional representative may wear a white suit in midsummer quite easily; so may his or her clients. But those working on Fifth Avenue or Wall Street in New York City are not very likely to be found wearing white suits in any season; nor will their clients in the New York area. And when *you* go to Atlanta on business in midsummer, you will be unwise to don a white suit, although you may leave your dark, pinstriped suit and Ivy League tie behind. A white suit would properly be perceived by local people in Atlanta as a phony, while the pinstripes and Ivy League tie would make you seem too alien to be comfortable with; the solution is somewhere in between.

You will find the most conservative business dress on the East Coast, especially in the corridor that runs from Boston to Washington, D.C., as well as at most corporate headquarters, regardless of geographic location. The basic business colors of blue and grey will work well virtually anywhere in the country, but clothing styles loosen up a bit in the Midwest, where more browns and tans are worn by men, and more bright colors by women. Short sleeves and light dresses are common in the South and Southwest. And the West Coast is far more casual than the East Coast, with California being the most relaxed of all. In general, it is best to stay within the conservative range for your region and industry, avoiding sartorial extremes.

Some basic guidelines are helpful when you are planning and upgrading a sound business wardrobe. Perhaps most important is to learn the look and feel of quality. Many people, when they shop, go through the racks until something catches their eye. If it looks all right and the price is acceptable, they buy it. They may check the label for fiber content as a second thought; they may never inspect the finishing and stitching.

If you are shopping for your professional "uniform," you should shop more carefully, with a purpose and plan. Do a little window shopping first. You will find the best quality in better stores; visit them and inspect their merchandise. Read the labels for manufacturers and for fiber content, and note prices. This will help you get the best value and quality at the best price when it comes time to do your actual buying.

Good quality garments are well finished. Most clothing is machine-stitched, with the exception of the finest suits, which are tailored and stitched by hand. Machine-stitching should be small and even. The pieces of a garment should be well joined; that is, collars should lay flat, sleeves should not pucker, and lapels should not pull. Buttonholes should be well finished, without loose threads. Check the inside of the garment for seams that are ample and finished, and that will not begin unraveling with wear and cleaning. Linings should not pull or pucker or droop below hemlines. Buttons, if not bone, should at least be a good quality plastic or a nontarnishing brasslike metal.

For quality, look for the real thing—natural fibers or blends with natural fibers for clothing, and leather for accessories such as wallets, gloves, shoes, belts, and briefcases. In general, avoid garments that are all synthetic and any material that is shiny or semitransparent. Some synthetic fibers have a shininess to them that looks cheap; they also feel rough to the touch. Above all, avoid all polyester knits, especially for outer garments. They are distinctly not upper-middle class, and tend to snag, stretch, and bag. The real thing costs more than substitutes and imitations, but it is far better to own a few good quality outfits than many cheaper ones. The difference in quality speaks for itself.

The best natural fibers are wool and cotton. Wool can be worn year-round, particularly if it is blended with polyester. Wool breathes and keeps its color and shape well. It adds richness and texture to a blend. Wool will keep you warmer in the winter and, believe it or not, cooler in the summer than synthetics. Polyesters, rayons, and acrylics, for example, do not breathe well. A lightweight suit that is 45% wool and 55% polyester is cooler during hot months than is an all-polyester suit. When buying wool-blend garments, be sure to check the fiber contents label; 45% wool is the minimum for optimum wear, durability, appearance, and texture.

Cotton is comfortable on the skin, breathes well, and is cool in the summer, but it is a fragile fabric that is much better blended with polyester. By itself, cotton shrinks, fades, wrinkles, and wears out quickly. In a blend, you can have the comfort of cotton with the durability of polyester. Some of the best and most expensive men's shirts, however, are all cotton. Buy these only if you are prepared to foot a weekly cleaning bill. Because of the way cotton wrinkles, you will need to send your shirts out for cleaning and pressing in order for them to look crisp.

Silk is a natural fiber that has been enjoying renewed popularity, especially in more fashionable clothing. Silk is especially appropriate, even preferable, for accessories such as ties and scarves. Good silk has a rich, quality look, but the fiber has significant disadvantages in clothing for business purposes: it is expensive, can soil and stain, generally requires dry cleaning, and wrinkles easily. In addition, the rich, lustrous look of silk may give garments—particularly suits—more of an evening wear look than a business look. However, many women have made silk dresses and blouses staples for business wear. Silk dresses may be better left for evenings, but silk blouses are certainly acceptable with suits and with skirts and blazers, if one is willing to bear the expense of caring for them properly.

Silk—good silk—can be wonderfully soft and comfortable and rich and shiny in appearance. Even though it is a thin fabric, it can absorb up to one third of its weight in moisture, which makes it very comfortable to wear on hot days. Not all silks are equal, however, and, unfortunately, most labels do not tell enough about the quality of the garment. Italian silks tend to be the best, generally very soft and quite lustrous—and they are the most expensive. Dyes vary greatly in quality; some are actually water-soluble, a disaster if they ever get wet. Others stain easily, and many will fade when subjected to strong sunlight. Many stores will tell you that you can avoid heavy dry-cleaning costs by washing silk in cold-water detergents meant for woolens, lingerie, and other delicate garments. But that may not be as practical as it sounds. Depending on the quality of the fiber, washed silk may wrinkle considerably and may not iron out well. It is safer to dry clean brightly colored silks and textured silks, such as crepe and taffeta. If you do opt to hand wash your silks, take care not to rub or twist the fabric, because the yarns can break and stretch easily. Also, be sure to iron the garments on the wrong side.

Since you can invest a lot of money in silk, it would be worth your while to do some research on the various silk weaves before buying any; there are nearly two dozen of them, all with different qualities and properties. When shopping for silk, remember that good silk is expensive. The popularity of silk has brought many cheap silks to the market, and a cheap silk is just that: cheap. It may not be dyed evenly, it may discolor unevenly, or it may separate or tear easily. If you cannot buy silk, look for silk and polyester blends, or good polyesters that look like silk. If you shop around enough, you will soon be able to recognize polyesters that are good imitators of silk.

Accessories are where many otherwise smart shoppers fall down. They pay top dollar for quality clothes, which they then ruin with cheap accessories. Your entire appearance must convey quality; do not skimp, thinking you can "get by" with something pulled out of a bargain basement. Do not buy imitation leather; buy the real thing. Be especially careful with shoes—inexpensive leather shoes look only marginally better than vinyl ones. Any jewelry should be simple, functional, and fashioned from real gold or silver. If you have an inexpensive watch, you may wish to dress it up with a leather band instead of a plastic, fabric, or metal one. Always carry and use a good gold or silver pen—never a "cheapie," no matter who else around you may use one.

As you do your window shopping, note brand names and their various levels of quality and cost. While you will find top brands in better stores, you will also begin to notice the brands that come next in quality and are less expensive. You need not buy the most expensive of everything you need. It is perfectly acceptable—and wise from a budget standpoint—to buy more moderately priced goods, as long as they look high quality. You will find some good quality, more moderately priced brands in department stores, but avoid discount chains. Discount chains often stock imperfect goods and overruns that have missed the market in their style. The same caution applies to factory and warehouse outlets. Many do sell name brand goods at marked-down prices, usually with the labels ripped out, but others sell seconds and imperfects that are not marked as such.

A word about name brand labels: as you become more familiar with the quality of certain brands, you will probably develop a list of favorites that you will trust. Many stores have their own labels, and these are often good bets for quality merchandise at moderate prices. Stores generally are careful when it comes to their own labels, as it is bad advertising to put your name on something that falls apart after one or two cleanings. A discount chain, however, may put its own label on an inexpensive loss leader item designed solely to attract traffic to the store. You must discover for yourself which stores are the most reliable.

A designer label once ensured good quality. With some designers, that is still true today, but other designer labels have become so diluted through mass manufacturing and merchandising that they really offer no guarantee of quality at all. In fact, the clothing may even be poorly constructed. Such designers license manufacturers to produce their designs, but they cannot possibly monitor quality. They sit back and collect royalties while you pay a premium price for their name without necessarily getting premium quality. The proliferation of designer labels in department stores, discount houses, and outlets has also reduced their status. Wearing such items is no longer a sure mark of upper-middle-class status and wealth. In fact, in the business world, designer labels can work against you, if the designer's name or initials are plastered all over your garment. Traditional, classic apparel is understated, and is not a walking billboard for someone else.

A second basic in wardrobe planning is to consider the importance of color. For people in most business situations, dark colors work best because they convey authority and power. The all-around general business suit color for men and women is dark blue or navy blue. Charcoal grey and medium grey are good, but dark browns are not universally acceptable. If you have limited funds for your wardrobe, it is best to build it around blues and greys; beige is an acceptable third color.

Women have more latitude to wear bright colors than do men; still, both sexes should take care to avoid trendy, fashion-oriented shades and styles, which make their wearers look frivolous in the conservative eyes of the business establishment. Women should also strike red from their business wardrobes—it is a boldly sexual color. At the other extreme, be careful with black; it is a very severe color, and can cause as much negative reaction as a frivolous color, like pink. Some colors—such as gold, pink, lavender, and certain greens—are best avoided in suits altogether.

The quieter your outfit is, the better. Solids work the best, especially for women. Pinstripes function well for men (as long as they are not reminiscent of the wide, "gangster look") but less well for women. Muted plaids and tweeds are acceptable if they are of very good quality; make certain that plaid patterns match where garment pieces are sewn together. Both sexes should avoid fabrics that have busy, dramatic, or distracting patterns, which diminish professional appearance and, consequently, status.

Shirts and blouses should contrast with suits; white and pastels (except pink) are the most acceptable shades for men and women. The pastels should not blend into the color of the suit, for that can create a dull, lifeless look. While women can wear dark shades with light-colored suits (a maroon blouse with a light grey suit, for example), men are best advised to stick to white with light-colored suits.

For important occasions, such as job interviews and key group presentations, it is wise to dress especially conservatively. The best colors for job interviews are suits in charcoal or light grey and navy blue, with contrasting shirts or blouses. When job hunting, women should forgo their freedom to wear darker colors in shirts and blouses, and stick with white or pastel blue, the most accepted contrasting colors in the business establishment.

The only kind of clothing for which bright colors are not only acceptable but expected is sportswear. You should not go overboard, however, and show up looking like a neon sign at your company's summer sales refresher workshop. Upper-middle-class sportswear colors tend to center around white, navy, maroon, and khaki, although many bright plaids are also acceptable. In this area, however, beware of light blue, which can look cheap, and bright yellow, which can look gaudy.

When selecting colors and putting together outfits, take into consideration your weight and build. Fortunately for most of us, the dark, "power" colors also tend to be slimming, while brighter colors tend to make people look larger. A plaid over a paunch can add to the rotundity. Dark colors on tall, large men and women can make them look too imposing, almost unapproachable, however, so if you fit into this category, you may want to build your working wardrobe around lighter shades such as light grey and beige.

The color of your overcoat is just as important as the color of your suit or dress. Camel and beige are good all-around colors in coats, followed by dark grey, navy blue, and black, which are somewhat more formal and severe. Furs may be a bit pretentious in the workplace, except for fur collars on coats, so women should save their fox and mink coats for evening wear.

When planning your business wardrobe you should carefully assess your professional environment. Your company, industry, even your geographic locale will influence your latitude in building your professional wardrobe. If you work for a conservative company such as IBM, you would be wise to stick to very traditional dress habits. Whenever you are in doubt when shopping for clothes, it is safest to go with the most conservative choices. You may have more freedom of expression if you are in a trend-oriented industry such as entertainment, fashion, or advertising, but in most corporate circles, you cannot be too conservative.

Dress customs vary around the country, too. Drop in at a mid-Manhattan restaurant during lunch time and you will see mostly dark suits. But in Los Angeles, you will most likely see brighter colors on both men and women, and even shirts open at the neck on men.

Look around you and note carefully how your peers and superiors are dressed, particularly the key sales management people at your company. You may want to pick out one or two successful superiors, analyze their styles of dress, and use them as role models to emulate. That does not mean you should copy them—you can make mistakes that way. For example, monogrammed shirts may be seen as fitting for a senior marketing vice president, but not for a youngish field representative. And certain affectations, such as linen handkerchiefs in breast pockets or diamond lapel stick pins, may work wonderfully for one person and look pretentious or silly on another. Use your role models as guides, wear nothing that makes you feel uncomfortable, and add your own distinctive personal touches.

Once you have planned what your business wardrobe *should* be, you should carefully and critically assess your present wardrobe. This is the moment of truth. How does your closet stand up to the test? Divide your clothes into seasons and assess each item—each suit, dress, blazer, pair of slacks, accessory, shirt, blouse, and pair of shoes. Be honest and ruthless, even though it may be painful to see just how much of what you own does not meet critical standards. If you are like most people, you have accumulated your wardrobe in a haphazard fashion, buying this on sale here, that on impulse there, including items that may not fit you quite right, but they were such a terrific deal you could not pass them up. Well, reform time is at hand. No point in lamenting past mistakes—just vow not to repeat them. Give everything in your closet a meticulous examination and be firm in setting aside everything that does not measure up. And that means *everything*. All of those items will eventually disappear from your working wardrobe; how quickly will depend on how much you have to replace, and how much money you can afford to spend over what period of time. What will you do with all your discards? Save what you can to wear around the house, donate them to charity, or—if they are in excellent condition—take them to a thrift resale shop.

As you assess your wardrobe, keep in mind that you will want to build your clothing around one or two main colors. Group those items that go together and then determine what you still need to round things out. Limiting your color schemes will help prevent you from buying something on impulse, only to seldom wear it because it does not go with many of your other clothes.

What if you feel you must start almost from scratch, but have a tight budget for clothes? In that case, at least eliminate the most unsuitable items from your wardrobe and gradually replace the rest. Work out a timetable with what you feel you can comfortably afford to spend, and start with a few basics that can do double duty for you, such as a dark, solid-colored suit that can be worn twice in one week but will look different with varying shirts and ties or blouses.

Rebuilding Your Wardrobe.

You are now ready to begin reconstructing your wardrobe. You should start by making a list of the things you need and ranking them by priority. Concentrate on the season at hand—if it is summer, focus on your lighter clothing needs. You should also make a list for your fall and winter needs, but you can postpone buying for the next season until it actually arrives. Eventually, when you get your core wardrobe established, you can begin buying for seasons in advance, in order to take advantage of sales. You can get some very good markdowns on clothes at the end of seasons.

But you must be careful, because it is easy to get carried away with sales. Do not buy something that is of mediocre quality or that may go out of style in a season or two just because it is on sale. Do not buy something that is not quite the right color or something you merely *think* will coordinate with clothes hanging in your closet, just because the price is right. The price may be appealing, but chances are the garment will not be quite right, and it will only go unworn—a quite expensive purchase when you consider the small use you get from a particular piece of clothing. A suit marked down $80 is no bargain if you wear it only once or twice a season. You may find that the labels you like to buy seldom go on sale (as is often the case in premium clothing), although you may get lucky and find something you are looking for at a reduced price. The important thing is never to sacrifice quality and practicality for price.

Your general rule of thumb should be to buy the best

possible quality you can afford. If you cannot afford a Brooks Brothers suit, buy a less costly brand that comes closest, in your estimation, to the quality you seek. If you cannot afford a good-quality silk blouse, buy one made from a polyester that closely imitates the look and feel of real silk. It is far better to have a smaller wardrobe of high-quality clothes than a large wardrobe of medium-quality or cheap clothes.

When shopping for shirts, ties, and blouses to go with suits or jackets, buy the items together rather than separately. You cannot rely on your memory to tell you accurately the shade of something in your closet; you may get something home and find it does not match at all. If possible, pick out shirts, ties, and blouses at the same time you buy a suit. Or, take a swatch of suit material with you. Better yet, wear the suit when you go shopping, or take the jacket with you. That way, you will be certain of picking out items that complement each other. The same idea applies when shopping for shoes. Do not try on business shoes while dressed in jeans or dungarees; wear an outfit you plan to wear with the shoes. It does make a difference. Remember, you are striving for a well-thought-out, unified, *total* look.

If you have done enough window shopping, and have examined the quality of merchandise offered at various stores, you will probably know which ones you want to patronize. You will probably get the best, most personalized attention at smaller shops that carry top quality lines, because part of their business is knowing the individual needs of their clientele. Most of these salespeople will not try to pressure you into quick sales; if they see you are serious about your shopping, they will generally take the time to help you assemble well-integrated outfits. Explain what you are looking for and what you can spend. Many of these shops will keep a card on file with your measurements and color and fabric preferences, and experienced sales representatives will keep an eye out for new arrivals that match certain customers' requirements. Many department stores also offer personal consultants to help you with your year-round clothing needs. Some such services are free, though others carry charges; they can be very helpful for busy people who have little time to shop.

At warehouse and factory outlets, however, you are on your own. Such outlets may have personnel available to direct you to the right racks, even assist you with a fitting, but beyond that, do not look for much advice. If you know what you are looking for, you can sometimes find good bargains at outlets. But you must know your outlets; be sure they sell store-quality goods and not seconds or irregulars.

When shopping for any type of garment, be sure to try it on and carefully check the fit, because no two manufacturers make the same size the same way. Even two garments of the same size, made by the same manufacturer, may vary slightly. Whether you are purchasing a suit, skirt, blazer, or dress, chances are you will need alterations. Although many women simply wear garments as they come off the racks, it is highly unlikely that clothing will fit well enough without changes. Do not just "make do"; have it altered. Unfortunately, many stores still charge women for alterations that they give men for free. Even so, the extra charge is worth it to get the best possible fit.

When the alterations have been made, buyers should always ask for—and insist on—a second fitting. You should check the fit from all angles in a three-way mirror, walk in it, and sit down. Be exacting in your assessment of the job done, and accept nothing that looks merely passable but not quite right. You, not the tailor, are the one who has to live in the suit, and you want to look and feel your best in your clothing.

Unless you have a lot of money to spend at one time, it will probably take you awhile—a year, maybe even two—to acquire what you feel you need. But your investment will pay off handsomely in a well-planned image, and your quality garments should last for several years, with proper care and cleaning. Even so, you will probably want to add a little to your wardrobe each season.

The general guidelines discussed in this chapter apply to both men and women. But each sex faces some special considerations regarding business dress. First, the women.

BUSINESS DRESS FOR WOMEN

Unfortunately, dress standards for women are often vague. While a company may have clear-cut, unwritten guidelines for men, women often have few or no female role models in higher positions from whom to take cues. Women have only recently entered selling in any significant numbers, and have in the process been confronted with conflicting advice on how to dress.

In the 1970s, when women began moving into the professional job market in earnest, they were admonished by consultants, both male and female, to adhere to conservative, tailored, mannish dress—dark, skirted suits, often with vests, which were cut in a masculine fashion. Many women, however, looked like imitation men rather than professional businesswomen; mimicking the dress of their male peers sometimes proved more distracting than helpful in establishing a proper business image. Such dress can be very comfortable and effective for some women, however. The key is for women to choose such styles only if they feel comfortable with them personally and in their work environment.

Toward the end of the 1970s, the female dress pendulum began to swing the other way. Women were told that they had established themselves in professional roles and could loosen up their conservative dress standards and be more "feminine." What that meant was the reintroduction of fashion in business dress. Women who were lawyers, securities analysts, and corporate vice presidents—among the most conservative positions in the business world as a whole— were pictured in women's magazines wearing new "business fashions" of bright colors, and high-fashion styles of skirts, dresses, pants, and even culottes. But these kinds of clothes harm more than help, too. Fashion is distracting, and the message it conveys is one of frivolousness. It is hard to take someone seriously if her attire does not look serious, or she looks like she is ready for an evening date.

Furthermore, fashion clothes have two additional disadvantages. First, they do not identify the wearer as a businesswoman. The classic, conservative suit identifies a man as a businessman, and he is treated as such wherever he goes. The well-dressed businessman is accorded respectful—often preferential—treatment at restaurants, hotels, and other service establishments. But any woman, regardless of her professional status, can dress herself up in the latest rage. And when you do not look like you mean business, you will not get the business—or the service or the respect.

Second, fashion clothes tend to be short-lived, holding sway for a season or two and then being replaced by something else that is completely different. That, of course, is how fashion designers and manufacturers stay in business. If their clothes looked the same year after year, women would have no incentive to replace them every season. So, it is to the fashion industry's advantage that clothes for business-women carry seasonal marks. The short-waisted, belted skirt suit in electric purple that looked so smart one season will definitely be *out* the next, and no one would be caught dead wearing it. Likewise with skirts and dresses that go up and down in length.

Changing your wardrobe every season is both costly and foolish. The smart professional woman builds a long-lasting wardrobe, adding to it each year. The well-constructed, high-quality man's suit lasts about five years, on the average, and sometimes longer. The same should be sought in women's business suits—in fact, in all garments. Clothes should be selected for their classic timelessness, quality, and durability. The professional woman who builds such a wardrobe achieves a polished, consistent, upper-middle-class look; she is not surprising her co-workers each season with whatever "look" the fashion designers have decided will rule the day.

While women should not let fashion dictate what they wear to the office, they need not totally ignore it. Many women pay homage to trends through their accessories— scarves, belts, shoes, and handbags. They should not, however, let fashion hold sway in choosing eyeglasses. Designer eyewear, as it is often called in advertisements, comes in odd shapes and colors, and can be as frivolous-looking and as distracting as fashion clothes. A simple plastic frame that complements face and coloring is the best choice. Many businesswomen, particularly those who are petite or very young, find that glasses *add* to their authority; in fact, some women who do not need vision correction have been known to wear spectacles with plain glass lenses just for the appearance of gravity and intelligence they impart.

Skirted suits, followed by skirts and blazers, are still the best all-around items of apparel for the professional woman. A tailored suit or blazer still communicates business and professionalism. Solid colors offer the most flexibility for combinations. Dresses tend to be too fashion-oriented, but they can combine very well with a blazer. A dress with a blazer can solve the problem of going right from the office to an evening social function; a woman can wear the blazer at the office and take it off for the evening. While men can still wear their daytime business suits on into the evening with ease, a woman is still better off with a tailored dress. Some women prefer to wear pantsuits, although such styles have, to some extent, become associated with clerical and secretarial help. Although many companies find pantsuits perfectly acceptable, others do not. Again, the key is personal comfort and an assessment of your environment. If pantsuits are frowned on, you may wish to avoid them as potentially distracting; remember that you are striving for a neutral, professional appearance, not one that calls attention to itself. Vests for women can also backfire, by looking either sexy or too masculine, and sweaters and sleeveless or short-sleeved dresses are definitely not professional.

For skirts or dresses, the best hem length falls right in the middle of the kneecap, which will not hike up excessively on sitting and will not look dowdy when standing. Pantyhose should be neutral, skin-colored shades, not opaque or dark, and certainly not covered with stitched designs.

Women should be sure that jackets do not bunch or roll across the shoulders or pull across the bust. Vents should hang straight and not stick out, and sleeves should end at mid-wrist. Skirts should allow plenty of room around the hips so that zippers do not pucker. And jacket lapels should lie flat; if they do not, a pressing will not help—the lining will need to be readjusted.

When choosing dresses and blouses, stay away from anything semisheer or sheer. The best blouses and shirts have a clean, tailored look, which can be dressed up with scarves if desired. A little bit of lace is all right if it is not excessively frilly. Necklines should be modest, never low. Dressy blouses are certainly appropriate for evening business functions, and can transform a dark tailored suit into evening wear.

Accessories should be selected similarly. Plain, leather, low-heeled pumps are the best, most practical shoe for women, and are healthier for the feet than high heels. Avoid open-toed shoes and sandals, even during hot weather, because their casualness detracts from a managerial appearance. Your shoes should be at least as dark as your clothes, not lighter; that includes white shoes in the summer, which should be avoided unless white also dominates your clothing. Silk scarves and leather belts can add nice touches to an outfit, as long as they do not bear designer names or imprints. Many women tend to go overboard on jewelry, as though more meant quality or status. However, jewelry—and that includes watches—is most effective when it is spare and functional, so resist the urge to drape several gold chains around your neck and put a series of bracelets on your arm. Women are better off with a few distinctive pieces of good jewelry than a multitude of less expensive pieces. It is often effective to have a "signature" piece of jewelry that you wear all the time, such as a tasteful locket, an unusual ring, or a single bracelet (one that does not jangle or clatter). Such a piece can add to your own individual look or style.

Briefcases signal business, and women sales professionals should carry one, even if it only contains the morning paper or their lunch. Brown leather is best for women as well as men, although women may wish to avoid the extremes of either a distinctively "masculine" attaché or a flimsy "feminine" envelope-type portfolio. With a briefcase, a handbag is unnecessary, although many women purchase a small, flat bag to put inside a briefcase. A handbag carried separately should be simple in design, made of good quality leather, and just big enough to carry a minimum of personal items. Nothing looks less professional than a luggage-sized bag dragging on someone's shoulder. The handbag should match—or at least not jar with—the shoes and the rest of the outfit.

Other aspects of appearance deserve similar attention. Hair should be short to medium in length, in a simple cut that tends to stay in place and requires little fussing. Long hair left to fall around the shoulders may diminish a woman's authority; conversely, hair that is too short can look mannish. Long hair may be pulled up on top of the head, as long as the bun or knot is neat and not odd-looking. Hair pulled back from the face this way can give a woman a sterner, more authoritative appearance. Hair that tends to get mussed at the slightest breeze calls for a light hairspray or perhaps another kind of cut. Hairdressers at top salons can cut hair to complement the way it grows, which helps it fall into place naturally. It may be worth spending a little extra money to get a good cut.

Although grey hair usually makes men look distinguished, particularly if the grey is premature, it generally only makes women look older. If desired, many rinses on the market can cover up the grey and keep hair looking its natural color. But frizzy permanents and offbeat tinting jobs, such as streaks of different color, are usually out of place in the business environment. Similarly, lacquerlike hairsprays, especially heavily scented ones, should be avoided; so should perfume. They have no place in the business environment.

Likewise, the less makeup the better. Makeup should never be obvious. Many people find elaborate eye makeup especially distracting. The last thing a woman should want is for someone to be wondering how long it took her to "put on her face" that morning instead of listening to what she has to say.

Polished talons may be in vogue in the fashion magazines, but they are very impractical for business. Long nails prevent people from grasping things properly and can impair handwriting; also, one broken nail on a hand of long ones does not look good. Polish requires time-consuming maintenance, and even a few chips give an ill-kempt appearance. It is far better to keep nails filed to a short or medium length, with cuticles manicured. Nails may be buffed for a sheen; if polish is desired, it should be a clear polish, which will not show nicks or chips as colors do.

Because there are few reliable guidelines, women must experiment and learn through trial and error just what works best for them. Note that what works well in one area or company may not at another, not only because of differences in corporate standards, but because perceptions and impressions created by dress are so subjective. Many men, sadly, are still threatened by the idea of a woman seller; a woman who sells to many such men may get far better results by softening her appearance. But whatever the situation, women will be safest in sticking to tailored, classic, conservative styles that have the look of quality workmanship.

BUSINESS DRESS FOR MEN

Men, luckily, do not face the confusion that women do in dressing for corporate success. Since men have always dominated commerce and industry, clothing standards have always been readily apparent and nearly universal; indeed, the business "uniform" has evolved over a considerable period of time. Even within the confines of customary male business dress, however, there is a great deal of latitude, and some men dress to better advantage than do others.

The key is to have a tailored, subdued, well-integrated look. That means colors and patterns should be complementary and not clashing; belt and shoes should match; tie, shirt, collar, and lapels should be at neither fashionable extreme—too narrow or wide; and nothing should stick out in an obvious or odd way. All parts of the outfit should blend together in a tasteful, but not monochromatic or dull, way.

Unlike women, men are generally provided with a free fitting, unless they buy suits at an outlet or on sale in a department store. Even if they must pay extra for it, the fitting is vital and should be done carefully and thoroughly. Never let the tailor try to hurry you through a fitting. Places where alterations are most commonly required include:

- Shoulders—there should be no bunching or rolling of jacket between shoulder blades;
- Lapels and collar—they should lie flat;
- Sleeves—they should reach the middle of the wrist bone;
- Jacket vents—they should hang straight and not stick out;
- Trouser crotch—it should fit comfortably for sitting, walking, and standing without pinching or bagging.

Trouser waists and lengths, of course, are usually fitted. When shopping, be sure to wear a pair of shoes you intend to wear with the suit so the pants can be accurately measured for the proper break over the shoe tops.

Except for people who are prepared to care for all-cotton shirts, the best bet for shirts is a cotton and polyester blend, in white, pastel blue, or ecru (a yellowish beige or light grey), with either button-down collars or collars with removable stays (stays that are sewn into collars turn the fabric shiny when ironed). Broadcloth and Oxford weaves are among the most common shirt material, as well as end-on-end, in which white threads are woven among colored threads. Solids are best for business shirts. Shirts that combine more than two colors should be avoided. That is, stripes should be of a single color—preferably dark—against white; likewise, tattersall, which is a kind of check, should also be a single dark color against white. Stripes or tattersalls that combine colors, such as red, blue, and white, or black, yellow, and white, should be reserved for sporty, casual wear.

In recent years, fashion has invaded men's shirts. Collar lengths change, from very wide to narrow and rounded, or collars and cuffs may contrast, as with solid white against a striped shirt body. These shirts go in and out of style and should not be part of your business wardrobe unless you are a high-fashion dresser, and are willing to bear the extra cost of replacing them as fashions change. French cuffs are certainly acceptable, however. White shirts with French cuffs have an elegant look, provided they are not diminished with cheap cuff links.

Think twice before you have monograms added to your shirts, even if the monogramming is free or advertised as a low-cost special, for fashion has taken over this former mark of distinction, too. First, assess whether or not monograms are appropriate within your company and for your position. If no one else in your company or at your level of responsibility wears monograms on his shirts, you might only look pretentious, or you may stand out for reasons other than your ability. Also, monograms have become fashionable in many circles and can appear on everything from crew-neck sweaters to a secretary's blouse. Catalogs and department stores advertise monogramming free or nearly free with a purchase, thus you may have little to gain by monogramming your shirts. If you do elect to have monograms, they should be small and tasteful, and stitched in uniform size above the left breast pocket or area. Avoid elaborate stitching or initials encased in diamonds or circles.

While putting together your suit ensembles, do not neglect your socks—they always show whenever you sit down. Sock colors should fit in with the color scheme of the rest of your outfit, of course; never wear brown socks with a blue suit, or vice versa, for example. And white socks are out for business wear. Skip the cheap, all-synthetic socks, which have a tendency to pull after several washings. Also, avoid short socks. Make sure your socks are over-the-calf length and are the kind that will stay up. Nothing looks worse than socks that have fallen down around the ankles, allowing bare flesh to poke out from under trousers.

The most important male accessory, which is really a part of daily business dress, is the tie; like many accessories, it can make or break an ensemble. Ties should be selected with great care, but unfortunately they are much abused. They are often purchased as gifts with little or no knowledge of what they will match, or what they are made of; or they are picked up en masse at sales and bargain tables. It is time to treat the tie with more respect.

Silk is the best material for ties, although thin, shiny silk will not hold a knot well unless it has a thick enough lining. Polyester and silk blends are the next best material, followed by polyester, provided it looks like silk or a silk blend. Textured or knitted wool is also acceptable, although these ties look more casual. When knotted—the half-Windsor knot is the most common knot for business—the tie tip should just reach the belt buckle.

Solid colors or solids with small polka dots are the most versatile ties, followed by rep ties, which usually have stripes running in a diagonal pattern. Club and Ivy League ties—those with small emblems, sports symbols, or geometric shapes—are distinctly upper-middle class but also can convey an Eastern stuffiness or snobbishness. If you are an Easterner, you may not want to wear such a tie when traveling to other parts of North America. Paisley is also a fine choice, as long as the pattern is not large and wild, although some people regard paisleys as less serious looking. Save bow ties for sports clothes and tuxedos. Avoid ties that mix patterns or have borders along the tips. Try to purchase tie, shirt, and suit or sports jacket together in order to get the best possible match. Do not put similar patterns right next to each other, as with a striped tie against a striped shirt. Solids on solids are fine, however.

Shoes should be constructed of good-quality leather and be of simple design, either tie- or slip-on, without fancy stitching or a lot of metal doodads. Wingtips are a staple in the business world, but they are a heavy-looking shoe, and a large, imposing man might look better in a more streamlined slip-on. Loafers are too casual, and higher heeled shoes are best avoided as a passing fashion. Half-boots are acceptable in many quarters, but shoes are more traditional. The shoe color should be as dark as your suit, if not darker—never lighter. Black is the safest bet because it goes with everything. Always make sure your belt color matches your shoes; do not wear a brown belt with black shoes, for example. A slim, leather executive wallet that fits in your inner suit breast pocket is better (and safer from pickpockets) than a hip wallet; neither should bulge, in any case.

Conservatism is the rule with glasses, too. Steer clear of trendy, oversized designer shapes and wire rims in favor of dark-colored plastic frames. Glasses should not call attention to themselves. The same is true of jewelry, including watches, collar bars, and tie bars. Jewelry has become more and more acceptable for men to wear, but it is best reserved for casual social time. A simple, masculine ring (in addition to a wedding band, if you have one) is fine, but do not risk putting someone off with a bracelet. Watches should be simple. Resist the urge for digital gadgetry, like those thick diver-style tanks that glow in the dark and tell what time it is anywhere in the world. If you do buy a digital watch, keep its functions unobtrusive. Most digital watches can be set to beep on the hour, which can be most offensive and annoying. Meetings invariably suffer a minor disruption when a dozen watches start going off, never in unison. And if you are in a one-on-one situation, a beeping watch gives the impression that you are either anxious about time or have something more important to do.

Hair requires the same approach of simplicity and unobtrusiveness. Hair should be neatly trimmed around the ears and never extend below the collar in the back. If your hair musses easily, try holding it in place with a light spray, but never with grease, pomade, or a lacquer-type spray. You should also avoid curly permanents, unless you want to look like a rock musician. Many men do not mind if their hair is all or partly grey, feeling that it enhances their image. Those who wish to trade a distinguished look for a youthful one, however, will find many preparations that will cover the grey, restoring the natural color.

Loss of hair calls for different steps. If your hairline is

receding at the temples, part it at the point of greatest recession for the neatest look. Never try to grow hair to cover bald spots and receding hair lines; invariably you will not succeed, and your attempt will look obvious and vain. Many good-quality toupees are on the market, and a surprising number of men are choosing them over their own thinning hair. Shop carefully, however, because even good hairpieces are fairly easy to spot, and bad ones look ridiculous. A bad toupee may curl strangely at the nape of the neck or stick out from the neck; it may not match the natural hair; it may have an unnatural, synthetic sheen; or it may have a part that looks artificial—or no part at all (everyone's hair parts in some fashion).

For the face, a clean-shaven look is still the most widely acceptable choice. Eschew cologne, however; it is distracting and inappropriate in a business environment. Moustaches have become more commonplace, especially among younger men. If you wear a moustache, keep it neatly trimmed above your lip, and do not extend it beyond the corners of your mouth. Waxed moustaches, as well as handlebars that extend up to sideburns, are not advisable for managers. Sideburns are best when they are short and trimmed. You need not look like an Army recruit, but do avoid muttonchops and cuts that extend far out onto the cheek or are slanted in a diagonal. Beards and goatees have more variable acceptance, being sported widely in some industries and rarely in others. Those considering a hirsute look will want to carefully assess their business environments before growing a beard—and then only on a long vacation, to have time to pass beyond the scruffy stage and to judge its effect privately, before putting in on public view. On some faces and in some settings, a beard can enhance a person's authority and intelligence; but sometimes a beard can make others uneasy, since it hides the face, and can make it harder for a person to gain the confidence of others.

For all professionals, the key to "dressing for success" is using the same type of discipline they apply in their daily business affairs—knowing their objectives and putting together a program designed to accomplish them in the most efficient, effective way. You should approach building your business wardrobe with the same diligence you might apply to preparing for a major presentation. Your business wardrobe can be your enemy, or it can be a most helpful ally in achieving your career goals. The right clothes and the right accessories, in the right combinations, can help you create and maintain a positive image, one that can influence others to respect you, listen to you, trust you, and buy from you.

EQUIPMENT

Sales equipment is an extension of personal appearance. You should no more appear before a prospect or customer carrying a worn, misshapen briefcase than you should wearing a stained, torn blouse or old, baggy pants. And you should no more reach into that briefcase and pull out tired, faded presentation materials than you should hold out a hand to be shaken that is in desperate need of washing and a manicure.

Sales equipment has to be new-looking, clean, crisp, and capable of being used to lovingly demonstrate the top of your line. It presents your company and product; it also quite significantly casts light upon and presents you to your customers and prospects. All marketing managements budget for sales equipment wear and breakage; no sales professional should be deficient in this area.

It extends to all the seemingly minor details, too. For example, the pen you work with when using an order form to move to the close should be one of recognizably good quality; inexpensive pens may write just as well, but a good pen is more reassuring to the buyer.

Similarly, but not quite as directly, your car, if you use one in the field, is an extension of your personal appearance. And although the stereotype of the successful sales professional as a cigar-smoking, fast talker driving a big car is long gone, what you drive and especially what condition it is in can, in some situations, make a difference to your prospects and customers, and can stand in the way of developing the kinds of relationships that build sales.

Unfortunately, in these days of high automobile prices and unreliable new automobiles, a battered ten-year-old station wagon that needs a new coat of paint but runs like a dream just will not do in the field. What will minimally do, though, is a well-cared-for, smallish automobile as much as four or five years old, that gets good gasoline mileage and has an excellent repair record. If you travel a good deal, you are unlikely to get more than four reasonably trouble-free years out of a car anyway, and the cost of missed appointments because of automobile troubles is usually far larger than the cost of a newer automobile.

Newer, but not necessarily new. Hardly anyone cares any more about trading in a car every year or two; in these times, economy has to a significant extent become a virtue, and conspicuous consumption is now rather suspect. The car you drive out in the field need not be new, or large, or expensive; but it must be clean, look well cared for, and be of a reasonably late model.

All of the above argues strongly for getting a well known and rather traditional American or foreign automobile just under the extra-laden top of whatever line it is part of, and one that is not in its first model year. It also argues for maintaining it well and preventively, and for planning to retire it from field use in the 80,000–90,000-mile range, at the outside. Many of us have second cars, and a car used in the field is often perfectly usable as an additional family car for years after it is no longer suitable for work purposes. It is quite possible to buy or lease a car every three or four years, and have two usable vehicles out of that pattern of purchases at all times.

Dress, grooming, sales equipment, automobiles—all the appearance elements together present a single image of you to prospects, customers, and colleagues; an image that can, if properly worked with, considerably enhance sales and career success possibilities.

CHAPTER 8

WOMEN AND MINORITIES IN SELLING

Despite all the movements for affirmative action, equal opportunities, and equal pay, and despite substantial advances made by women and minority group sales professionals in recent years, the world of selling is still dominated by white males. To a considerable extent, women and minority group members seeking to enter and move up in selling careers are still seen as novices by many seasoned sales managers and field sales professionals, and are very likely to continue to face unthinking prejudice as well for a long time more. It continues to be true that women and minority sales professionals must generally work harder and be more skilled and competent than their white male counterparts to achieve full acceptance and equal opportunities for advancement. Similarly achieving white male sales professionals often have a much wider range of action; they can often "get away with" behavior that would be devastating to the career of a woman or minority sales professional. Despite all the changes of recent decades, women and minorities must still work doubly hard and overprepare to meet and overcome social obstacles to successful careers in selling. For sales management, this state of affairs implies the need for extra attention, not to provide special support for any group, but to see that an operation is run in a fully professional manner, unaffected by sexual or racial questions. This chapter is primarily directed at those minorities, women included, who are still working to gain that fully neutral, professional acceptance in the selling world; and secondarily to those sales, marketing, and general management professionals who wish to run organizations free of discrimination.

In selling, the heart of the matter is empathy. Yes, prospecting, selling the interview, approaching, presenting, handling stalls and objections, and closing are important. But underneath it all—empathy. The ability to put yourself into the other guy's shoes, to find the buying motives, to come together to the close.

That poses a problem for women selling to men in this society. For men selling to women, too—but much less so, for men have not been sex objects in the same way, have not been sexually exploited in the same way, and do not run the same risks that women do of being misunderstood in selling situations.

The problem is that the reach for empathy can very easily—and very often quite willfully—be misunderstood as a sexual approach. And sex and selling do not mix. The selling situation that becomes confused by sexual signals, undertones, overtones—any tones at all—is a selling situation that is headed in the wrong direction and is highly unlikely to result in a sale. It is much more likely to result in a totally unwanted and thoroughly insulting sexual approach by prospect or customer to a woman sales professional.

Most women in selling know how to avoid this, and more and more men being sold to are coming to understand quite well that selling situations are not also sexual situations. Still, it does not take too many sexual approaches or near-approaches to sour a day or week, and women in selling usually take great care to dress and groom in nonsexual signal ways, and to project entirely businesslike attitudes in business situations.

The less obvious, but in the long run the more important, sales success question is that the heart of the selling process is still the achievement of empathy, and that the need to back away from any action or attitude that might trigger a sexual approach in a selling situation can make it considerably more difficult to achieve empathy in cross-sex selling situations. Yes, tens of thousands of women do sell successfully to men—just as successfully as men sell to men—but only by surmounting the sex and empathy problem. It takes care and skill not to project what may easily be interpreted as a set of sexual signals while reaching for empathy—but to be able to do so is also an indispensable selling skill.

There are still double standards routinely applied on and off the job to women and minority group members in every profession and trade, and selling is no exception. That is odd, in a way, for selling is so results-oriented a profession that it would seem logical to assume that it would be very easy to see who was successful and who was not regardless of sex. Indeed, that is a very attractive aspect of the profession for many; either you sell or you do not, and all the political maneuvering, nepotism, and plain old bootlicking in the world is useless if you cannot sell. The trouble is, sex prejudice and other bigotries are by their nature not at all reasonable or logical, and women and minority group members often have to prove themselves in the field over and over again, as sales leaders, trainers, customer relations experts—whatever it takes to demonstrate professional excellence—before that excellence will be recognized. They are all too often not even considered, much less considered and rejected, for senior status, top territories, national account jobs, and management, even though they may be by every rational standard top contenders for advancement. All too often, the woman, black, or Hispanic somehow "doesn't fit," "is a little too independent," "may not really be a team player," or "might cause some problems out there." Of course, management itself never carries the virus of bigotry—not much.

All to be expected, dealt with, and turned into a better set of attitudes over the years. It may have seemed otherwise to some during the very hopeful early years of the modern movement against business bigotry, but the truth is that bigotries die hard and deeply held attitudes take generations to change. Laws have helped—and helped a good deal—by providing a new set of contexts within which the move toward real equality in the business world continues to work itself out. But experience, not laws, changes attitudes. New experiences now accrete; attitudes are slowly changing as women and minority group members move into and become fixtures in selling and other professions; but it still changes very slowly, sometimes hardly even seeming to change at all. When a woman moves into a male prospect's office, and he immediately first-names her, and goes on to call her "honey" and "dear," all the while visibly sizing her up as a sex object, not too much has changed in the mind of that prospect, whatever else has occurred in the larger society. Nor will it, for him; his son may feel quite differently, though. *May,* not *will;* the returns are by no means in yet on the rate of change regarding those bigotries built into American society.

Meanwhile, all this has to be dealt with. And although women and minority sales professionals seem to have gained considerable ground in recent decades, much of the remaining prejudiced behavior is not overt, but very subtle; often it is even unnoticed and unrecognized by those who feel they are relatively enlightened. That very subtlety poses real problems for women and minority sales professionals trying to establish the kind of recognized professionalism that will serve them so well both in the field and within their own companies.

How to establish that kind of professional status? Most of all, by looking and acting the part of a sales professional at all times and in all situations. Many customers, prospects, and colleagues will not take seriously women and minorities unless they put forth a special effort; they often have to earn the respect that white male sales professionals may be accorded almost automatically.

Appearance is often crucial in quickly establishing the proper professional image. People form first impressions based on appearance, and those whose dress is not conservative and professional may be automatically discounted.

Whatever else they do, women and minority sales professionals must maintain their composure, even when faced with difficult situations in the field and in their own companies. This is generally important for women, who are often expected to be emotional and flighty. A male may succumb to pressure in the field and let impatience with a difficult customer or prospect show without risking loss of professional status and the respect that comes with it; a woman who does so runs great risks. Similarly, a male may fly off the handle in a difficult intracompany situation and be regarded only as a "little off his feed today," while a woman who does so may all too easily be seen as unstable and in need of coddling and coaxing. This fits perfectly into previously held stereotypes and becomes a stone a woman may have to push uphill for years.

Profanity, likewise, should be used with extreme caution, especially by women. Better yet, not at all. Yes, an occasional well-placed expletive may get proper attention and help restate strength of character. On the other hand, many are likely to be shocked and strongly disapprove the use of profanity by women, and will use that to reinforce their previously held prejudices. Profanity can also backfire, drawing attention to itself and away from the point you are making; that continues to be true for all of us.

It is also important to speak up at sales meetings. As a sales professional, you are likely to have to attend many sales meetings; do not take them lightly. Field people are constantly being sized up for possible advancement at such meetings, and those who do not speak up may considerably harm their chances of moving up. It is especially important to take the time to prepare for each meeting and to do your best to contribute something of value. Merely agreeing with others or offering thoughts that do not add to the matter under discussion will not do, however; to be meaningful, the contribution must be substantive, or you may be seen as a lightweight and a time waster.

ENTERTAINING AND TRAVELING

The double standard pervasive on the job also applies to the social side of business life. Behavior that is tolerated, sometimes even admired, such as an ability to socialize at a bar for hours, is scorned in women and minority group members. They must always be aware that, whether it is apparent or not, their behavior is being observed and noted, and negative impressions are formed easily.

Women have a particular problem in business entertaining, such as over lunch. It does not matter who does the asking, what their status is, or how big their expense account is, many men still do not like women to pick up the check. It makes them feel very uncomfortable and embarrassed. Increasingly, men are coming to accept equality in check paying, especially when the woman puts the whole situation on a firmly professional basis. Occasionally, however, a man appears to be truly distressed at the idea of having his lunch paid for by a woman. In that case, after a gentle protest, the best course is to smile graciously and thank him. A fight over the check will only increase his discomfort and undo any goodwill established with him in the business relationship.

Many women avoid such scenes by making arrangements with the waiter or waitress in advance to have the check placed on their side of the table, so the check will not automatically be given to the man. In that situation, it is a good idea for them to have a credit card ready in advance, in a handy pocket or right on top in a purse, so they can immediately place the card on the table when the check comes. It is far better to pay with plastic than with cash, for riffling through bills seems to make men even more uncomfortable. The guest may still protest, and if he insists, the businesswoman will have to judge whether the price of lunch is worth his distress. Many businesswomen, especially those working in city business districts, have learned to avoid the check scene altogether by arranging to pay in advance, so that a check never reaches the table. They search out one or two restaurants to patronize, go there regularly, and get to know the staff. Generally they present their credit card in advance of a lunch date, specify the tip percentage (a generous one, so there are no slipups), and sign the check. If they patronize an establishment and tip well, the staff will be only too happy to accommodate them. The same procedure holds for entertaining while traveling out of town. It is wise to check out in advance restaurants where you will likely eat, introduce yourself to the maître d'hôtel or head waiter, and explain how you want things handled when you bring your guest in.

Women also have a special problem with dinner dates, because too often they can lead to something else. People tend to be a little more relaxed over dinner, and after a few drinks or a bottle of wine it is all too easy to retire to the bar or a nightclub for a nightcap—and perhaps a proposition. If a male business acquaintance suggests dinner, the wise woman will decline and suggest lunch or drinks instead. If she meets someone in a bar for drinks at the end of a working day, she can always excuse herself after one or two drinks, citing other plans or an appointment. In a place where there is music and dancing, she should decline invitations to dance, for then she would become a sexual object, not a businesswoman.

The area of social drinking poses hazards for all sales professionals, but especially for women and minority group members. Even the practice of meeting associates for drinks after work should inspire caution. Whether you are drinking with your peers, superiors, customers, or prospects, never try to keep up with the others, and never allow yourself to get intoxicated. If you match them drink for drink, they may cheer you on at the table, but remember you as a hard boozer the next day at the office or in the field. The last thing you want is a reputation as a barfly. That caution applies especially to women. It does not matter that Charlie downed six doubles without looking any the worse for it; the standards that apply to him and his male associates do not apply to women. If you feel yourself getting intoxicated, excuse yourself immediately and leave. It is far better to leave early than to risk slurred speech and sloppy coordination.

What you drink is as important as how much you drink. More and more people are steering clear of hard liquor. It's a good idea—let others drink scotch and bourbon if they wish. One alternative is sherry, a drink you can sip and nurse for a long time. Beware, however; sherry's alcoholic content is greater than wine, and will affect you more quickly. Beer is another alternative. Wine is probably the safest alcoholic drink, and can also be sipped very slowly. A wine spritzer, which is wine mixed with soda or seltzer and served with ice, is even better, though you should be careful not to drink it quickly just because it is diluted. Of course, you need not drink alcohol at all, either at lunch or after work, and many today do not. Mineral water with a slice of lemon or lime is perfectly acceptable and health-conscious. Not only will you keep your mental alertness, you will be doing your figure and your health a favor.

As a sales professional, you may be expected to attend evening functions or to entertain at your own home. If you are entertaining at home, such as a dinner party or a cocktail party, do it in style with hired help and a caterer. Nothing reduces your professional status faster than to run around fixing and serving food and drinks. Besides, you cannot really entertain your guests if you are preoccupied with kitchen and bar details. Hiring help will enhance your image and is well worth the cost. A single woman should never invite a lone male business acquaintance home for dinner, because it implies seduction.

Single businesswomen always have a dilemma of whether or not to bring an escort to business-social engagements. Wives may tend to resent a single woman, and if she is alone, she may appear to be even more of a predator who will snatch their husbands away. Yet, an escort may be a handicap, requiring introduction, entertaining, and inclusion in business-oriented conversations. For these reasons, many businesswomen have decided it is best to forgo the escort. However, it is a good idea for single businesswomen to go out of their way to meet the wives of co-workers, of superiors, and sometimes of their best customers, and to try to put them at ease; they will seem less of a threat that way.

Although wives have the freedom to dress up for evening functions, and some of them will go out of their way to look sexy, conservatism should be the rule of thumb for businesswomen. That does not mean wearing a navy blue business suit, but it does mean wearing modest, high-necked, and nonclinging clothes. Anything remotely sexy will counteract a professional image—and increase resentment from wives.

Traveling also requires special attention for women and minority group members. If they are traveling alone, they may well encounter some discriminatory treatment in service establishments, which are used to catering to the white male business traveler. Hotel clerks may slight them, reservation clerks may put them in rooms they would never dream of giving their preferred customers, and restaurant help may treat them like pariahs. It may be infuriating, but getting angry will accomplish little. If you are placed in such a situation, be polite and firm; do not accept second-class treatment. Refuse the table by the kitchen door, speak up when the service is slow, and do not hesitate to insist on another room if you do not like the one you were given. It will help if you always dress like a professional and tip well.

For women, traveling alone on the road can be an extraordinarily lonely experience. All too often, the end of the field selling day is also the end of all real human contact. You cannot have an "unwinding" drink alone in the hotel or motel bar; that only invites unwanted attention. You dine alone, often with a book, for invitations to dine with customers and prospects have almost always been very wisely turned down during the course of the day in the field, and invitations to dine with strangers are turned down reflexively. You then go up to a very, very empty room, to a pile of work, a television set, a book, some personal letters, and perhaps an all-too-brief long-distance conversation with those left at home. Then to sleep—if you can. Tomorrow it will be the same.

All of this can make the most stable of us do some very foolish things, such as going down to the bar late at night just to be with people, and even winding up spending the night with a perfect stranger in a fit of extreme loneliness. Like finally accepting a dinner invitation from a very nice male customer or prospect, and ending the day fighting off his advances in the politest possible way, and perhaps alienating him as well. Or worse, not fighting him off, and winding up with a "reputation" in his small town—or the county, or state. People talk; men talk about their "conquests."

There are no easy solutions to the problem of isolation women face on the road. You can help yourself somewhat, though, in two ways. First, cultivate women friends. Men cultivate men friends to overcome the problem of isolation, and often make a beeline for friends and a home-cooked dinner in every town in their territories. Women are wise to cultivate women similarly. There are more and more women in business, and women sales professionals are just as capable of making friends with women customers and prospects on the road as men are with men.

Second, be sure to work nights, setting yourself in attitude, tools, and hotel or motel environment to do just that, as we have discussed at length in Chapter 5.

Traveling with males, whether they are superiors or equals, is often a touchy situation for women in selling. Men often feel ill at ease, and some are downright resentful that they cannot really "cut loose" while they are away from wife and family. Because some men will naturally feel obliged to look after women companions while traveling, women must make it clear, politely, that they can shift for themselves. They should not drag along too much baggage, but pack the

minimum and make sure they can handle it easily themselves. If they are fearful fliers, they should not admit it, no
matter how terrified they are and no matter how much their
traveling companions may rattle on about their own flying
jitters. Women's behavior must be impeccably businesslike
for the entire trip.

The woman who does not wish to dine with her male
associates should decline with a simple but vague "I've
already made plans for the evening," even if it's only eating
alone in the hotel room. If dining with one or more associates
is unavoidable, she should do so, but excuse herself at the
end of dinner and not be enticed into going out on the town
for a night of drinking, which is asking for trouble. At some
point in her career, almost every woman will take a trip with
someone who assumes that an out-of-town trip is reason for a
one-night stand, someone who would never think of proposi-
tioning her back at the home office, but does it quite matter-
of-factly on the road. If you are a male, such behavior should
be considered strictly off limits. If you are a woman in that
situation, do not puff yourself up indignantly and make a big
deal of it, for you may have to travel with this person again.
Decline politely and firmly in a nonpersonal way. You might
add either that you are happily married or, if you are single,
that you are involved with someone else, even if you are not
at the moment.

THE BUSINESS ROMANCE

That raises the question of the business romance. No matter
how you look at it, those who engage in business romance,
no matter what their professional level, stand to lose more
than they gain. The risks are enormous. News of such
romances has a way of getting around, no matter how careful
or secretive people think they are. It is gossip that spreads
easily and quickly, especially because people are still all too
willing to believe that women in selling routinely try to make
sales and advance their careers through the bedroom.

In selling, the business romance is most damaging when it occurs between people selling in team fashion, or between sales manager and sales representative. At the very least, such a romance can be distracting and disruptive, not only to you and your partner, but to those you work with. Corporate policy may severely discourage such sexual entanglements; both the man and the woman—although sometimes only the woman—may be disciplined, let go, or transferred. Even without such action, the affair may run out of steam and leave both parties feeling extremely uncomfortable at having to continue to work together. Many people argue in defense of such romances, saying they are inevitable as long as men and women are frequently thrown together. Attraction and sexual tension naturally result. Although it is true that some people manage to successfully carry off an office romance, affairs still backfire far more than they succeed. In general, you are better off leaving sexual tension unacknowledged, for acknowledgment requires some sort of action, either acceptance or refusal.

While affairs among peers are difficult, affairs between superiors and subordinates are even more so—for both parties. The superiors risk at least loss of professional image, which can be disastrous for a woman or minority group member. Subordinates in such affairs are in an even more precarious position. Some think this will benefit their careers, and sometimes it does temporarily, although the benefits may be undone in the end. Co-workers will resent them for having an unfair advantage over others. If the lover departs, for another division or company, the new superior may swiftly throw out the remaining party. Or, if the affair dwindles, a superior may get rid of an ex-lover, who is an embarrassing reminder of a former dalliance. By far the worst kind of romance involves partners who are married to others. The gossip can be far more malicious, and the consequences worse.

But, say some single women, how is it possible to have a social life without dating those you work with? What if you do not like to go to bars, and your job keeps you too busy for involvement in clubs or organizations? It is a dilemma, and a tough one, without a ready answer. Still, the risks of such romances must be carefully weighed before you become involved in one. If you do become romantically involved with a co-worker, you are better off with someone with whom you do not work closely every day.

No matter how attracted you are to someone you work with, do not react impulsively or rashly. Keep a cool head and carefully assess your situation, lest you undo a lot of hard work and years of effort to advance your career.

If you work for a company in a highly competitive industry, you also must be careful about seeing people who work for competitors. You may never breathe a word about business when you are together, but if your company finds out about your relationship, you may be out on the street before you know it; at best your position may be compromised.

HANDLING PREJUDICE AND CHAUVINISM

Women and minorities may have come a long way, but chauvinism is still pervasive in the business world. Some of it is obvious and overt, and some of it is very subtle and difficult to counter. Some of it is even disguised as chivalry, as with the strongly prejudiced man who believes a woman cannot handle responsibility as well as a man, that she must be closely supervised, that she is just "biding time" in the job until she quits to have children or to spend more time with her family, and that she is really just a sex object. Other men may not have such extreme sentiments, but may still treat women differently due to an upbringing and years of cultural conditioning that have taught them that women are not equal to men. These attitudes may be irritating, even enraging, but taking an aggressive posture against them will get you little more than an "angry feminist" label. That does not mean that women should have to put up with any demeaning behavior; they should just be cool in their counterattacks.

One of the most common sexist behaviors is the use of endearments, such as "honey," "sweetheart," and "doll." It may seem harmless enough, but every time a woman lets someone get away with it, she has allowed herself to be reduced to a sex object. She should stop it immediately and firmly with a reply such as, "My name isn't honey, so please don't call me that," or "My name isn't doll, it's Susan," repeated—always coolly—as often as necessary. Some men are chivalrously chauvinistic. They constantly remind a woman that she is not equal through little courtesies such as helping her on with her coat, holding open doors, and making comments in meetings such as, "Well, Roberta's here now, so clean up your language," or "Here comes Denise, now we can't tell any more dirty jokes." Women on the receiving end of such remarks should simply smile pleasantly and tell them it is not necessary to alter their behavior for her. If someone holds her coat or opens a door, she should accept the courtesy graciously but say, "Thanks, Tom, but that isn't necessary." She should never make a big deal out of it, especially in front of others. Men who have these habits are not even aware of what they are doing; they are not deliberately attempting to demean women. Some even think they are being casual and friendly, which is why it is inadvisable to leap down their throats. Attitudes do not change overnight; that takes a long, slow process of reeducation. It is up to women—and really to all enlightened professionals—to see that the reeducation takes place. Laws alone will not do it.

Fortunately, laws have gone a long way towards reducing sexual harassment in the workplace. Once it was quite pervasive, and women who complained about it were usually fired, while the offending men were unscathed. However, demanding sexual favors—regardless of whether a man or a woman is doing the demanding—is against federal law, and many companies today are swift to react to it and stop it, punishing or firing the guilty party. Alert managers should be sensitive to any such harassment in their organizations, and should take steps to stop it, rather than leaving a victim to handle the situation alone.

Sexual harassment usually occurs at the lower levels in a corporation, and most often is directed against the lowest level of female employees, such as secretaries and clerks. Women sales professionals will probably experience propositions, but little overt and persistent harassment. If, despite a professional attitude and dress, a woman receives a proposition, she should try to deflect it without striking out at someone's ego or personality, no matter how much she would like to; she can always plead that she is married or involved with someone already—and then change the subject. Even if the situation turns more difficult, the harassed party should always try to handle it on a one-to-one basis. He or she should remind the offender that asking for sexual favors is against the law; if that still does not work, the situation should be referred to the offender's superior. Court should be the last resort in seeking redress for sexual harassment. Court suits take a long time to settle and create many bad feelings on both sides. The parties involved should ask themselves if they can continue to work in an organization together, as the proceedings get messier.

In recent decades, minority managers have become less subject to overt kinds of harassment. But both women and minorities are subject to a wide range of covert actions stemming from prejudice or chauvinism.

What if you are in a meeting or a group and someone deliberately tries to embarrass you with an insulting joke or remark, for example? You are in a tough spot, because you can lose either way—if you speak up and challenge the offender, or if you meekly let it go by. One response will make you look like a militant with no sense of humor, and the other will make you look like a spineless jellyfish. If you are lucky and smart, you will have cultivated some allies who will speak up for you. It is far better for an offender to be censured by others, making clear that that sort of behavior is unprofessional and unbecoming. If you have no such ally present, the best thing you can do is ignore it. You may be being baited, and your refusal to take the bait may make others uncomfortable enough to discourage such remarks in the future.

But what if someone persists in trying to discredit or embarrass you with rude remarks? You would be best advised to speak to that person privately, and say something such as, "I'd like to establish a good, cooperative working relationship with you, but I'm a bit put off by the remarks you make about _____ (fill in the blank) whenever I'm around." This approach is risky, because it can make the person very defensive; if the person is nasty enough, he or she may keep trying to undercut you in that or some other way. But a direct approach may jolt the person out of that behavior.

Another form of chauvinistic treatment that can be quite frustrating is to be discounted or even ignored. It usually happens in meetings. A woman or minority group member speaks up with a suggestion or idea, and no one seems to pay much attention; perhaps no one even responds directly to those remarks. Then, a few minutes later, someone else pipes up with almost the same idea, and everyone applauds the suggestion. That person takes the credit, and the originator has been discounted. If that happens to you, there is not much you can do about it but keep silent. If you try to point out it was your idea originally, you will only antagonize people and look like a whining poor sport. Instead, try to prevent it from happening in the future. That means making sure that others notice you when you speak. Women, especially, are often easy to overlook or ignore because they speak softly, sometimes even timidly. Practice projecting your voice, as you would do in a group field presentation, so that it commands more attention. Be careful not to raise the pitch because your voice will begin to sound unattractive or screechy, and others will tune you out in self-defense. Keep the pitch low, but your voice strong. Get right to the point. If you are sitting in an audience, stand up when you begin to speak so that others can see you and focus their attention on you. And on days when you know you will be attending important meetings, wear a dark-colored, conservative suit, which will lend seriousness to your image.

The position of women and minorities may be undercut in other ways, too. For example, they may be assigned secretarial duties at a business meeting. If asked in advance to take notes during the meeting, to be written up as minutes, the best course is to demur, citing lack of shorthand knowledge and suggesting a secretary might be more appropriate. If that is met with the insistence that you "just jot down a few notes," you may agree to do so, if the duty is shared by others at future meetings. If asked at the start of the meeting, in front of others, they should agree pleasantly, but should tell their superior in private that they do not wish to be exclusively delegated the task. Similarly, you should not accept a "fetch-and-carry" role. If asked to see to the coffee before a meeting begins, you should turn that job over to a secretary or assistant. But whatever you do, never bring in the coffee, and never clean up the empty cups and dirty ashtrays after a meeting.

MOVING UP

All professionals must actively pursue their own career interests. Women and minorities must do so even more than most. It not only is acceptable to actively seek raises and promotions, it is expected. No professional should for a minute sit back and think that his or her strong performance will be noticed and automatically rewarded. Even if noticed without assistance, they may not be rewarded financially. Companies try to hold personnel costs down as much as possible, and if people are willing to work for less than their true market value, so much the better for the company. That is the employer's gain and the professional's loss. Do not be shy about tooting your own horn, because no one else is going to do it for you. The longer people work for less than they should, the more it hurts them. It does not take long for percentage raises and bonuses to widen the gap between what you earn and what you *should* earn.

In order to make the most out of opportunities for advancement in pay and position, you must have a clear idea of your own career plans. What are your goals with your company? Do you want to change territories? Move into national account selling? Move into sales management? Once you know exactly where you are headed, tell your superior and remind him or her periodically of your aspirations. Do it in a low-key fashion at the right moments, of course, such as when you sign up for a training course. If your advancement hinges squarely on your superior's advancement, you must be especially sensitive about making your plans known. No one likes to think that someone is out to get their job—especially while they are still in it and perhaps uncertain of their own promotion prospects.

If a slot opens up that you want, and you qualify, do not hesitate to speak up for it; otherwise no one may think of you as a candidate. Women and minorities are far more likely to be overlooked for advancement than are white men, who more or less take upward movement for granted. Many males still have a hard time thinking of women as ambitious. Be able to explain, with concrete examples, why you deserve the job and what you have to offer. Saying you have been in your present job long enough, or that it is time to move on, will not suffice. Cite your past performance and accomplishments, and the contributions you have made to the company's operations.

Even so, you may find yourself held back for no apparent reason. If you are routinely skipped over, and management seems to turn a deaf ear to your pitch to move up and on, give notice that you are going to take the matter up with higher levels of management. If you do take your case to the next level again and again, and still get no results, prepare yourself to look for another job—you may be working for the wrong company.

If you are basically a salaried employee, and if it is a

raise in your current position you are after, be aware that there are good times and bad times to ask for more money. The best time is right on the heels of a major accomplishment, which has earned you favorable recognition or attention. Do not wait for the glory to grow cold, hoping that you will be rewarded; step up and ask for it. Make your request at an appropriate moment, when conditions are favorable and time is available to consider the matter—not right before a major meeting or near an important deadline.

No matter how much you may deserve a raise, your chances of winning one will be sorely diminished if you choose to ask just when the company's earnings are down. Better to wait a few weeks. Never, however, let more than a year go by without asking for a performance review and raise. Most companies have regular schedules for such matters, but some smaller ones do not; as long as you let it slide, an employer is likely to let it slide, too.

On the other hand, mistrust excuses that put you off until another time, or justifications for small raises. Arguments that company profits are down or that a ceiling has been placed on raise amounts are often not completely true. Management somehow always finds a way to adequately reward the good performers. Chances are, the gullible employees will buy the argument and settle for less or nothing, while the funds available for raises go to those who make a strong case for them. Be persistent and firm. Do not, however, be hasty in delivering an ultimatum—"If I don't get a raise, I'll quit!"—because an ultimatum may backfire and work to an employer's advantage. Do not deliver one unless you are prepared to follow through on it. As with promotions, be sure you can back up your argument for more money by citing examples of performance; never plead financial difficulty or give the lame reason that you just "deserve" more money.

When discussing salary for a new position, do not be afraid to negotiate. Many relatively inexperienced people fear that if they try to negotiate they will lose out altogether, but negotiation is a natural and expected part of the process for setting salaries. Know what your market worth is. You can keep current on this in a number of ways: through classified job ads in the Sunday newspaper, professional organizations, and executive recruiters. In order to negotiate the salary effectively, you must know what your general market worth is.

Decide on a minimum figure you are willing to accept, and then ask for a figure higher than that. Give ample room for negotiations but do not name an astronomically high figure; remember, both sides will want to feel that they have won something. As always, be prepared to show why you should be earning the amount you are seeking.

If you are interviewing for a new position and your interviewer asks what you expect to earn in that job, never reply, "What does it pay?" Such an answer starts you off in a weak bargaining position. State firmly what you expect to make. Do not be surprised if the other person protests that your sum is too much; that is a common negotiation practice. Once the other person has named a figure, you can work out a compromise in between. Women and minorities often get caught in a low-pay trap in salary negotiations. Most of them are underpaid for what they do; some are severely under-paid. An interviewer who asks what they are currently earning as a basis for calculating an offer will keep them in a low earnings trap, claiming the size of increase they are looking for cannot possibly be justified. Make it clear that your compensation must at least equal the compensation of others doing comparable jobs in your own company and throughout your industry.

If a salary ceiling on a job is firmly lower than desired, it is always possible to try to negotiate extra "perks" or a salary review within three to six months. Whatever arrangement is made should be confirmed in writing; otherwise a promised review can easily fall by the wayside because of a personnel change or for any number of other reasons or excuses.

Remember that the more money you command, the more you are valued by a company. People who work cheap do not get the same respect as those whose price is high. If an employer has to pay well to get a sales professional, everyone will feel that he or she must be good at the job. It is automatic for the men who still do most of the hiring in the nation's corporations to expect women and minorities to be happy working for less than other sales professionals. A prospective employer should know right from the start that competent, serious professionals expect to be paid fair market value for their worth.

CHAPTER 9

JOB SEEKING

Changing jobs well requires a good deal of preparation and the application of vitally important personal selling skills, whether the change sought is voluntary or involuntary, part of upward career mobility or a defensive move away from a troubled situation, inside your current company or to another company.

Professionalism, balance, integrity, personal warmth, a wealth of relevant skills and experience—all this and more we try to project to others during the course of our careers, as we move up and around in the world of American business. In one way or another, we project those images every day as we pursue our careers. When we are involved in selling situations, we are very careful indeed to do so. And when we are seeking employment elsewhere, finding and meeting people who may or may not know something of us and our work, and who have not really worked with us before, we do everything we can to sell our prospective new employers on the immense benefits that will result from hiring us. Putting it a little differently, in all these kinds of situations we engage in persuasion, with the attention, time, and effort we put into them depending largely on how important they are to us and how difficult it may be to persuade others in the situation.

250

JOB SEEKING AS SELLING

The essence of job seeking—whether within or outside your present company—is that you are involved in a selling process, with you as seller. That description in no way vulgarizes or oversimplifies the process; it is a precise description of the main content of the transaction between you and whomever you are trying to convince. Nor is the process simply analogous to selling; it *is* selling, ultimately face-to-face selling. The successful job seeker uses precisely the same procedures and techniques as does the successful face-to-face sales professional.

Job seeking involves several kinds of preselling activities, many of them alternatives that depend on where you are starting from. It also involves a set of selling processes, again often alternatives, aimed at selling someone or a group on the desirability of seeing you face to face. And it involves a second set of selling processes, this one rather straightforwardly applying equally to almost all face-to-face selling situations, in which you and a prospective employer come together to sell and be sold on the desirability of hiring you above all others. In-house personal evaluations differ in that you are not always seeking to make a sale, but many of the persuasive techniques used face to face are indistinguishable from those used in the job-seeking selling process. In-house job seeking often involves some preselling activities, normally takes little interview selling, and involves essentially the same face-to-face skills and understandings that outside job seeking requires. Two significant features make in-house job seeking special: you are likely to know a good deal about company, division, and operation. You also may know those who make the hiring decisions, which is a real advantage because empathy is often a good deal easier to achieve this way than with strangers or near-strangers.

Throughout these job-seeking processes, you should bear in mind some basic selling approaches. One is that what you are selling are the *benefits* that hiring you will bring. No, you are not selling *you;* it is both self-denigrating and inaccurate to think of job seeking as a process by which you sell yourself. You are not for sale; further, nobody should have any reason to buy you. Some, in their eagerness to sell "themselves," lose both the image and the substance of personal integrity, and that is a personal and business disaster. What is for sale is not your time, loyalty, skill, or talent, either; those things have to do with you, not with the benefits that come from hiring you. That you have long and relevant experience is a *feature* of the product that is you; that your experience, as part of a constellation of skills and qualities, will bring profitable sales is the *benefit* that you bring with you. That you have a wide range of government contacts is a *feature* of the product that is you; how you will use the contacts to sell lucrative government contracts for your new company is the *benefit* that hiring you brings. In short, as in all selling, it is a matter of "putting yourself into the other guy's shoes," and responding empathetically and specifically to that other guy's wants and needs. Those who want to hire will say: "This is what I think she (or he) can do for us." In contrast, "This is her (or his) background and experience," is the language used by those who have not been sold on the benefits that hiring you will bring. *Will* bring, not *can* bring. People hire the sales professional they believe will do the job. If there is an element of doubt in their minds, they will probably keep on interviewing. That is especially true in hard times, when competition is keener and hiring standards stiffen.

This question of selling the benefits that hiring you will bring is central, as it is in all selling, whatever is being sold. It is an understanding that should permeate every aspect of the job-seeking process, providing a proper basis for first approaches with potential job contacts, recruiters, personnel people, and those who hire, whether those contacts are face to face or in writing. And it should provide a takeoff point for all self-description, as in résumés and covering letters. People tend to take you at your own self-evalution; they see the image you habitually project, so will more easily see the truth of high self-evaluation if there is truth in it. But they need help in seeing how to apply your virtues to their business wants and needs; that is why selling benefits is so important.

These questions of understanding and personal attitude lead to another central matter in job seeking. Put simply, you have to be up and ready for every relevant job-seeking personal contact. The old song has it that "nobody wants you when you're down and out." Quite right; nobody does. Nor when you're tired, ragged, affected in the slightest degree by alcohol, defeated, or down in any discernible way.

In one very significant way, job seeking is not like professional selling. In professional selling, you have to be able to close sales, day after day, year after year, never losing the sparkle that professionalism brings. In job seeking, you need only make a single sale; you may not have to make another such sale for a decade or perhaps even for the rest of your life.

The sales professional knows how to stay "up"; it is a basic career need. But as a job seeker, even a seasoned professional is all too often in a series of unfamiliar situations—in a hurry, sometimes in urgent need of a job change, or unemployed—and easily becomes disoriented by repeated, seemingly personal, rejection. It is very easy to lose your "edge" when job seeking, to become perceptibly negative, and to thrust yourself upon potential employers as supplicant rather than as large potential asset. All of which results in more negative responses, more self-doubt, and a downwardly spiraling attitude from which it can be very difficult to recover. For it is not so simple as "pumping yourself up" for every interview or contact; real attitudes show, whether we want them to or not.

The essential understanding is that you need only make one sale, and that each situation is new. As an excellent sales professional, you know that, and take great care to treat each new prospect as a brand-new ball game; the same goes for each employment interview or personal contact. In job seeking, the last interview is just as important as the first. In each, you need to be calm and cool, warm and eager, professionally distanced and capable of being deeply involved with whomever you are dealing. You need to have researched well enough and to empathize enough so you can put yourself into "the other guy's shoes," and apply your prepared benefits story to your prospective employer's wants and needs. That is the language of selling; it is also the language of successful job seeking.

Another basic is your physical appearance. As in all selling, appearances convey first what you are and the attitudes you carry to others. The person who arrives in an office or a restaurant on a hot city day somewhat wilted and sweaty, and who does nothing to freshen up before the meeting, will probably unfavorably impress an executive recruiter or prospective employer, stacking the deck in the direction of failure. It is far better to be a few minutes late, those few minutes having been spent in freshening up, than to move into a situation looking and feeling less than your best. It is better yet to arrive early, cool off, and freshen up, providing yourself with a chance to review your research and your benefits story.

Clothing matters are also important in job seeking. In this context, we should stress that flamboyance is out, conservatism in dress and demeanor is in. In short, the old rules still apply here, and especially for sales professionals, who must be assessed in terms of their ability to deal with all kinds of people in many different situations.

Do not, under any circumstances, arrive with even one modest drink under your belt. For some hirers, the slightest hint of alcohol having been taken before arriving at a job interview is a complete disqualifier, the kind of red flag that cannot be disregarded. It is good to remember that, from the prospective employer's point of view, there are all too few personal keys to be perceived in an interview, and many have learned to treat alcohol as the kind of key negative that should not be disregarded.

At a luncheon or after-hours interview, it is wise not to drink anything alcoholic, if possible; stress may cause even one drink to have an unusually strong impact upon your system, and especially on an empty stomach. Sometimes abstention turns out to be impractical, as when a prospective employer really presses you to take a drink as an "ice-breaker," and you assess that it is he or she who really wants the drink and would probably feel uncomfortable drinking alone. Then the lightest drink possible is indicated—a glass of wine, or perhaps a tall scotch and soda, to be sipped, rather than swallowed. A second drink can and should almost always be refused. Even if it soon becomes apparent that it is not you, but your interviewer, who may have a drinking problem, it is entirely inappropriate to have more than one drink. That may sound a little rigid, but interviews are easily spoiled by drink, and it takes too much time, trouble, and expense to get an interview with a qualified prospective employer to let a couple of drinks ruin a job opportunity. Even when drink seems to be helping the situation a great deal, as you and your interviewer seem to get on extraordinarily well in an alcohol-induced haze, you are probably ruining your chances; many a job offered the night before has been withdrawn the morning after.

Smoking is not appropriate, either, unless your interviewer makes it perfectly clear by smoking that it really is all right. The nonsmoker who gamely invites you to smoke is highly likely to remember only that you did smoke, and that it was bothersome. That is especially true of the virtuous, recently converted nonsmoker, who may be particularly bothered when you smoke. And if you generally smoke cigars, do not do it during an interview; the smell lingers and sours, and all too often so does your prospective employer's recollection of you.

PRESELLING MOVES

A great many things can happen before you even try to sell a prospective employer on having you in for an interview. Depending on such matters as positioning and career status, it can be as easy as showing up at a recruiting session or responding affirmatively to an executive recruiter's or friend's call. Or it can be as hard as instituting a full-scale approach to hundreds of strangers via letter and résumé, while answering as many advertisements, some seemingly appropriate, as can be found.

The best way by far to look for any kind of job is from a position of employed strength. That is something that "everybody" knows. On the other hand, it is not something that everybody, or even most of us, take as a guide to action. Again and again, in these times, we see people "hanging in there," in situations that they know very well are fragile, to put it gently. We see companies that have been doing badly for years finally going under in generally worsened economic circumstances, their assets sold off, their employees, including their sales staff, given rather brief notice, and thrown out on the street to make their way as best they can. Our comment is often some equivalent of "Ain't it awful!" Yes, it is.

For sales professionals, staying on is one of the avoidable disasters of modern life. Some will, of course, but you need not. It is far better to seek new employment from the strength of current employment. The same applies for those who are facing adverse circumstances that may block advancement or lead to firings. And so, too, for those who want to make a move as part of career-building, rather than defensive, strategy. The key idea is to move from a position of strength.

Under such conditions, preselling moves include activation of previously made contacts outside the current company, and in some instances cultivation of new contacts, as when you very carefully arrange to exhibit at industry meetings and shows, become active in local industry and professional organizations, and attend professional development courses —*after* making the decision, or tentative decision, to seek new employment. Those are all things that should be done routinely in all seasons and in all years; but, being human, many of us tend to do them less than we should, so a swift catch-up is indicated. It can be done in that kind of catch-up way, and work well; but it is hazardous, given the pace of business change in these times. The danger is that you will be caught unprepared by adverse business circumstances and, when you should be activating a host of contacts to swiftly move out of a bad situation while still employed, events will overtake you while you are still trying to catch up. Then, as so many have found to their painful surprise, the contact who would gladly have recommended you yesterday as a prime acquisition will suddenly find that no openings exist, and will warmly urge you to "keep in touch." The old saw has it that "success builds success." In terms of job recommendations and referrals, that is certainly true. People like to hire and recommend success, or at least seeming success, and all too often have doubts today about unemployed people that yesterday they would have loved to "steal."

Bear in mind that—as every sales manager knows—good sales professionals are hard to find. So hard to find, in fact, that it is often necessary to settle for someone who seems fairly competent rather than the top producer they are really looking for. When you arrive on the scene, highly recommended by another known and respected professional, most good sales managers will feel remiss unless they talk to you. It is part of the sales manager's job to search constantly for people just like you. If you look strong enough, the astute sales manager will make a place for you. But also bear in mind that referral selling in this area usually takes time and planning. And it almost always requires being employed while you are looking.

Preselling moves from an employed position often include talking to professional recruiters. It is best here to be talking to recruiters who have called you, rather than approaching those who have not, although most recruiters will assure you that it makes no difference at all who approaches whom first. The fact that previous conversations did not lead to a job is not a bar here; for most recruiters, it only means that the valuable time and effort expended to get to know and sell you can now be made to pay off. And if you have previously turned down job offers obtained through recruiters who have approached you, so much the better. You are often viewed as a commodity of greater value under those circumstances, as long as you are still employed.

All this places a considerable premium upon talking to recruiters who approach you, even though you have no current inclination to seriously consider a job change. You can never know what career-building offers may be out there; and in these times, you never know when you will have to change your mind about the desirability of making a move. An approach to a recruiter is as easy as a phone call, whether to someone you know or to a stranger. So is a broadcast letter approach to recruiting firms, although that is usually an unnecessarily time-consuming approach for people currently employed.

Some of your closest business and personal friends—outside your current organization—can also be approached directly, as they would expect to be able to approach you. But job-seeking contacts with less close business and personal friends and acquaintances require considerably more care. They are not casual matters, for a bad first impression, a bad introduction, or the choice of a bad time may destroy an otherwise promising job contact. Most people know very well that these are difficult times for many, and know that although the basic thrust of your job approach may either be career-building or defensive, it is quite likely in this period to have strong defensive aspects. Even so, and even with most business and personal friends, it is wise to remember that people feel most comfortable selling and hiring strength. When one of your friends recommends you, it feels far better to be able to say something like "I have someone really great for us; hope I can convince him (or her) to move" than "One of my friends is in real trouble over at AYZ Corp; think we might have anything open?"

If your friend is willing to say anything at all, that is. Or if that treasured job contact you've been associating with week after week at chapter meetings of your professional organization is really eager to hire you. You will seem more desirable to both if they see you as an asset ready to make a move up than as someone about to be fired. A caution here: even your best friend may have second thoughts about hiring or recommending you if your approach comes over a couple of drinks at the end of a long, dispiriting day, week, or month, and in the form of a desperate plea for help. *The job-selling situation starts at the moment you raise the question of a new job face to face with a friend, recruiter, or prospective employer*. Therefore, it has to start when you are entirely up for a new situation, have thought through your benefits story, look your best, and are in all respects ready to make this sale *the* one—and remember, you only have to sell one.

As a practical matter, that often means making a very difficult decision in private, often in considerable anguish and in a state of mind quite closely approaching despair; or, if it is a basically career-building move, in a state of considerable excitement, accompanied by a couple of celebratory drinks. It is not every day that you decide to make a major job move; the day you do so is not usually a good time to try to do anything about it. Wait, at least until the next morning, before you tell anyone, except perhaps those so close to you that they have helped you make the decision, such as your spouse and closest friends. Then think it over again, in the cold light of day. If it still looks like a good decision, it then becomes time to update your résumé, develop a benefits story adapted to each of your current best job prospects, reexamine your wardrobe and the rest of your personal appearance, and begin to make your moves. For while it is true that you only need to sell one, your first few moves are likely to be toward your best prospects, and any one you lose early because of inadequate preparation may have been your best opportunity. In some ways, then, the first few job contacts may be more important than most of the others you may have to try farther on down the line.

ADVERTISEMENTS AND AGENCIES

Beyond existing networks, possible referrals, and known recruiters are a great many easily qualified prospects; they are as close as the host of newspaper advertisements and the employment agencies. A good sales professional is indeed hard to find, and there are always a great many people out there looking for one.

Many companies believe it best to hire sales representatives directly through newspaper advertisements. Some of your best prospecting will therefore be done directly from the want ads.

Many will be blind ads, with a number to call. (Sometimes these numbers are in a different city and can be called collect.) The number will often be that of a hotel or motel, and the person you're calling may well be your prospective hirer and perhaps future sales manager, out in the field on a hiring trip.

Thousands of American companies sell nationally, have offices in very few places, and rely on far-flung selling organizations and sales managers who travel a great deal of the time. These managers often hire, train, supervise, and handle some major accounts. In short, they are the marketing organizations of those companies in their sales regions.

When you call that kind of sales manager in answer to a direct advertisement, you're calling a prime prospect. Moreover, you're calling a prime prospect who has held up his or her hand and asked for help. That sales manager wants to hire a solid sales professional, preferably someone who will be a star. Someone who will require little training and retraining, a magnificent closer who will stay on for years and years, making money and building careers for everyone. In short, a money-making top producer—you.

Convincing that sales manager that you're precisely the right person for the job starts the moment you pick up the phone. Yes, you want to know a little more about the job, and the manager wants to tell you more, but the main object of your call is to start the process of selling yourself into that job. You need to sell the interview when you pick up the phone— not yourself, the interview. You can always turn down the job later if offered; what you want is the opportunity to meet that sales manager face to face in a selling situation, just like any other prospect.

The sales manager, in turn, is trying to find out whether your experience and telephone personality warrant further investigation, whether or not the face-to-face selling interview is worth going into. Over the phone, he or she will want to know a little about you and your experience, and will be listening hard to what you say, even harder to how you say it. Your clarity, maturity, and vibrancy are all capable of being communicated over the phone, and can be key factors in selling the interview. There are always general knockout factors a manager has in mind over the phone—too little and the wrong kind of experience chief among them—but most such knockout factors evaporate when a seasoned sales manager hears someone over the phone who sounds good. It's usually rationalized by the manager with "A little light on experience, but sounds great! Can't hurt to take a look." And you've sold the interview.

A few direct advertisements will ask that you send a résumé. By all means, do so, although it is usually an inexperienced manager who goes about hiring that way. If you do get a callback in response to your résumé, respond to it as if you hadn't sent a résumé at all; sell the interview as if you were starting a brand-new selling situation. You probably are.

Managers with open selling jobs also often place them through employment agencies. Many employment agencies specialize in sales and marketing jobs; others have specialists within general agencies who deal exclusively with sales and marketing openings.

Agencies often advertise selling jobs. Promising-looking jobs advertised by agencies may turn out well. On the other hand, they may be come-ons aimed at getting you in to offer you a far less desirable position which the agency is finding hard to fill. In any case, it never hurts to treat agency ads as you would leads supplied by a home office, which must be investigated and qualified. And, as with any lead, the sale starts as soon as you enter the agency office. Although the strength of an agency recommendation rests mainly on the placement person's desire to make a commission by filling the open job with you or someone else, you are the one who supplies the agency person with what to say about you.

Agency representatives, in most instances, are commissioned sellers, working either on straight commission or on a draw against commission. If they are agency owners, they get income from results, just as do their representatives. They want to sell you into a job and need some selling tools to work with. It's up to you to give them those tools—the ability to describe your appearance as superb, your experience as just right, your motivations as those of a winner. And very often, agency representatives are not as good at selling as the sales professionals they're trying to place; they need a lot of selling help from you. Therefore, when you move into an agency situation, move in ready to sell.

Some agencies are worth prospecting for leads even when they haven't advertised any jobs that look right for you. The right ones to visit are easy to find. They are those that advertise that they specialize in sales jobs. They are the agencies that obviously specialize in the industry you've been working in or want to enter, and that clearly have a sales and marketing specialist. You'll find the right agencies to visit in the general newspapers, in the business newspapers and magazines of your region or city, and in the trade magazines of your industry.

Most agency-advertised selling jobs today are fee paid. That is, the employer picks up agency charges in full, at no cost to you. Others split fees between you and the employer. Others charge agency costs entirely to you, usually to be paid as a percentage of salary over a specified period of time. Be very, very careful to understand precisely what the agency fee basis is for any job possibility you're sent out on. Know just how much you'll have to pay the agency, if anything, should you get the job. Be particularly careful not to get caught with a fixed agency fee that must legally be paid even if you quit the job soon after you get it.

Some "agencies" are really executive-search organizations, which will charge you a fee, often a rather large one, for helping you look for a job. Such organizations often render real service, with tests aimed at identifying your most salable talents and skills, and offer real help in finding the kind of selling job you want. Others are of questionable value. Occasionally, one will turn out to be an outright fraud. If you do hire this kind of help, treat it as you would any major purchase—check directly with others who have used it, or with the Better Business Bureau. Ask a lot of questions and be skeptical as to the answers. Above all, don't be stampeded into signing anything you don't understand. The foregoing seems like odd advice to have to give to sales professionals, but a great many sellers are very easy to sell, and too many sales professionals with their buying hats on turn out to be victims.

Often, your knowledge of the industry you've been working in can supply you with the names of several companies you might like to prospect for a selling job. Research will often turn up more.

When you do have the names of some companies you want to prospect, treat them as you would other prospects. Get the name of the national or regional sales manager from directory sources or from the switchboard operator at the company. Call the right prime prospect, using much the kind of telephone interview selling approach described earlier. Do your best to sell the interview. Usually some variant of "I'm calling you because you're the best" works well.

Again, as with any cold calling, you may find yourself with some time between other calls, and may want to do a little cold calling on company employment offices. It's generally the least fruitful of job-hunting techniques, but occasionally turns up a reasonably good prospect you might otherwise have missed.

RÉSUMÉS

Another preselling requirement, really part of the nuts and bolts of job seeking, is a good basic résumé, which will properly include work and personal history cast in a selling form attractive enough to help you secure an interview. Rather too much is made of résumés, really. They do not ever get you a job; at best they help you, with appropriate covering letter and other approaches, to get in the door and face to face with a prospective employer.

Résumés have a basic role to play, however. A good résumé certainly does not merely tell an amorphous group of potential employers something about you, so that they will be able to see whether or not they want to interview you. A résumé that does only that—and that includes by far the overwhelming majority of résumés—does you an enormous disservice. Such a résumé performs approximately the same function as an operating manual or a similar piece of background or how-to-use material; and you do not sell very well from that kind of material.

A good résumé *sells*. It is not general, for all possible industries or functions, but directed at specific industries or functions, and sometimes both. It aims to cast you, your previous training, and your career to date in the most favorable possible light for the kind of job you are seeking. It tries to provide specifics that can be alluded to in your covering letter, which will cause a prospective employer to want to see you in relation to a specific job. But both should sell. The résumé and your covering letter are a single selling package, rather than your résumé being a straight broadcast document, leaving your covering letter to do all the selling.

That is why the general broadcast résumé, with or without a broadcast covering letter, is generally ineffective. By its very nature, it is very hard to develop as a selling tool, being general. Its frequent rejection by prospective employers tends to make you think that you have used up possible employers, when in fact you usually have not even begun to approach them. And it can make you think that something must be wrong with you, when in fact what is wrong is that you have not begun to sell. To send broadcast résumés to hundreds of potential employers can be a waste of time and effort; to cover them with letters that in no way specifically reach for the employer's wants and needs may merely waste good prospects. The broadcast résumé should only be considered in two types of situations. If you are rather well known in a field or industry, the broadcast letter and résumé serve to alert your contacts quickly as to your availability; even so, the technique is to be used very cautiously. However, one who has used up many of his or her best prospects might lose very little by using it.

Rather than a broadcast résumé, you should develop a *series* of résumés tailored to the different industries and responsibilities that interest you. There is everything right about developing more than one résumé, whether you are looking for your first job or have years of experience as a sales professional. As a practical matter, it will in most elements be a single basic résumé, with adaptation to different kinds of employers and, in some instances, to a single employer, when time and situation allow. A basic résumé will be used for certain purposes; for example, it may be sent in response to advertisements asking that applicants include résumés, or to prospective employers turned up through research on whom insufficient data has been developed to "customize" the résumé. But whenever possible, and however much work it entails, that basic résumé should be adapted for a particular purpose. And the résumé should always be topped by a personal letter to a prospective employer, unless your résumé has moved through a recruiter or some other employment organization, in which case they will supply the covering letter.

Figure 3 shows an illustrative résumé, one that does its best to sell, rather than to merely list. This résumé is not done in the only form we think workable; there are several available résumé forms and approaches, and some works focused solely on job hunting suggest as many as a dozen. It is illustrative only; Vaughn Smith might be a man or a woman, is a composite, and is not a real person.

What follows here is the résumé of a sales professional who has had considerable practical experience in several different areas. It starts with name, address, and telephone numbers; moves immediately to a summary statement of

(Text continued on page 268.)

FIGURE 3

RÉSUMÉ

Vaughn Smith
2222 Smith Street
Chicago, Illinois, 11111
(987) 1212
(987) 3131

Objective:

The opportunity to help profitably grow a substantial company into an even more substantial one, using the proven skills developed during the course of a very successful career in sales and marketing. Major qualifications and experience include over 15 years of senior sales leadership while profitably developing companies all over the country. Have very successfully accomplished national account, regional, and territorial selling functions, as well as regional sales supervisory functions. Fully equipped to apply the tools and techniques of modern selling and marketing to the widest possible range of problems and opportunities.

Experience:

1975 to present   PRS Corporation, San Francisco,
                                                   California

Senior Representative, National Accounts Representative, and *Field Sales Representative* of this large, multiline industrial equipment manufacturing company.

As Midwestern regional Senior Representative, headquartered in Chicago, handled a wide variety of special account and sales promotion functions, as well as many field training functions. Was Acting Sales Manager of region in absence of regional sales manager. Helped plan and execute regional expansion from 10 to 18 representatives, while introducing several new lines and products and increasing regional sales by 34% over a two-year period.

As National Accounts Representative, headquartered in San Francisco home office, was responsible for expanding sales to existing national accounts handled by over 50%, opening up many new accounts in the process.

As Field Sales Representative, handled Atlanta, Georgia, territory. Was National Field Rep of the Year in 1977, and sales leader (top 10 in country) in 1976, 1977, and 1978.

1970 to 1975   TPT Corporation, Atlanta, Georgia

Senior Field Sales Representative and *Field Sales Representative* for this well-established regional distributor of office equipment.

As Senior Field Sales Representative, worked out of Atlanta home office selling and servicing major accounts throughout the Southeast. Increased major account volume in this area by over 20% in each of three years, for a total of 68%, and increased number of major accounts sold by 41%.

As Field Sales Representative, handled New Orleans territory. Was contest winner and sales leader throughout period in which territory was handled.

1966 to 1970   GHI Corporation, Detroit, Michigan

Field Representative and *Sales Support Liaison* for this regional restaurant equipment dealer.

As Field Representative, handled Chicago Center City territory. Grew territory billings by a total of 54% over a three-year period, and was sales leader every year.

As Sales Support Liaison, handled a large variety of sales administrative and support functions in Detroit home office, including the development of promotional materials and sales contests, and assisted in the preparation of several sales meetings and training classes.

Education:

B.A., Michigan State University, 1965, top 10% of class, majoring in Business Administration, with special emphasis on Sales and Marketing.

Continuing Professional Education includes courses in Advanced Selling, Modern Marketing, Public Speaking, Speedreading, and Persuasion, for a total of 24 Continuing Education Credits (CEUs).

Community Activities:

Vice-Chairman, Community Fund, Skokie, Illinois, 1986, 1981.
Vice-Chairman, Toastmaster's International, Atlanta, Georgia, 1977, 1976.

Hobbies:

Tennis, golf, public speaking

Personal:

Married, two children, excellent health.
References and personal data on request.

---

objectives cast as benefits resulting from the hiring of Vaughn Smith; moves into a chronological account of work history, which continues to stress achievements and imply benefits; and then outlines Smith's education, nonwork accomplishments, and relevant personal data, ending with a promise to furnish references and supporting information as necessary on request.

It is as long as it happens to be. The many who counsel short résumés and the few who counsel relatively long résumés are reminiscent of those advertising people who argue interminably about whether ad copy should be "short" or "long" for maximum effectiveness. The truth is that excellent copy sells, whatever its length, and that bad copy does not work, whatever its length. If a résumé is intrinsically interesting—if it sells well—then it will be read, no matter how long or short it is, or how busy its reader. A too-short résumé may not take the time to sell as well as it should; a long, badly written résumé may not be read at all. What does matter is that a résumé be written clearly, tell its benefits story, and serve as a basis for an interview. You are wisest to adopt the selling style that works best for you, however short or long the resulting résumé.

This example is a basic résumé, attempting to specify a sufficiently varied array of accomplishments. It can be turned in whatever is the desired direction by recruiter, by business friend, by Vaughn Smith's own covering letter, or during the face-to-face interview.

It does not state age, although age is implied by length of work and related history. "They're either too young or too old" is a response you need not court. The résumé helps sell the interview; a prospective employer's preconception about age (which might be a knockout factor, if age is stated in the résumé) can often be easily dealt with face to face. It states nothing about sex, race, religion, or ethnic origin, recognizing that those matters are irrelevant to the central selling questions involved in the hiring situation. Nor does it include earnings history; the question of price is here entirely premature, as the sale has not even started. If absolutely necessary, you can include some earnings history data in your covering letter. It does, however, include data indicating a high level of energy and community involvement, matters of considerable importance to many in making interviewing and then hiring decisions.

Finally, the résumé presented in Figure 3 is that of a seasoned sales professional who has taken great care to accrete wide experience and build success on success. This is a person who very clearly and from the first has been successful and growth-oriented, unafraid to move into new areas and take up new challenges, and who can be relied upon to make a substantial contribution to any company.

Note the continuing emphasis on profitable growth, sales professionalism, and continuing sales leadership. These are the key matters, underlying all the mechanics of résumé, covering letter, contacts, and appearances. The promises you make and the attitudes you bring with you are central hiring matters. Your success in job seeking depends in large measure upon how well you convey those promises to others, first while selling the interview, and later face to face in the direct job-selling situation.

PREPARING FOR THE INTERVIEW

However the process of selling the interview starts—whether through your mailed letter or by telephone, as in response to an advertisement, through the referral of a business friend, by action of a job searcher in your employ or a recruiter engaged by a prospective employer—there will be some interviews.

Before those interviews, however, two other things are likely to happen. The first is a phone call, which may either set an interview or serve as a screening device, and you cannot know which it is when you pick up the phone. The second is your own research on the company and, when possible, on the individual with whom you will be meeting.

The screening call is easy enough to handle, if you bear firmly in mind throughout the conversation not to go off the deep end and try to sell yourself into the job while on the phone. That hardly ever works, and very often sets up barriers between you and your prospective employer that either cause cancellation of the projected interview or make the interview far more difficult than it should have been. On the telephone, just as when you are answering an advertisement, all you are doing is continuing to sell the interview, and after that has been done, trying to leave the most favorable possible personal impression, as preparation for the actual face-to-face interview. Be as brief as you reasonably can, answer whatever questions are asked as best you can, make it clear that you look forward to the interview and the possibility of working with the company and individual enormously, but never take that one step beyond and try to sell yourself into the job on the phone.

With the interview sold, it is time to do some research. When the firm involved is one you have been interested in, you may already know a good deal about the company, its key personnel, strengths, weaknesses, future prospects, and where you would like to fit in. Otherwise, all that must be accomplished between the time an interview is set and the time it takes place. Try to leave yourself enough time for that kind of research. Clearly, if someone you want to see is eager to see you immediately, you will make the appointment, scant the research, and hope that your prospective employer's eagerness to see you can be used far more effectively than the selling tools any research would have yielded; but if some research time can be arranged, take it.

Some of your most valuable insights may result from a series of calls to your business friends, inquiring about the company, its situation, and its people. It is not at all unlikely that one or more people in your web of contacts will know a good deal about your prospective employer. You may also get a good deal of hard and detailed information relating to what your prospect may be seeking, information that can help you turn your background and skills into a solidly effective benefits story, which you may use to sell yourself into the job. Indeed, you may find yourself talking to a good friend who is capable of paving the way for you with a glowing recommendation to a friend of long standing who is about to interview you for that job.

On the other hand, your friends may be able to make it clear that you would be unwise to touch prospective job and employer with a ten-foot pole and that, too, is extraordinarily valuable insight, although you are likely to want to make up your mind for yourself by going through with the interview. You cannot know what you will get from your business and personal friends until you ask, and you should never be shy about asking for information. That is what friends are for, and a lot of what networking is all about. And if you ask them now, they will be encouraged to ask you later, which only solidifies friendships.

There are formal sources of information, too. One of the best of such sources is really not a single source, but a vehicle more and more in evidence on desks and in libraries. It is the computer terminal, hooked into one or more massive distributed data networks, such as Lockheed's Dialog, which taps hundreds of massive data bases. Through such a terminal, it is possible to secure corporate disclosure statements filed with the federal government pursuant to the securities laws;

yearly and quarterly financial statements, such as profit and loss statements, cash flow statements, and balance sheets; lists of directors and officers; business press articles relating to the company and its people; and a wide miscellany of other quite relevant materials capable of helping you build a job-getting benefits story.

There is another such vehicle, too, the time-honored one. It is the nearest specialized business library or large public library, which will have many similar information sources in their print-on-paper forms, and sometimes on computer terminals, as well. They will also have trained business and general reference librarians, who can be invaluable in helping you frame the right questions to ask about your prospective employer and in finding the answers to those questions. Here, as with your friends, you must not be shy about asking. Librarians will help a great deal, if you let them.

These on-line and print sources can yield a great deal of basic information, and even sometimes yield—as through an astutely researched and written article on the company—a lot of what you need to know about the company, as to both selling yourself into the job and whether or not you want the job. A series of financial statements and accompanying materials can tell you how the company is doing and is likely to be doing in the near term. Company people are likely to paint a rosier picture than is justified by the hard facts; you need to try to learn something about those hard facts before you go into that interview.

CHAPTER 10

GETTING THE JOB

And so to the face-to-face interview, where it all comes together, and where you and your prospective employer are involved in the process of deciding whether or not you want to work with each other.

The best job interviews involving two sales professionals—one as seller and one as buyer—are also a good deal of fun, as the best selling interviews always are, but in a sense even more so. For good job interviews have a certain resonance, a kind of double impact. You are presenting the benefits that hiring you will bring; at the same time you are both sizing up your potential employer and assessing how well he or she appreciates the art and craft you are demonstrating in the selling situation. Your prospective employer is assessing the benefits you are describing, and at the same time watching you sell, perhaps with appreciation for the art and skill of a real professional, perhaps with some dismay. That all makes it interesting, as much as any selling situation you will ever be in. All the more so if you successfully close, but interesting either way.

We have so far cast this discussion in selling terms. That is proper; when you seek a job, the essential transaction that continues to take place throughout the process and until a job offer has actually been made is a selling process, with you as seller and your prospective employer as buyer. The fact that seller is sizing up buyer quite as actively as the other way around is not relevant to the central transaction. Be aware that if you spend too much time and attention probing and sizing up a prospective employer, it may indicate less than the active interest in the job you may otherwise be expressing, possibly harming your ability to close the sale. There are questions to raise, many of them, but they should be raised seriously only after a job offer has been made, so as not to interrupt the flow of the selling process before and during the face-to-face interview.

THE FACE-TO-FACE JOB INTERVIEW

That face-to-face interview may be one or many. You may meet with the person to whom you will report only once, and get a job offer. Or you may meet with someone from a company personnel department, then with several members of sales and marketing management one at a time, and finally even with a member of top management, who can make or break a decision tentatively made by others—and all before you have a firm job offer. Aside from the personnel department screening interview, it matters little how many times you are interviewed, and by whom; the basic situation changes little from interview to interview. You still need to "put yourself in the other guy's shoes" in order to empathize successfully and thereby become able to adapt and focus your benefits story so that it properly speaks to the wants and needs of your prospective employer. Achieving empathy is really the key to the face-to-face job interview with someone who will be your superior or peer in a new company, just as empathy is the key to all selling success.

In job seeking, as in all selling, empathy building is more than anything else relaxed and responsive listening, signaled to others by every nonverbal and verbal means at our command, and conveying that we care a good deal about what they have to say, and want to hear it. It requires knowing what you plan to say extremely well—at least in its general outlines—so that you can focus hard on what "the other guy" is communicating to you verbally and nonverbally. Then it is relatively easy to find the specific insights you need to fit yourself so well into the situation that you are clearly the person for the job. And underneath, it requires real human sympathy for those with whom you are meeting, for sham almost always is apparent, and especially to people who are just as experienced as you. Real empathy requires real human sympathy.

Operationally, it starts with as simple a move as a calm, warm, friendly handshake, and an icebreaking comment about the restaurant you are meeting in, a trophy on the office wall or outside in the reception area, and a straightforward query about what the company and interviewer have in mind for the job in question. After all, the interviewer has your résumé and may know a good deal more about you besides. Many will respond to that kind of approach; people do like to talk about their work, their companies, and their own careers, and it is always a good idea to encourage them to do so. For then you stand a very good chance of learning what you need to know to later secure the job offer. You are also likely to painlessly pick up much of the basic insight you need to make your own decision as to whether or not to take the job if offered. All depending, of course, on whether you listen responsively enough so that the flow of talk will continue.

Then, and usually fairly soon, it will be time to tell your story. The opportunity then lies in casting your personal and work history as a series of potential benefits that will accrue from hiring you, each facet meeting employer needs and desires as squarely as possible. The hazard lies in forgetting about benefits, and merely telling your story as a series of incidents in which you are the prime figure, thereby ensuring that you seem narrowly self-centered. It can be compounded by focusing on negatives, such as how unfairly treated you were on this job or that, but few of us are so naive as to do that. The main danger is self-absorption in the telling, rather than careful focus on what hiring you will do for your interviewer's company and, if possible, for the interviewer as well.

You are best advised to "assume sale" throughout. When you walk through a prospective employer's door, you expect to get the job. You really do; it sticks out all over you. You are relaxed, but ready to go, eager to get started on what promises to be the job of a lifetime. You want to hear all about it, are ready to tell your interviewer all about yourself, but regard all that as a mere formality, because once the company understands what you can do for it, you will be offered the job. No, not as rawly ebullient as that, but almost. A quiet but firm assumption that you are going to get the job will very often during the course of an interview build precisely that view in the mind of your interviewer.

You will be ready for such standard questions as "Why are you leaving your present company?" or "Why do you want to come and work with us?" or "Where do you see yourself in five or ten years?" or "What do you see as your key strengths and weaknesses?" Those kinds of questions are easily handled, if prepared for; their answers should be as much a part of your planned presentation as your basic résumé and covering letter story, as adapted during the interview. As a sales professional, you sell with a completely thought-through presentation, complete with the basic answers to the standard questions, stalls, and objections raised by prospects; so, too, when you function as a seller in a job situation. By all means write the answers to what you feel will be the basic questions you will be asked; memorize those answers, if you feel that will help. At the very least, memorize the key words and phrases you will need in dealing with such standard questions.

It will help to learn how to "take the prospect's temperature," that is, to trial close. It is not really an attempt to get a firm decision; in an interview, that is rarely appropriate. Rather, it is such a query as "Does that make sense to you?" or "Does that square with your view of the matter?" It is an attempt to find agreement between you and your prospective employer on matters key to the hiring decision; to the extent that you successfully find common ground, you have moved closer to a favorable decision.

From a selling point of view, the interview generally consists of an early introductory and empathy-building period; a presentation period in which you tell your benefits-laden story; a wide-ranging discussion period, in which you handle questions and possible reservations about hiring you, while continuing to build empathy and find areas of agreement; some trial closing along the way; and the close, in which you get as close as you can to a firm job offer. As to the last, this situation differs somewhat from that encountered in most selling situations. In selling, you usually try very hard to close the sale during the interview, knowing that the sale deferred is usually a sale that has to be made all over again later; in the job interview situation, it is quite likely that no decision will be made on the spot—unless you are at the end of a whole selection process, in which instance you will be best advised to fight hard to close the job then and there.

We are not describing a fixed sequence of events. You may find yourself engaged in a wide-ranging discussion of business events from the moment you move into the interview, never sequentially present your benefits story, and find yourself with a firm job offer half an hour after you meet for the first time. You may meet a compulsive talker and self-aggrandizer, who hardly lets you get a word in edgewise, talks uninterruptedly about his or her own family matters for two hours, ultimately regrets that you did not have more time together, and does not hire you because you somehow "failed to impress." Or you may find yourself in the middle of a well-oiled, multimeeting hiring process, in which you never really get to first base with whomever counts, although you meet with a whole series of sales managers and personnel people over a period of months.

When you are talking to someone who will make a hiring decision, it is quite often the first few minutes that count the most. These are those utterly crucial moments in which you make a first impression, begin to develop empathy with your prospective employer, and begin to show to an experienced eye who and what you are. That is what the experienced eye looks for first, after all: who and what you are, not where you have been, what you have done, how you have been educated, and what you know. All those things can be put on paper, weighed, and analyzed, but they are not why you hire sales professionals. From the viewpoint of the experienced manager who is deciding whether or not to bring you on board, all the paper is background—essential background, but only that. It is the face-to-face interview or series of interviews that tells the experienced manager who and what you are, and determines whether or not you are the one for the job.

As always, the first few minutes are crucially important. Putting it a little differently, most job offers are lost in the first few minutes; most real contenders for jobs are born during the first few minutes of the face-to-face interview. Yet whether or not those first few minutes go well or badly is not a matter of chemistry (often used as a synonym for accident), as so many think. The kind of chemistry that occurs between seller and buyer has little to do with accident, and much to do with the seller's art. Those first few minutes together provide—or fail to provide—an excellent first impression and the beginning of empathy, and that is the formula that gets job offers.

You should bring to the interview copies of your résumé, letters of reference, and key supporting documents, and be prepared to use the résumé as the basis for a connected life history. Very often, you will not present that life history, or any large part of it, during the interview. On the other hand, you may find yourself being interviewed by someone who wants you to do just that; when that happens, you must have the best-prepared presentation you can muster. There are those who will want to hear you talk about yourself for a while, while they orient themselves and "size you up." Others will come to the interview unprepared, and need to hear your story even to begin to assess your possibilities.

The interviewer who says, "Why don't you tell me a little

about yourself?" should not then be treated to an off-the-cuff, undirected discussion of family, childhood dreams, and miscellaneous unconnected professional accomplishments. That question should never be treated casually in an interview; it should be seen as opening up an opportunity to tell your carefully prepared benefits story, in which personal and business histories together point to a series of substantial benefits flowing from your hire for the job in question. An experienced interviewer will normally expect you to be able to do that, and failure to at least start to make a highly professional presentation can weigh heavily against you.

That presentation should clearly show a career-building line of previous jobs, with you going to continually greater pay and responsibility. Where there are breaks in that line, clear, sharp, and positive explanations should be ready. For example, trying to go on your own and failing can be seen as a negative—but if cast properly can be seen as proof that you are entrepreneurially minded and, in many ways, are therefore better able to make a contribution than many who have played it safe and never struck out on their own. A caution here, though: those who hire are usually at least as experienced as those who come to be hired. If you have had a bad career break and it shows, say so, indicate how much the experience helped you to learn proper career directions, and move on. It will seldom then be seen as a negative in the hiring situation.

Your presentation should include the reasons you made each move, and focus strongly on your reason for leaving your current or last employment, if at all possible casting that move as a positive career builder. Here is where the desirability of moving from currently employed status to a new job becomes particularly apparent.

It is enormously important not to be seen as a restless job-hopper, one who moves around from job to job not for good career-building reasons, but rather out of impatience, boredom, and perhaps incompetence, never stopping long enough to build anything anywhere. Nobody really wants one of those around, no matter how good the formal educational and work records look on the surface. Even if you have made a fair number of moves—as many as four or five in 10 to 15 years—you may have been pursuing a firm career-building line rather than job-hopping. Here it is the explanation that makes all the difference. The prospective employer who is convinced that you are basically stable and capable of moving ahead strongly will usually have no difficulty with several previous job moves, if they make good career sense. On the other hand, if those moves convincingly indicate a pattern of instability, and you are unable to dispel that impression face to face, your cause is probably lost.

Throughout your presentation, you should find opportunities to link up what you have learned during the first portion of the interview with your past history and current job objectives—that is, if you have properly developed information and started building empathy in those crucial first few minutes. Bear in mind that the job presentation that goes most smoothly and with the fewest interruptions is the one that is probably going worst. Without interruptions and the ability to build areas of agreement, you are probably not making any significant contact and are getting nowhere. Contrary to how it is normal to feel while presenting your story, interruptions are good for you, and passive and seeming acceptance is bad. If you have done your early work well, and started to build empathy early, you will be interrupted, be unable to finish your story, find yourself building agreement, be able to assume success easily throughout the interview, and stand a good chance of getting the job.

Similarly with questions, especially during and after you have told something of your story. The engaged prospective employer will very often ask searching questions, demand clear answers, and go back again and again to matters of particular interest, hearing you on the same subjects from different vantage points. When that happens, what you are getting is enormously important insight that can help you get the job, for then what you are seeing is the exposure of the employer's own concerns and interests, which makes it possible for you to sharply adapt your selling story to perceived employer needs.

Getting the Offer.

Although most job interview situations will not result in an opportunity to try to make an on-the-spot close, some will. There are times when you may find yourself meeting with someone who can make the hiring decision and is ready to do so, then and there. On rare occasions, it will be at a first interview; but the manager who hires that way will seldom hire well. But it can come on a callback interview, when most applicants have been weeded out, and it is down to you and very few others; or at a time when there are still many applicants under consideration, but you strike someone who has a hiring decision to make as particularly right for the job and perhaps personally very compatible.

Sometimes it is quite clear that the person you are meeting with cannot make a hiring decision, as when you are meeting with someone from a personnel department, rather than a sales manager. Often, though, you do meet with someone who can hire, and the question is whether or not he or she is willing to make a hiring decision now. Often, the question seems to be "When do I ask?" Well, if you have done your selling job well, and built real empathy between you and your interviewer, it never hurts to ask, and it never hurts to ask again and again. On the other hand, if it has not gone well, and your first asking runs into a stone wall, you will know it. Then it hurts a good deal to ask again and again, for then you are likely to be regarded as pushy. There is never any magic about closing, no foolproof technique that works particularly better than any other technique to get a job or make a sale, no way to force or trick anyone into hiring you, and no optimum number of times to ask for a job during an interview. Closing techniques in this context consist only of a few ways of asking for the job, some of which will be more appropriate in one situation, or with one person, than another.

Sometimes it is most appropriate simply to ask. If you have built empathy, told as much of your story as seems desirable to both of you, discussed whatever needed to be discussed, agreed a good deal on important matters, and have been together doing all this for a good while, it may be perfectly natural to say something like "It all sounds wonderful to me, and it's beginning to sound to me as if you feel the same way. Do I get the job?" Or it may seem better to put it a less baldly, given the situation and the people involved. Then you may simply assume sale, and ultimately say something like "Great! When do I start?" Alternatively, you may want to put it in terms of a post-decision choice, assume that a favorable decision has been made, and say something like "Fine. I can start on the first of next month, if that suits you. Or, if you like, I can give a little less notice, and start two weeks from today. Which would you prefer?" A caution here: The choice close works well in selling goods and services, but should be used cautiously in the hiring situation, and only if you are quite sure you are dealing with someone very close to a favorable decision and yet so indecisive as to need a bit of push in a direction he or she really wants to go. For the really undecided, this kind of push may be counterproductive, causing an almost committed interviewer to back up and want to think about it all over again.

Sometimes, you will not say anything at all, using the weight of silence—and silence has a great weight—to work for you. For example, far down the line at the end of a hiring interview, you might say something like "It looks good to me. How does it look to you?" and wait. Then, as silence grows between you, so does a certain kind of confrontation, and with it considerable pressure to make a decision. A caution here, too: these are pressure tactics, and can rebound to your disadvantage.

On balance, it is usually better to play this kind of close rather conservatively, with "Do I get the job?" or "When do I start?" or "Which would you prefer?" These are the better closing choices, when you do have a chance to try to close.

And close you will, whether during or after the ultimate hiring interview, for if you learn how to move from job strength to strength, build your network of contacts well, research and prospect effectively, develop sound written materials and prepared presentations, and above all sell empathetically as well in the job-seeking situation as you do in the field, you will be far better equipped than most to build your career through a series of increasingly satisfying jobs.

NEGOTIATION AND DECISION

As a prospective employee, you will have many questions about job, company, and related matters. Many of these will be answered during the course of the interview or series of interviews, often as part of the interviewer's discussion of the job in question. Some will not, and will need to be answered before you can decide on acceptance or rejection of the offer. It is often tempting to raise some of those questions during the course of hiring interviews, but it is wiser to wait until you have a specific offer, even if it means going on through and spending time that might ultimately prove to have been unprofitably spent. It is very difficult to put questions so well that none of them will be seen as objections or premature negotiations, and the last thing you want to do during the job selection process is to shift focus from the enormous benefits to be derived from hiring you to your own possible objections, or to begin to negotiate terms before receiving a firm offer. If there are really major objections, such as a mandatory relocation when you will not relocate, or an income range that at its top is far too low for you even to consider, then you should stop the job selection process as soon as that is known, which will usually be very early. But if the job is worth considering, then let the focus continue to be the hiring decision, and that means going through to the end of the hiring process and receiving a firm offer.

Once you do have a firm job offer, then negotiations are very much in order. For then all has reversed; you are wanted, rather than wanting. The seller has sold and, with firm offer in hand, has become the buyer. Prospective employer is now desirous employer, engaged in selling you on the wisdom of taking the proffered job, and therefore almost always willing to make some concessions on top of the firm job offer in hand. Now the company has time and money invested in you, and a decision has been made that no one is likely to want to remake. And whoever has made the hiring decision has ego and hopes invested in you, too. It is very much like dealing with someone who has spent a good deal of time agonizing over which of several boats to buy, who then waits with ill-concealed impatience for delivery. Your bargaining position is small before the hiring decision has been made, but it is never better than just after, and before you have accepted, the job offer.

Note that this is a time when you may have new bargaining power in your current job, as well. Some current employers will not negotiate against a new job offer, as a matter of policy; but many will. A good sales professional is hard to find, and just as hard to keep; when someone else has recognized your worth, the new offer may remove blinders and unlock previously locked doors in your current company. No, we do not suggest soliciting an offer from another company to use as a lever in negotiations with your current company. That is a very dangerous game indeed, and can rebound to your very great disadvantage. But when you do have a firm offer and are quite ready to take it, then by all means consider giving your company a chance to make a better counteroffer. The way to do it is to be very simple and straightforward. With satisfactory new offer firmly in hand, tell your current company that you have an offer and that, although you hate to leave, you are very seriously considering taking it, and plan to respond affirmatively tomorrow or the next day. Say no more; your attitude will indicate clearly enough that you might respond favorably to a counteroffer. Then wait. If no counteroffer is forthcoming, take the new job, for you have very likely burned your bridges by informing your current company of your readiness to make the move. On the other hand, you may get a counteroffer; if so, it must be specific and immediate, rather than a general promise to somehow take care of you later on. Of course, if you cannot wait to get out of an uncongenial situation, the whole question is moot; then it is a matter of going when the going is good.

Negotiating ability varies, of course, as does available flexibility on the part of a prospective employer. For most experienced people, though, it is possible to do a good deal of negotiating between the time you say "That's wonderful! When can we talk about the details?" and when you say "Okay, that's it; I'm satisfied if you are. I'm giving notice Monday morning."

A prospective employer will usually go to considerable trouble and expense to see to it that you have the kind of information and incentives you need to be able to make a favorable decision on the job offer. Many elements of the total compensation package will be negotiable between offer and acceptance. Here we will discuss the kind of information you need to be able to make a balanced decision to accept, reject, or negotiate an improved job offer.

Some of that information is precisely the kind of insight you may have been able to discover through business friends and published sources before going into the interview. Whether before or after the interview, though, you will certainly want to know as much as possible about prospective employer and company prospects before accepting a job offer. That may involves trips to home offices and sometimes to other locations at company expense to see facilities and talk with company people. It may, in the instance of international relocation, mean a trip abroad, again at company expense. It is very difficult to size up a job offer from a distance; the possibility of making a major mistake becomes very large if you are interviewed, negotiate, and accept a job offer far from your eventual operations base. And even when your job move is within your present geographical area, or to an area you know well, it is wise to size up company and people on-site, rather than taking anything at all for granted. That is particularly true in difficult times, for yesterday's affluent, growing company may be today's company in deep trouble, and yesterday's "plum" of a job may be today's personal and business disaster.

RELOCATION

Relocation questions can deeply affect both your basic decision as to the desirability of a proffered job and your negotiating stance on several elements of the total compensation package. Sometimes it is as basic as being delighted by the prospect of a move to San Francisco or Phoenix from New York or Detroit, or dismay at the thought of trying to cope with New York's extraordinarily difficult living conditions and cost factors. Sometimes it is a matter of realizing that one area may be far more expensive than another, in terms of your quality of life requirements, whatever the Consumer Price Index indicates as to relative price levels, generating the need to negotiate a higher income offer before an otherwise desirable job can be accepted. Sometimes it is the quality or kind of schools available, or cultural life, or recreation, or professional opportunities for a spouse. All require careful examination before effective negotiation and decision making can eventuate. No, you will hardly ever have as much insight as you would like in accepting or rejecting a job offer involving relocation, but you can try very hard to get as much insight as possible before making a decision.

Happily, the corporate job-moving styles of the 1950s and 1960s are less and less prevalent. Few corporations in this period attempt to routinely move their people from installation to installation every few years. Some do; whenever possible, those should be avoided, for they provide only a fragmented, corporate-dependent life, with little opportunity for real professional growth and no opportunity to put down satisfying personal and economic community roots. That corporate transfer style causes enormous personal difficulties; rootless families are, far more than most, disoriented and may have deep problems. So are rootless employees, for that matter.

One large reason for the demise of the corporate transfer style is the emergence of the movement for women's liberation and sexual equality. Many women today reject the role of nonworking wife and mother, much preferring to pursue satisfying and lucrative careers. Many transfers that formerly would have been accepted are now refused, because the career dislocation and loss of income resulting to a working spouse is often an unacceptable price to pay for a corporate transfer, even when that transfer involves a substantial promotion and raise in pay.

It makes very little sense to trade two careers for one by accepting a corporate transfer that effectively puts one spouse out of work or sets back that spouse's career development by many years. A psychologist or lawyer who has spent many years developing a practice cannot redevelop that practice at will, and quickly, in another location, perhaps even in another state with different certification requirements, and should not be asked to do so just because her husband has been transferred or promoted. That goes either way, of course; women in business today find themselves facing the same transfer and promotion questions as do men.

In terms of family and professional security, two careers are far better than one. Two professionals in one family can together build some savings and investments, and thereby develop a "cushion" against such adversities as the loss of a job or serious illness. Two professionals with such a cushion can afford to make job moves that involve a certain degree of risk, or venture into their own businesses; the result is a flexibility rarely available to one worried person with a mountain of bills, children to educate, and a nonworking spouse. With fewer transfers, companies may have somewhat more difficulty meeting changing staff requirements, but for individuals it is usually far better to stay in place, develop two lucrative careers rather than one, and reap the benefits of putting down roots into a community, as well.

Sometimes, though, a relocation seems right, as for a promotion within your own organization, a step up to a better job in another organization, or a move from unemployment to employment. When that occurs, you will want to explore personally several related cost and quality of life factors, if at all possible on the spot and, if you are married, with your spouse. For even your best friends—sometimes especially your best friends—will shade the truth when they are trying to convince you to make a move. Before deciding to accept a job offer, you will want to see for yourself several things:

  • Where you and your family, if you have one, would like to live, within reasonable distance of your home base. Within *reasonable* distance, that is; the community that is "only" an hour away in the suburbs of a big city may turn out to be an hour and a half away in most rush hours and two hours away in rush hours in midwinter. There may be several such communities; there may be only one; there may be none. There is often a balance to be struck between quality of life and cost factors, and negotiations that must be undertaken before a job offer becomes acceptable. It can also happen that careful examination of an area makes it clear that you want no part of it, and then it may not matter how good the job offer is in other ways; you will either reject it, or spend some very, very unhappy months or years before you decide to give up on what turns out to have been a bad job-changing decision.

Within compatible communities, you will have some quite standard, quite indispensable explorations to pursue, including:

  • The nature and cost of the housing available. That means consulting with local realtors on home and mortgage prices and availability. By all means, visit some homes for sale, so that you can see what is really available at indicated prices. The same for rentals, if you plan to rent rather than buy, including visits to available rentals. And since realtors are in the business of selling homes, it is wise to doublecheck their information on mortgage rates and terms at some local banks.

Some of this information becomes important when finally negotiating the job offer, if you indeed decide to take the job. You may need to negotiate the sale of your current home guaranteed by your transferring company or new employer, with purchase of your old home at a guaranteed base price a condition of employment. You may need mortgage assistance in your new location to get any mortgage credit at all, with company payment guarantees if mortgage rates and points are over guaranteed maximums. You will be very wise, for example, to try to get the company to pick up mortgage interest payments over a guaranteed maximum interest rate, if you take a flexible rate mortgage, which can rise over the years and ultimately become far more expensive than you had anticipated.

- What the schools are like, if you have children. That, too, needs a personal look, which can usually be arranged without any trouble with local school officials, who are quite used to such requests. The schools may indeed look fine to you; on the other hand, you may decide that expensive private schools will be necessary or desirable for your children, with the very large additional costs that are involved. Such costs, measured in after-tax rather than pre-tax income dollars, can make a big difference as to income needs, and may have to be figured into negotiations.

You may also find that no available schools are acceptable, and that may be a knockout factor, making the job offer unacceptable. That is especially important if you have a child who needs special education that may be available in your current location, but is unavailable in the area to which you may be relocating.

- What the cultural and social amenities, which have so much to do with the quality of life, are like. Concerts, theaters, sports facilities, local libraries, churches, and synagogues—such organizations can have a profound impact upon the quality of life as perceived by you and your loved ones, and therefore upon your job decision.

- What commuting conditions will be like from compatible communities. A long, difficult commute from the nearest compatible community in an area can be daunting; perhaps it should be daunting more often than it actually is, for in the long run it can disastrously affect the quality of your own life. Once again, there is no substitute for actually doing it; take the drive or the bus or train, and more than once if possible, and carefully consider it as a major job-decision element.

▪ What educational opportunities are available in the area and state for you, your spouse, and your children. You may want to pursue additional formal professional education, for example. The existence of a major business school nearby can then have a significant impact upon your job decision. Or your spouse may want to either pursue additional education or get some basic education; what is available can become very important in career development terms. And one state may offer your children fine state colleges, at small cost, while another has a rather poor state college system, necessitating large college costs at private colleges. The difference to them and you can be tens of thousands of dollars.

▪ What professional and other career opportunities are available for your spouse. That lovely home in a parklike setting may turn out to be very lovely indeed—but if it is located 50 miles from the nearest fair-sized city, your tax accountant or psychologist spouse may have an impossibly difficult time making professional connections, making the move unacceptable. On the other hand, you and your spouse may long have dreamed of doing some farming, and a move into a country setting may be an opportunity to make that dream come true—and perhaps an alternate career for one or both of you as well. A major job move requires considerable self-analysis on the part of all those moving.

Relocation is a particularly difficult problem when it involves an international move, and especially for those with families. For then a spouse's career can be in very serious jeopardy, and the related quality of life and cost-of-living questions as well as tax and foreign exchange factors must be examined with extraordinary care. Before you accept a post abroad, by all means take at least one trip to the proposed location, as an indispensable part of the decision-making process. Accept with thanks the advice and materials furnished by your prospective employer or current company, and then read about and discuss the proposed place and situation with everyone you know and respect, including your accountant and lawyer, before and after you make that trip abroad and before you make the job decision. Then, if your decision is affirmative, seriously consider going on ahead by yourself for a considerable period, to pave the way.

Many do decide to hedge their relocation bets, whether they are going abroad or staying in their home countries. Some commute long distances to their new jobs for a period. Some return home only for weekends for a rather extended period of as much as a year or more. Others come home less frequently, as in the instance of an international move. That is often a quite necessary set of arrangements, as when it is important for children to finish a school term or year in place, rather than suffering the dislocation of a mid-term move; or when the process of selecting, closing, and readying a home for occupancy takes months, and begins only after the job has actually started. It is also a very prudent approach, for no matter how carefully a job move is considered before it is actually made, many a move goes sour soon after. Unanticipated internal moves, business difficulties beyond your control, even allergies surfacing in new climatic conditions—a score of things can turn a job move bad, even if the original decision was a correct one. Sometimes the move is simply recognized too late as a mistake, for whatever the reason. When a job move does turn out badly early in the game, the ability to return to your previous community and business environment can make a relatively painless correction out of what might have been a family disaster if you had picked up stakes and moved entirely to the new job and community.

Single People.

For those who travel alone, relocation questions are often just as difficult as for those with family ties. Even those just starting out, having been hired for their first jobs right off college campuses, can face difficult and potentially very expensive career decisions—and before they have any experience to fall back on.

Some of the potential problems faced by beginners are

economic. A 25-year-old may be single, but is rarely unencumbered in these times of huge college costs and shrinking family ability to pay. Young people are quite likely to have large debts; have little or no capital with which to acquire such goods as automobiles, clothes, and furniture; and command not very large after-tax incomes. It may be difficult, under those circumstances, to make ends meet anywhere, and particularly difficult in such expensive cities as New York and Houston. Yet housing must very often be obtained in the most expensive portions of center cities, as working hours for beginners may be extraordinarily long during the years of apprenticeship, and commuting costs and the automobiles necessary to live in suburbs in themselves add large expense items to modest budgets. And beyond the pure economics of the matter, it can be terribly lonely, and therefore demoralizing, to be young and virtually friendless in a new town, and stuck out in the suburbs. Most young people need to be where other young people are to be found, and where the action—such as it is—functions as an icebreaker and group-maker for people like themselves. It is not at all unusual, therefore, to find young people living over their heads in center cities, while seeming to command rather large incomes that should guarantee immediate solvency. The young person who "can't save anything" is not to be censured; that is merely normal in our times.

But lack of solvency can cause career problems, for this is a time when mobility is a must, and early solvency therefore is far more than a prudent approach to savings and investment. Young people need money to be able to move from job to job and from industry to industry, as apprenticeship needs and desires on the one hand, and defensive needs on the other, demand. A young person who has been fired because of company cutbacks or failure, and who has neither a strong track record nor financial reserves, can be someone in deep personal trouble, for he or she is probably also carrying a sizable education debt and may need to relocate to find a new job. A young sales professional who clearly sees that a move should be made, and wants to gamble, for example, on a move to a small, untried company in a growing new industry, must have some savings to fall back on if the gamble does not work out. Otherwise, in all probability, he or she should not and will not make what might otherwise be an excellent career move.

Given the economic conditions of this very difficult period, it may be unwise to go heavily into debt to finance graduate business education. Some may profitably continue to do so—an MBA from a top business school, such as Harvard or Stanford, may lead to a fast and very lucrative career track—but many may be better off to take their MBAs after moving into the business world. Many companies will pay all or part of tuition for employees, and will cooperate in other significant ways to help their people through graduate school; as credit becomes even more difficult to get, the high cost of education may indeed make company assistance essential for many.

Similarly, economic factors may cause young people just starting out to reach for jobs in major metropolitan areas, where many potential employers exist, and where job moves may not require relocation. It is all very well to get relocation help when taking a job, but when leaving a job you may have to bear the costs of relocation yourself, and those costs may prove prohibitive. A recent graduate who took a job in a single-industry town, lost that job, and has had to relocate to a big city, broke and jobless, has little bargaining power. Without realistic severance arrangements—and that means more than a return airplane ticket to the campus from which you were recruited—the enticing job in a fine but isolated physical location may be a career and a personal mistake.

For any single person, and for a good many married people as well, relocation can bring loneliness. The easiest and most attractive country or small-city life style may be a personal disaster for someone who is a confirmed city dweller used to the cultural and social amenities available in a major metropolitan area. The church-centered social life so attractive to some may be a stone wall for the agnostic or atheist. For the devoted small-town churchgoer, on the other hand, life in a big center city may be wholly unacceptable. For all of us, a long, searching look at the social and physical environment within which we are going to work in a proffered new job is just as important as our assessment of the job itself. We are whole people, and must try to view business and personal needs and desires as an intertwined whole.

In sum, then, it is wise to regard most aspects of an offered job as negotiable, including income, moving expenses, house-selling and mortgage assistance, insurance plans, club memberships, and vacation arrangements. All after the offer and before acceptance, none before the firm offer; and all cast in terms of helping you to best do the job you are now setting out to do. You should not have to be worried about a less-than-adequate income in inflationary times, about being unable to sell an old house or properly finance a new one, or about inadequate incentives—not when you are setting out to do the job of your life in the opportunity of a lifetime.

INDEX